RADICAL JACK

By the same author

R. S. SURTEES
HAVELOCK

THE FIRST EARL OF DURHAM

From a portrait by Sir Thomas Lawrence

RADICAL JACK

The Life of
JOHN GEORGE LAMBTON
First Earl of Durham, Viscount Lambton
and Baron Durham
Member of Parliament for Durham County
LORD PRIVY SEAL
Ambassador at the Court of St. Petersburgh
GOVERNOR-GENERAL
and
CAPTAIN-GENERAL OF CANADA
1792 – 1840

BY
LEONARD COOPER

━━━━━━

LONDON
THE CRESSET PRESS
1959

First published in 1959 by The Cresset Press, 11 Fitzroy Square, London, W.1
and printed in Great Britain by The Camelot Press Ltd., London and Southampton.

To
THE VISCOUNT LAMBTON, M.P.
with deep gratitude

Le Jour Viendra

PREFACE

Through the generosity of The Viscount Lambton, M.P., I have had full access to the Lambton Papers and I can only offer my sincere, though inadequate, thanks to him for this privilege, as for his constant kindness, help and hospitality. I must also gratefully acknowledge the help and kindness which I have always had from Major Grey and his staff at the Lambton Estate Office, and to the staff at both Lambton and Fenton.

As ever I have drawn continually on the resources of the Leeds Library (a library which, I believe, was a few years old when Radical Jack was born and which, I am told, Brougham may have visited). I cannot measure the thanks which I owe to Mr. Frank Beckwith, M.A., and to all his staff, especially to Mr. Bumby and Mr. Walker. Their time and labour have always been generously and courteously given. I count myself especially lucky in being able to draw not only on the Library's immense collection of reference books but on Mr. Beckwith's learning and scholarship and most of all on his specialized knowledge of the period of which I was writing. I am indebted to the City Librarian of Leeds, who kindly took much trouble to get me some vital and rare works of reference.

The late Professor J. W. Williams, of St. Andrews University, was unfailingly helpful with advice and criticism and took enormous trouble in suggesting revision and instilling his own standards of scrupulous accuracy. He was a great admirer of Melbourne and the only tribute which I can now pay to his memory is the hope that I have abated, in this respect, somewhat of what he used to call my 'pejorative eloquence'.

I should be churlish not to record my gratitude to the many friends who have given me help and encouragement and, as ever, to my sisters, Lettice and Barbara, and my friend Glen Inglis, with all of whom I have discussed my work at all stages of its progress; to Mark Hamilton, and all his colleagues at A. M. Heath & Co. and to John Howard of the Cresset Press for valuable suggestions. My wife and family have had Radical Jack for breakfast, lunch, and tea for the last few years without apparent resentment. I am as grateful to them for this as I am for everything.

AUTHORITIES

Professor Chester New's *Life of Lord Durham*, published in 1929 is, and must long remain, the standard work on the subject (modern jargon would call it the 'definitive' Life, a word which I cannot bring myself to tolerate). I have made constant use of it and to it, for a bibliography, I can only refer any reader of my own book. Like Professor New, I have had the good fortune to have the use of all the Lambton MSS., a collection consisting, as he feelingly says, of 'several thousands of letters and other manuscripts', which were also used by Mr. Stuart Reid for his earlier Life. No writer can include by quotation more than a fragment of that immense store and he can only choose what seems to him essential for his purpose. Professor New, an eminent historian, naturally used much which I have omitted. I, working on a smaller scale and being absorbed by Lord Durham's home and family life and the strange complexity of his nature, have relied more on the personal letters and on nearly everything which Lady Durham left. If I cannot claim to have added much to the general store of knowledge of Lord Durham's career, I believe that I am the only man who has worked out his batting average.

It would be presumptuous for me to reproduce Professor New's bibliography and the only books which I ought to mention are those which, by reason of the date of their publication, he could not have seen when he was writing. The most valuable, to me, of all these, was Sir Reginald Coupland's *The Durham Report*, an admirably concise summary and appreciation, published in 1945.

I ought not to omit Mr. St. John Packe's life of John Stuart Mill or Miss Frances Hawes' of Lord Brougham, nor the pleasure and profit which I have derived from all the writings of the late Sir Philip Guedalla, especially *Palmerston* and *The Duke*, and those of Mr. Michael Sadleir and Sir A. Bryant. For getting the political atmosphere of the time I know nothing to compare with the novels of Lord Beaconsfield and Anthony Trollope and surely one of the best elections in all fiction is in Stanley Weyman's *Chippinge*.

Contents

Illustrations

ix

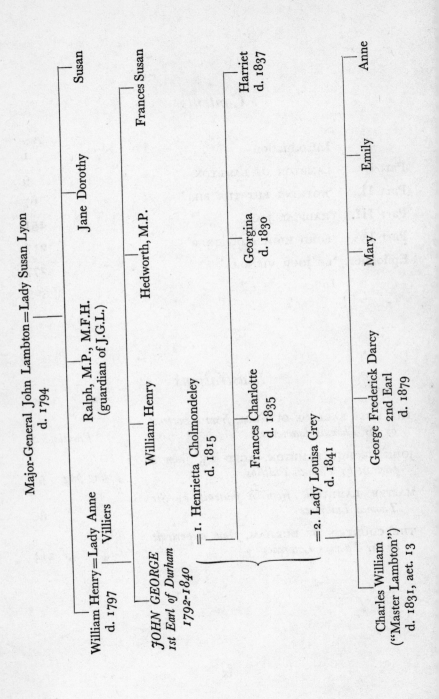

Major-General John Lambton = Lady Susan Lyon
d. 1794

William Henry = Lady Anne
d. 1797   Villiers

Ralph, M.P., M.F.H.
(guardian of J.G.L.)

Jane Dorothy

Susan

JOHN GEORGE
1st Earl of Durham
1792-1840

= 1. Henrietta Cholmondeley
d. 1815

William Henry

Hedworth, M.P.

Frances Susan

= 2. Lady Louisa Grey
d. 1841

Frances Charlotte
d. 1835

Georgina
d. 1830

Harriet
d. 1837

Charles William
("Master Lambton")
d. 1831, aet. 13

George Frederick Darcy
2nd Earl
d. 1879

Mary

Emily

Anne

INTRODUCTION

Cleveland Row is a short street near St. James's Palace and its solid, dignified houses run westward towards St. James's Park, but there is no plaque to tell that No. 13 was once the town house of John George Lambton, First Earl of Durham, and that it was the birthplace of the First Reform Bill of 1832 and of the Durham Report of 1840.

There is little record of any sort in London today of the man who was known to his contemporaries as Radical Jack and to Mr. Creevey as 'King Jog' and 'The Angry Boy'; who was Lord Privy Seal, Ambassador to Russia, High Commissioner for and Governor-General of Canada. There is no statue outside the Houses of Parliament, or before Canada House; nothing but two public houses which were named after him in the first rush of enthusiasm over the Reform Bill. One of these, near the Oval, has so far forgotten its origin as to bear on its signboard the arms of the Diocese and City of Durham. The other, in the Maida Vale district, has been more faithful and its board shows the arms of Lambton—Sable a fess between three lambs passant argent. In the bar there are booklets which tell of its origin and naming, but so far has Radical Jack passed from general memory that any taxi-driver knows the inn better by its common name, 'The Drum and Monkey'. His own county, the County Palatine of Durham, has done a little more for him. Lambton Castle, though it is no longer the family seat, still stands on the bluffs from which the trees run almost sheer down to the windings of the River Wear. A traveller by train, going north to Newcastle and looking out of the right-hand window of his carriage, can see, eastward of Chester-le-Street, the graceful temple which the Freemasons of County Durham raised in his memory. His county, which loved him, has not forgotten him.

The Durham folk of his own time loved him less for his public work, his lifelong championship of the weak and oppressed, than because he was an honest and generous employer and most of all because he was their Squire and a familiar figure. There had been Lambtons at Lambton for the best part

I

of a thousand years and they had always been men who loved their home and shared in the work, the life, and the sport of their countryside. Radical Jack was no less the squire for being the first Earl. His duty took him to London, to St. Petersburg, and to Toronto, but his heart was always in the tall house above the Wear. In that he was like his father-in-law, Earl Grey, who, even as Prime Minister, was always sick at heart for Howick and his own land.

It was so with many of their fellow-aristocrats, to whom court and camp, embassy and mission were only interludes in the real life of country house and hunting field. Lord Althorp, when he was a Junior Lord of the Treasury, used to keep relays of horses on the road to Leicestershire and to ride all night so that he might enjoy a day with the Quorn and ride back to London at the end of it. That attachment to the country was the real difference between the French and the English aristocrats and it was to save the British when their people, in their own slow and, on the whole, good-humoured way, began to accomplish their own revolution. The great French lords looked always to Paris as to their heaven and to Versailles as to their sun. To them the country was exile and the peasants were a source of income and a pool of labour. The great English families—Lambton, Grey, Spencer, Cavendish-Bentinck, Mowbray—may have blossomed in London but their roots were in the country. They regarded the court at Windsor or St. James's with just as much respect as its master could command by his own character, which was not very much in the early nineteenth century. They were, many of them, improving landlords, and, nearly all of them, sportsmen. As boys they ran wild on the estate, wrestling, swimming, ferreting with the sons of grooms and keepers. At Eton or Harrow or Winchester, they were fed and treated worse than most grooms' sons. After their schooling and perhaps their years at the University, they came back to the country to hunt, to shoot, later to administer summary, but seldom tyrannical justice from the county bench, to read the lessons in the churches where they had been baptized. The tie between them and their people was lifelong and was not to be broken by years of absence in Navy and Army and Foreign embassies, or months in Westminster.

So, when the revolutionary years began in France, there were violence and terror and the French lords fled before it or looked through the little door on the Place de la Concorde. In England there was rioting, some burning of houses, and a little breaking of heads. Some of the aristocracy opposed the new ideas, a few were indifferent but many not only sympathized with them but cheered on the reformers, as they cheered on the hounds in their home pastures, and led them as they had led the field over hedge and water.

Such was the tie which bound the people of Durham to the man whom the outside world knew as Lord Privy Seal and Earl of Durham, but who, to them, always remained Squire Lambton. The tenants knew him as a family man and as a generous host. They had watched him at cricket on the old field where the new castle later stood and knew him for a sound opening batsman—as indeed the records of the matches show—and a useful fast bowler. They had seen him with the hounds and on the race-course which he had laid out in Lambton Park. They followed his fortunes further afield on the turf at York and Doncaster, and when, in 1817, his mare Borodino, failed to win the St. Leger, they were many of them the poorer by a few shillings. A wider circle of country folk had known him by his all but regal progresses about the county when he drove abroad—he was always a lover of state and splendour—with postilions and outriders in the Lambton livery. They had seen and heard him on the hustings, when he stood as candidate for the County of Durham, and in the streets of Sunderland when he went there to attend meetings of colliery owners. His workmen in the collieries had come to recognize in him an employer who would always give fair pay and treatment and as a man who cared about them as men, worried about their accidents and gave his time and money to promote their safety.

Inevitably the domestic staff at the Castle, where there were seldom fewer than forty indoor servants and sixteen gardeners, beside coachmen and grooms, knew more intimate details about him. They had a glimpse of that side of his nature which brought him so many and such bitter enemies in public life, his arrogance and domineering ways, his occasional fits of terrifying anger and of hardly less terrifying remorse. But the staff knew, too, how frail was his health and how often such

3

outbursts were brought on by the neuralgic pains which attacked him so that he had to stay for hours, sometimes for days, in a darkened room and could find no relief from his suffering, which laudanum only dulled.

These, after all, were family matters and all good families hide their troubles from the rest of the world until some malicious outsider like Creevey lifts the curtain. There are accounts of life at Lambton Castle by guests who were happy there and saw only the courteous and gay host which he could be—guests such as Harriet Martineau, Sydney Smith, and Lady Holland, who are quite as reliable witnesses as Creevey without his talent for magnifying any incident into a good story. All these must be taken into account and carefully scrutinized because it is impossible to understand Lord Durham's character without a knowledge of the family and home life which were so vitally important to him. He was before all a family man. His wife and children and home were everything to him. They were the source of that immense compassion which was to spread beyond home and county to country and colony and to seek for the oppressed and desolate wherever he found them. His vision was always of a family, whether it was the little group at Lambton or the great conception of a commonalty of nations under the British Crown. The idea of a family implies a father and it was perhaps the faulty part of his vision that he cast himself for this role—a father loving and compassionate but unquestionably autocratic.

It was that autocratic side of him which he showed mostly to the colleagues with whom he worked in politics and diplomacy, and it may be for that reason that he has no visible memorial outside his county and holds only a small place in the memory of history. What he helped to achieve remains and time has confirmed and perfected it. His Reform Bill was completed by the Universal Suffrage Act, as the Durham Report was the seed which came to flower in the British Commonwealth of Nations. But history has never given him enough credit for either— certainly not as much credit as he claimed for himself in the matter of Reform, for he was never a man to undervalue his own deserts.

It would be easy to say of him, as it is of so many visionaries, that he was born before his time and that he thrust his ideas on

4

a world which was not yet ready for them, but it would not be the truth. The French Revolution set free a great wind of new thought and aspiration and, all over the world, men were ready to seize and examine any idea that differed from the old beliefs. He was in many ways ahead of contemporary thought but not so far ahead as to lack a hearing. His difficulty was, as usual, in himself, in that division in his inmost being, so that he was both ahead in thought and obstinately rooted in the past, revolutionary and traditionalist, reformer and autocrat. His mind was always active and far-ranging and had flashes of real genius, but at heart he was as self-centred and intolerant of other mens' opinions when they conflicted with his own as any feudal baron. It is not given to most ordinary men to be known by the contradictory names of 'The Dictator' and 'Radical Jack'. That contrast made his work doubly hard, since even men who were willing to go a long way with him in theory hung back in action because they could not reconcile themselves to doing exactly what he wanted at the moment when he wanted it. Few men doubted that he cared most passionately for the reforms which he advocated, but many could not escape the feeling that a reform was desirable not primarily because it was needed but because he wished it. Historians have appraised and recorded his work but have given little space to the man himself. His two biographers, Mr. Stuart Reid and Professor New, have dealt mostly with his public life and necessarily so, since what he did was important and worthy of record. To do this and at the same time to devote equal space to his private life would have resulted in books of intolerable length. Mr. Reid is a wholesale, Professor New a discriminating admirer. Professor New makes no attempt to hide or gloss over the darker side but he was absorbed by other problems and naturally, as a Canadian, concerned himself largely with the Canadian mission and its results. His picture of the man is fair and dispassionate but he makes no attempt—it was not within the scope which he set himself—to examine and to try to reconcile those two sides of his nature which were always at war and which produced such astonishing results.

A later biographer who attempts this need not feel presumptuous. He cannot hope to improve on Professor New's work but may, albeit with diffidence, aspire to add to it. It is now more than a hundred years since Lord Durham's death and in that time much new knowledge is available which may help to an understanding of him. Medical science may shed some light on the ill health which was always with him, psychology may point to some sources of the stresses and agonies of his mind, and a biographer, though he may himself have little of science or learning, can profit by the discoveries of wiser men. But his excuse for attempting the task, if excuse be needed, must be the fascination of the problem—the problem of a man who made so much stir in his own day and has since been so disregarded; who achieved so much and might have achieved so much more; who was by turns, Michael and Lucifer, noble and petty, compassionate and arrogant, tolerant and intolerable; who was so deeply loved by his family, so heartily detested by his colleagues, so profoundly trusted by the ordinary people of two countries and so suspect to the fellow-aristocrats of his own; who was not only 'Radical Jack' to his followers and 'King Jog' to Creevey, but 'Lord High Seditioner' to *The Times* newspaper, 'The Dictator' to Brougham, 'Robert le Diable' to King William, and always to his wife, 'My dearest Lambton'.

The task which any later biographer sets himself must be hard, and success can at best be only partial since no man can wholly understand another's soul and it is impossible for an ordinary mind to rise to the heights of one which has in it more than a trace of genius. It is worth the attempt for, whatever he did or failed to do, whether men loved or hated him, he was one of the most vital and fascinating personalities in a time which was rich in them. So much has been written, so much is known about his great contemporaries, Wellington, Palmerston, Melbourne, Canning, Castlereagh, Russell. Their memoirs and letters have been published, their conversations reported, their motives probed and their success and failures assessed. Lord Durham published nothing, left no memoirs. His conversations were not noted, only a fragment of his letters has been made public. His contemporaries seem to stand in the full light of day, while his figure is dimly seen against the sky of a stormy night, to be glimpsed only as a star whose light is pure but flickering and is too often obscured by drifting cloud. Such a simile may seem over-fanciful today. It did not seem so to the men who, over 300 years ago, wrote in the indictment which they were drawing up for the trial of Sir Walter Raleigh:

'He hath been as a Starre at which the World hath gazed; but Starres may fall, nay, they must fall when they trouble the sphere wherein they abide.'

PART ONE

Lambton of Lambton

1792–1830

In the meantime we are born only to be men. We shall do enough if we form ourselves to be good ones. It is therefore our business carefully to cultivate our minds to rear to the most perfect vigour and maturity, every sort of generous and honest feeling, that belongs to our nature. To bring the dispositions that are lovely in private life into the service and conduct of the commonwealth; so to be patriots as not to forget we are gentlemen. To cultivate friendships and to incur enmities. To have both strong but both selected; in the one to be placable; in the other immovable.

EDMUND BURKE. *Thoughts on the Causes of the Present Discontent.* 1770.

Men in great place are thrice servants; servants of the sovereign or State, servants of fame and servants of business. . . . The rising unto place is laborious; and by pains men come to greater pains. . . . The standing is slippery and the regress is either a downfall or at least an eclipse, which is a melancholy thing.

FRANCIS BACON. *Of Great Place.*

CHAPTER I

After the Second World War, a number of British traitors were brought to trial and Miss Rebecca West reported the cases in her book, *Trial for Treason*. One of the accused was a young man of good family and of him she wrote that, throughout his eccentric life, his family must have been constantly saying to themselves: 'He can't be doing that. But, my God, he *is* doing it!'

Something of the same baffled bewilderment as constantly afflicts the student of Lord Durham's life and, over and over again, he feels impelled to cry out: 'He can't have done that. But, my God, he *did* do it!' The contrast in him is so violent and so incessant that the brain reels under the storm of questions that demand an answer. How could he, the mind cries despairingly, do first this and then that, take a step in one direction and two in another, set his hand to something and, with the other hand, wreck it in the doing? How could he set out on his colossal task of pacifying and restoring Canada and at once spoil his chance of succeeding by wantonly defying the Government about two quite unimportant appointments to his staff? How could he, having come so near to success there, put it all in peril by holding up to open contempt the Government whose representative he was? On the other hand—for the contrasts are not all or even mostly in his disfavour—how could he return from Canada with the consciousness of having been betrayed and abandoned and put away all thought of revenge or even of personal justification to give himself wholly to the task of bringing peace to a distracted colony?

The same antitheses exist in his private life. It seems as unbelievable that a man of his breeding should have boasted of his wealth as it does that a man who spent £90,000 on rebuilding his house should have given dinners at which there was not enough food to go round his guests; that an aristocrat of such old and honourable lineage should have complained so noisily when he was given a barony and not the expected earldom; that a man who loved his wife, as he undoubtedly did, should have behaved so outrageously to her father. Yet—for here too the contrasts are not all against him—few men could have suffered the political eclipse which he suffered after the brief triumph of the Reform Bill and have surmounted their troubles to do better work than ever before. Still fewer, in the disastrous end of the Canadian mission, would have refrained— as he did on the evidence of his wife and his friends—from letting fall a single word of abuse of the men who had failed him.

Such contrasts are only evidence of the strife between Michael and Lucifer which every man has to endure. What made the struggle in him so painful and so incessant was the extraordinary strength of his feelings and the power of his intellect. Dr. Beddoes, his first schoolmaster, recognized it when he wrote of the six-year-old child: 'The character of John is very uncommon. I think he is as capable of going as far in good or bad as any human being I have ever beheld', adding three years later: 'John's disposition is extraordinarily peculiar. In fact he has the greatest sensibility I ever observed in a child.'

That is the first piece of contemporary evidence about him, and every scrap of such evidence is needed for the attempt to understand him. The contemporary diarists, Croker, Creevey, and Greville, are uniformly unfavourable, partly because they deal mostly with his public life and partly, in the cases of Croker and Greville, through political prejudice. Of the three the most enlightening is Thomas Creevey, who was a Whig and would therefore have preferred to speak well of him. Creevey, too, knew him in his earlier and more carefree years and gives invaluable glimpses of him as a host among the splendours and occasional discomforts of Lambton Castle. Creevey is often malicious and always a snob, but he is generally truthful, though he occasionally exaggerates for the sake of making a better story. In his account, unkind though it is for the most part, there are sudden reflections of that charm of manner and warmth of heart which Lord Durham showed so often at home and less often in London. There is admiration, too, for his intellectual powers, and especially for that gift of lucid speech of which its owner, perverse in that as in everything, thought so little. It was characteristic of Lord Durham, whose speeches Canning considered 'quite perfect' and who was, in Brougham's expert opinion, as good a speaker in the House as anyone and better than anyone at a public meeting, should have been so diffident about his ability that he seldom spoke in either House if he could avoid it.

Cam Hobhouse, afterwards Lord Broughton, wrote of him critically, but not on the whole unfairly, and often with shrewd understanding, as when he remarked that 'Lambton had many good qualities but was spoiled by wealth and too much home indulgence'. Brougham, who was first his friend and then his enemy, thought much ill of him, but spoke and wrote not a little good. Lord Melbourne's letters to Lord John Russell are full of references, generally slighting, often tinged by the political necessities of the moment, but sometimes showing a curious awareness of the reasonable side of his nature, while Russell's replies show honest admiration for a colleague with whom he could not go all the way, but whom he respected and admired. There is much in the letters of the lively and curious Princess Lieven which throws light on him and on the rapid changes in his political fortunes and in the esteem in which he was currently held.

All these and many less important contemporary witnesses must be examined by the student of Lord Durham's life, but the most important and unimpeachable sources of information are, of course, the unpublished manuscripts in the Lambton and Grey collections. It may almost be said that the key to an understanding of his nature lies, if anywhere, in his relationship with his father-in-law, the second Earl Grey. Set beside it are the letters of Lady Durham and of her mother, an irrefutable proof of his goodness as a man and a husband and father and, to supplement them, are the natural and wholly delightful letters which he exchanged with his children. Mr. Morton, the agent for the estate and the collieries, bears witness to his excellence as an employer, and the lively and often acrimonious correspondence between his mother and his guardians provides an agreeable scherzo which helps to an understanding of a childhood to which nothing was denied but the love and companionship of father and mother.

It is only to be expected, Lord Durham being what he was, that the evidence about him should be as sharply divided as was his own nature and the perpetual antithesis adds to the student's excitement even while it increases his difficulties. Fortunately there is a common ground of agreement which may serve as a basis for the search, certain qualities in Lord Durham which even his most bitter enemies did not deny.

His personal life was immaculate. In an age which thought lightly of sexual irregularities, no breath of scandal ever touched him, though his wealth and his exceptional personal beauty must have provided him with any number of opportunities. Yet he was never censorious of other men's morals and was as free from the growing prudery of the Victorian age as he had been from the grossness of the Regency. Had there been a suspicion of a scandal about him, it could hardly have escaped the unfriendly vigilance of Creevey or Greville, but there was none.

Another quality which no one denied was his courage. His physical courage was never questioned, but it was probably never severely tested apart from the one duel which he fought and the common risks of the hunting field. It was his supreme moral courage when, as often happened, he found himself in a minority or alone which never failed him and extorted an unwilling admiration from his opponents. Almost everything that he did in Canada was debated and hotly—often justly—criticized, but no one questioned the courage which he showed in accepting and carrying through his lonely and thankless mission.

His compassion was genuine. That too has never been seriously disputed. His own people at home and his adopted family in Canada, both French and English, could testify that his sympathy was not of words alone, but took shape in rapid and decisive action. When he was Ambassador at the court of St. Petersburg he risked his personal popularity with the Tsar and consequent failure of his mission to try, though with little success, to win mercy for the ill-treated Poles.

Lastly there was his honesty—not merely financial honesty, though that, too, he had. He was enormously wealthy, which is always a help, though not a complete safeguard against the more obvious forms of dishonesty. In a world of politics which, in his day, was seamed with corruption, in which seats in the House of Commons and political constituencies were bought and sold like any merchandise in a market, his hands were clean and if he fought hard he fought fairly. Even his more outrageous doings in Canada were done openly and in defiance of higher powers. None of his worst enemies ever convicted him of a deliberate lie or a broken promise.

It is possible then and may be helpful, even at the beginning of the search to strike a rough balance from the briefest summary of the opinions of his friends and his enemies—a balance which will necessarily have to be adjusted after proper scrutiny of evidence and may even be found to be too premature and hasty to last very long. But we may at the beginning throw into one scale without reservation all the evil which his enemies thought and spoke of him—his arrogance and ill-temper, his passionate addiction to his own way, his extravagance and childish love of display, his pettiness and vanity and his occasional outbursts of insolence and cruelty. We may add his few but appalling failures in judgement, his ruthlessness when opposed and his tendency to see all questions of public policy from a purely personal standpoint. The load is a heavy one and that scale might sink to the ground and stay there, were it not that into the opposing scale we can throw those great qualities which even his enemies admitted: decency, courage, compassion, honesty. We can get no nearer to a true balance until we have minutely scrutinized every available piece of evidence for and against him, and even then we may fail. At the end we may find that there is no more fitting word to be said of him than that of his own people. 'He was an honest man, he was.' 'Ay, he cared about us.'

CHAPTER II

If there is anything in heredity and validity in the belief that much of what a man will become is decided before his birth, it is necessary to look back as far as possible at Lord Durham's ancestry and try to pick out those threads which run unbroken through the family history till they appear in him. It is a comparatively simple task, since the history of the Lambtons is recorded for many hundreds of years. Robert Surtees of Mainsforth, in his *History of Durham* traces them back in direct male line to the twelfth century and quotes charters of almost 200 years earlier to which Lambtons set their hands as witnesses, so they must have been people of some consequence in the county at the time of the Norman Conquest and perhaps before that. Their name appears in early folk lore and song in the story of the Worm of Lambton, a monster which lived in the River Wear and put a curse on them because some unrecorded Lambton had the impious habit of fishing on Sunday.

There were two family houses at Lambton before Lord Durham built his castle there and the men who lived in them had enough in common to allow at least a guess at the family characteristics. If there is truth in the guess, it shows how Lord Durham differed from all those who had preceded him. They seem to have been, for the most part, typical country gentlemen, owning large estates in Durham and Northumberland; devoted to their homes but willing to take their part in their country's service abroad on sea and by land. An earlier John Lambton went as a Crusader to the Holy Land and came back as a Knight of Rhodes. In the Civil War, a William was knighted by the King for whom he afterwards died at Marston Moor, as his heir died a few months later in a skirmish near Bradford.

Apart from these two, the family obstinately remained without titles or decorations for nearly 800 years, while other families, no older, no wealthier and certainly no more honourable, attained to baronies, earldoms, and dukedoms. Lord Durham's grandfather, General John Lambton, was offered an earldom but refused to be indebted to Pitt for what he would gladly have accepted from Fox, had Fox been in a position to offer it. It was of that that Lord Durham was thinking when he spoke of 'the earldom which has for too long been denied to my family'. Indeed that avid desire of his for the trappings of nobility is one of the signs of his difference from the generality of the Lambton men. They had royal blood in their veins, which they could trace back to Edward II and to the sister of Henry VIII through marriage with the Eures and the Lumleys. With their own lambs argent, they quartered the popinjays vert of Lumley, the cinquefoils gules of D'Arcy and Hedworth the Fitz-William lozenges and the Fitzroger lion rampant.

They wanted nothing else. Doubtless they were content with their breeding, but also it would seem that they were not in any way ambitious, nor, it may be added, very enterprising. In that too, Lord Durham, who was both, stands in sharp contrast to them.

They were King's men but never courtiers, Knights of the Shire but never ministers. Above all they were representatives of their county in Parliament. Professor New, writing in 1929, calculated that between the year 1675 and his own date, there had been an aggregate of forty-four years during which there was no member of the family in one or the other House of Parliament. It is difficult to think that they could not have cut more of a figure in politics if they had wanted to, for they were not only of good stock but wealthy, and traditionally they were Whigs. After the revolution of 1688 the Whigs enjoyed a long tenure of power and it would not have been hard for one of their name and their wealth to win his way to high position if he were set on it.

It would seem that they were not. General John Lambton was typical of them. He served in the Coldstream Guards, commanded the 68th Foot (later the Durham Light Infantry), and represented his county in the Commons. When he gave up his seat, he was thanked by his constituents for his unvarying defence of their rights and liberties. He was succeeded by his son William who was an ardent supporter of that Parliamentary Reform which his son, Lord Durham, was to do so much to achieve.

William Lambton had been at Eton with Charles Grey, afterwards the second Earl Grey, and with Samuel Whitbread who, because of his brewery, was known to his contemporaries as 'Fermentation Sam'. They were among the founders of the Society of Friends of the People, whose object was, as their manifesto stated, 'Firstly to restore freedom of election and a more equal representation of the People in Parliament' and 'Secondly, to secure to the People a more frequent exercise of their right of electing their own representatives'. The manifesto was published on 11 April 1792, and on the following day William Lambton's first child, the future Lord Durham, was born in the family's town house in Berkeley Square.

Up to his time, then, the Lambtons were very much like other country gentlemen, different only from their neighbours in that they were always a little more receptive of new ideas, as they showed when they were among the first of the great families of the North to adhere to the Reformation. Many of their characteristics obviously lived on in Lord Durham, in his devotion to his home and his people and his absorption in politics. Where he differs from them so fundamentally is in his ambition and his ability. While they were, for the most part, content to follow traditional ways and to rest on their local importance, he had both the burning desire for a more active life and greater distinction and the will and the ability to win them.

Many families produce an oddity from time to time, but it is always worth while and often rewarding to search for some strain latent in the blood—it may be from a long way back—which suddenly erupts and breaks the normal pattern. In Lord Durham's case there is no need to go back for many years, for new movements were stirring in the Lambton blood in the two previous generations.

General Lambton, his grandfather, married Lady Susan Lyon, a daughter of the eighth Earl of Strathmore. The Lyons —who afterwards took the additional name of Bowes—were among the oldest and most distinguished families in Scottish history. Moreover their own history shows them to have been men who lived always strenuously and often dangerously and not seldom died violently. Sir John Lyon was killed in a duel in 1383, the eighth Baron Glamis in a fight between his followers and those of Crawford in 1578, the sixth Earl of Strathmore in 'a scuffle' in 1725. They died not only in their own quarrels, for two were killed at Flodden and one at Sheriffmuir in 1715, and a later Lyon was murdered in India by the Nabob of Bengal in 1763. The sixth Lord Glamis, dying early, left a widow and a son who were accused of plotting the murder 'by witchcraft or poison' of King James V of Scotland. Lady Glamis was burned alive at Edinburgh and her son was also condemned to death. He was a minor at the time and, by the curious mercy of his day, he was ordered to be closely confined in prison, there to contemplate the approach of the day which would bring both his majority and his execution, but happily he was saved by the discovery that the whole plot was a fabrication.

Unlike the Lambtons, whose devotion to the House of Stuart did not survive the Catholic James II, the Lyons were Jacobites and tradition tells that the Old Pretender had eighty beds made up at Glamis Castle for himself and his suite in 1715.

Such a world of darkness and violence with the romantic devotion to a fallen dynasty and with the dim shape of Glamis in the background seems a long way from the tranquil daylight of Lambton, but it is not altogether fanciful to see in it a possible source of one side of Lord Durham's character. As it was he fought in one duel and, had he lived a few centuries earlier, he would undoubtedly have been involved in quarrels between his own supporters and those of his enemies. Nor was he without a streak of such romance as might have brought him to Sheriffmuir or Culloden.

William Lambton, his father, married Lady Anne Barbara Frances Villiers, a daughter of the fourth Earl of Jersey. The Villiers were no fighting Scottish chieftains but courtiers and administrators who held such high positions as Master of the Horse, Ambassador Extraordinary and Lord Marshal of the Household under both Stuarts and their successors. They were men of culture and affairs, citizens of the great world, and, again, it may be something more than fancy that sees in Lord Durham something of their qualities.

Lord Durham's wealth may have been less important than his heredity, but it plainly had its effect upon him. The family had for many years been large landowners and well-to-do, and, though they had suffered some loss of land and fortune for their part in the Civil War, the rising prices of land and corn after the Revolution restored them to all of their former substance and more. But the main source of their increased wealth was coal and, as the demand for it rose all over the country, their incomes rose with it. It was a golden age for those families like them and like the Stuarts and the Fitzwilliams who had rich deposits of coal under their farmlands and, before the end of the eighteenth century, the Lambtons were among the richest commoners in England. Their ideas grew with their resources and, like so many of their fellow-aristocrats, they developed a taste for building large and lovely houses. The old halls of Lambton and Harraton had sufficed for earlier generations but William Lambton no longer felt them to be suitable residences for a man of his standing. He began to pull down Harraton and to erect on its site the huge house which his son finished and, characteristically, renamed Lambton Castle. For the first time in their history, they showed a liking for that display of wealth and personal splendour which Lord Durham was to carry to such absurd lengths. William Lambton nursed and increased the family fortunes, sinking a new pit at Lambton in 1792. It was in that year or near to it, that the plans of the new house were drawn and next year Mr. Lambton started a pack of hounds of his own. His brother, Ralph, also a Member of Parliament, was a master of hounds in the neighbouring country and until then the Lambton men had hunted with that pack, but a pack of his own was a desirable addition to the consequence of any country gentleman, and by this time he knew that he might hope for an heir to carry them on after him. So kennels went up near the new house and the brothers came to an amicable agreement to divide the country between them.

But that was the material side of it and, though it was bound to affect the heir, it need not do so fundamentally. He might have inherited a half-built castle, a pack of hounds and an income of some £80,000 a year and have lived more luxuriously, more carelessly perhaps than his predecessors and yet not have differed very much from them. It was his nature not his circumstances that drove him to set out on new paths. Something in Lord Durham forbade him to be satisfied with his castle and his hounds and with all the simplicities which had contented his ancestors. They had been Knights of the Shire, but in him there was something of the Knight Errant and it sent him out into the world, looking for dragons to kill. He was never to have far to look in that tortured world in which he came to manhood. Only a few months after his birth in Berkeley Square, a Paris mob swept into the Tuileries and let loose a terror whose effects had not ended when he died, nearly fifty years later. His life was to be spent in an age of revolution and counter-revolution, of war in two continents and of the stirring of new ideas throughout the world.

He would live to see his own country on the brink of revolution and to save her greatest colony from the same danger, for his whole life was to be spent in a time when the old was at war with the new, privilege with democracy, tyranny with liberty, Michael and Lucifer struggling for victory in all men as they would be in his own heart. Before he was a year old France had known the September massacres and had seen her King and Queen on the scaffold, and in Britain the powers of re-action under Pitt were massing for the counter-attack. He was still a baby when Lieutenant-Colonel Buonaparte's batteries opened fire on Toulon and the first dark shadow began to spread over Europe and out into the New World beyond the Atlantic. It could never be an easy world for the men who were to grow up to grapple with its problems, least of all for him, in whom heredity had already planted the seeds of sympathy with both old and new, the desire for fighting and great affairs with the underlying love of the tranquil life of his home and country-side. But that tranquillity and the sure support of a settled home he was to lose before he had come to know it, for when he was only four years old his father died.

CHAPTER III

Lord Durham never really recovered from the effect of those first years which robbed him of the love, the companionship, and the discipline of his parents and especially of his father. It is natural for children to want praise and admiration and to look for them to their parents. Had the boy's father been there to applaud his acting in childish plays, to watch him take his pony over his first jump, to admire some toy or piece of handi-work, he might well have been less clamorous for admiration in later life. 'Watch me!' is an innocent and natural request from a child, but in a grown man its repetition soon becomes weari-some and ridiculous.

It was not only admiration that he lacked nor even com-panionship, but also that discipline which only parents can give. Children, as is well known, need restraint and not only need it but long for it, being frightened of their own aggression, so that if it is withheld they become worse and more persistent in their offence, knowing that they cannot stop themselves and terrified because no one will stop them. There is a good deal of such childish aggression to be seen in the later obstinacy with which

Lord Durham persisted in some chosen course against all reason and in face of all opposition.

No later discipline, at school or elsewhere, can replace that earliest sort which is the outcome and the proof of love. Nor indeed can the discipline of the averagely happy nursery, which he lacked, be overrated, for nowhere are more home truths spoken and less resented than between brothers and sisters. William, the younger brother, was all Lambton, a placid, pleasant child who soon became completely dominated by his tempestuous elder and must, on the evidence of their earliest reports from school, have had to endure not a little bullying. Hedworth, the other boy, was little more than a baby when the elder boys were sent away to school, and Frances, the only girl, was brought up, as girls then were, very much apart from her brothers. When Mr. Lambton died, John, the heir, was five, William Henry four, Frances Susan three and Hedworth under a year old. Even John's position as the heir set him a little apart from and above the others so that he lacked not only the checks which he might have had from his father but much of the outspoken criticism which is the prerogative of brother and sister.

William Lambton died of that consumption which was to be a more fatal curse to the family than any that the Lambton Worm may have laid on them. For the last few years of his life, he was with his wife and children in Italy, where the doctors had hoped that rest and sunlight might restore him or at any rate prolong his life. During that time he took all possible steps to see that his children should be properly cared for and educated after his death. He left them in charge of his wife and of two guardians, Ralph Lambton, his brother, and Mr. Wilkinson, a solicitor of Newcastle, his oldest and closest friend. All of them are important figures in the story of the next few years and much of their voluminous correspondence has been preserved. Lady Anne's part in the story is a little pathetic since she meant so well by the children and did them unwittingly so much harm. She was always a loving though seldom a judicious mother, but her children were not her first interest. She was still young when she was left a widow and had no mind to retire for ever into the obscurity of the nursery or of that home in the cold and remote north country. She came from a gayer and less secluded world than her husband and soon returned to it, for when John was nine, she married the Honourable Charles Windham and later became Countess of Egremont. She never lost her interest in the children nor they their love for her, but it was a spasmodic interest and much complicated by her impulsive nature and her chronic inability to manage her own finances. Her erratic attempts to intervene in their educational problems, amusing as they are to read of in her letters, soon became a burden to the guardians and something of a danger to the two older boys.

As far as the guardians were concerned, Mr. Lambton could hardly have made a better choice and Mr. Wilkinson, especially, emerges in the correspondence as the best friend and wisest counsellor whom the boys were ever to know. He had been closely connected with all Mr. Lambton's affairs, with his estate, his collieries, and his more private finances and he knew exactly what his ideas for the children were and was determined to see them carried out, though this often brought him into collision with Lady Anne and with his colleague. Ralph Lambton was honest and conscientious in his discharge of his duties but, when mother and guardians differed, he was always ready to take Lady Anne's side, probably because they were both members of the family. Wilkinson, not being a Lambton, looked upon all questions affecting the trust with a dispassionate eye and was free from the feeling which occasionally affected the others that because they wished for something it was right and necessary that they should have it. Lady Anne was often occupied with her social engagements and her own private life, Mr. Ralph had his hounds and his Parliamentary responsibilities, so, fortunately, it fell to Mr. Wilkinson to do the heavy work of the trust, to correspond with schools and tradesmen, and to arrange such details as journey money and the purchase of clothes and other necessities. The far larger number of his letters in comparison with any others is a proof of the devotion with which he carried out the wishes of his dead friend.

The first question to be dealt with was that of the boys' education until they should be old enough to go to Eton. Their father, who had been at Eton as a very small boy and had suffered untold misery there from bullying and near-starvation, had determined that none of the boys were to go until they were old enough to take care of themselves, which, for the elder two, meant until John should be at least ten. They were growing too big for the nursery and something had to be found for them to fill in the gap. As usual it was Mr. Wilkinson who found the answer, when he remembered his old friend, Dr. Beddoes of Clifton.

Beddoes had been Professor of Chemistry at Oxford but had been forced to leave after having expressed himself too freely in favour of the French Revolution. He had gone to Clifton where he set up the oddly named Pneumatic Institute, whose main object was chemical research into problems connected with gases. One of his assistants there was Humphry Davy, who later came to great distinction as the inventor of the Davy Safety Lamp for use in coal-mines.

Davy's correspondence suggests that he was not happy at Clifton and no doubt his double role of usher and laboratory assistant was tedious and ill-paid. He liked Mrs. Beddoes, whom he described as 'Gay, cheerful and witty. She is one of the most pleasing women I ever met with.' He was more severe on her husband—'short and fat with little elegance of manners . . . extremely silent and in a few words, a bad companion.'

Again the boys were fortunate. Beddoes, whatever his faults as an employer, was not only a distinguished scientist and physician, with a growing medical practice in Clifton, but also an intelligent and humane man with wide interests. His wife was a sister of Maria Edgeworth, the novelist, and had many friends in the literary world, so that the boys were introduced at an early age to a wider and more cultured circle than would otherwise have been their lot. Southey and Coleridge were among the literary figures who visited the house at Clifton, where the course of studies went far beyond the conventional Latin and Greek of the age.

This was Beddoes' deliberate intention. He wrote to Wilkinson: 'If in such times we may depend on the stability of property, it would be a matter of some consequence to give a young man of immense fortunes some inclination and power to be useful.'

He did not neglect the Classics—Lambton learned to write graceful Latin verse—but he added to them mathematics,

algebra, botany, physics, French and a curiously named subject, Moral Relations, which seems to have been a form of elementary economics. Beddoes was an educationalist far in
advance of his time and his aim was, as he said, 'to prepare the
boys to be men of public and private business'. Undoubtedly
they profited by this unusually liberal curriculum and the elder
especially had cause to be grateful to Beddoes when the Lambton Collieries became his responsibility.

Beddoes was diligent and sensitive in his dealings with the
children and gave them far more individual care than they
would have got at an ordinary school. He reported regularly to
the guardians and the letters, which have been preserved, show
how keenly he appreciated the signs of the difference in the two
characters. William, the younger, was a pleasant and normal
boy, who presented few problems, but John was much more
difficult and complicated.

The boy had been outrageously spoiled in his earliest years
and came to Clifton obviously expecting the whole establishment to be run for his exclusive convenience and his will to be
paramount. Most schoolmasters of the day would have tried to
cure him with the birch and might well have ruined him in the
process. Beddoes soon realized that he was a boy who would
respond to reason and persuasion and that force would only
make him stubborn and might drive him to some act of desperation. 'There are times,' he wrote, 'when his eyes are on
fire, his cheeks flushed and, in the paroxysm, I have little doubt
but he would run against a drawn sword or jump down a
precipice.' He remarked, too, that when one of Lady Anne's
rare visits was imminent, John became so excited that he was
almost uncontrollable.

Dr. Beddoes was not only an acute observer of a child's mind,
but he was a skilful physician and, when John was nine, he
wrote a grave letter to Ralph Lambton warning him that the
boy already showed a marked tendency towards consumption. He
insisted that for many years to come John and all who were connected with him would have to exercise the utmost watchfulness.

In 1800 the symptoms which he described were enough to
terrify both Lady Anne and the guardians. 'There are in-
dubitable signs about John of a constitution prone to consumption. Though stout and healthy, the bleeding from the nose and

the state of glands with other appearances demonstrate the necessity of persevering to guard his constitution against the fatal calamity.' Again, in the following year, he writes of 'frequent and large bleedings at the nose and a swelling of glands in the neck', adding, 'You have observed perhaps the length of his neck and how his shoulder-blades stand off like wings.'

Lady Anne's alarm took the form of irrationally blaming Dr. Beddoes for not having discovered and reported the weakness earlier, though probably she did him less than justice, for few schoolmasters could have watched their pupils' health with more anxious care. Apparently Ralph Lambton agreed with her and also with another suggestion, which she had made, for he wrote:

> 'I agree with you in thinking the Doctor may consider more the advantage he may gain by their stay than their health and most undoubtedly it appears strange, as you observe, that he never till now informed us that John was likely from his Form to be of a consumptive Habit.'

If Lady Anne did Dr. Beddoes less than justice, Mr. Lambton was positively unfair, for the advantage which Dr. Beddoes was gaining at the moment was limited by the extreme difficulty which he was experiencing in getting his bills paid. At the very time when Mr. Lambton was so gravely traducing him, he was vainly appealing to Lady Anne for a payment on account of what she owed him. In May 1801, she wrote indignantly to Ralph Lambton:

> 'I told him a few days ago he should have 580 £ on the 30th of next month, which is all I can give him and will nearly (when you have paid for expenses), pay everything up to March. He never would send in his a/c regularly, or this would not have happened. When the boys went home, I told him you had nothing to do with the payment of any one thing belonging to them. I am *quite vexed at him*—God knows the state of my *finances at this moment.*'

Money for the boys' education had been left in trust, but there was an extraordinary arrangement by which the trustees paid the fees to Lady Anne, who was supposed to pay the school. It was at this point that the arrangement broke down, for Lady

Anne was perpetually hard up and had no scruples in keeping the money for her own use. In this same year of 1801, Dr. Beddoes had complained to Mr. Wilkinson: 'Of the remittances from her Ladyship, not one was ever referred to any particular object and altogether, they do not amount to what I have advanced on the joint account.' Nor were the expenses which Dr. Beddoes had to advance a light matter, since they included the cost of journeys to and from Lambton, which he calculated, 'as in 1798, at eighteenpence a mile all included. I mean this to be rather below the mark. The distance I make 287 miles— £43.1.0. a head.'

When the boys grew older and went on to Eton, there was no improvement in the financial arrangements, and when they left in 1808, the Lambton Trust owed the College over £1,200. This was shocking to Mr. Wilkinson who was an honest man of business and he wrote bitterly to his fellow-trustee:

'If henceforward she should (as unfortunately and un-expectedly she hitherto has done), apply the money allowed for them to other purposes than those intended, in what disgraceful situations will the children be placed? What a stigma and a reproach will it be to the Guardians, what culpability indeed must attach to them if they wink at and allow such proceedings—I speak not from what *may* be. I reason from what *has* been. Is it to be credited that Lady Anne should have been behind in her payments to their Dame for board and lodging, to their Tutor, to their Trades-men, etc. at Eton upwards of £600 and that this Christmas, on their final departure from school, she should owe on the like account upwards of £1,200?'

It was an unfortunate thing for the boys that their guardians were not always in agreement and that Lady Anne could often count on the support of Mr. Lambton against his fellow-trustee. Mr. Wilkinson at least realized what harm might result from these differences, when he wrote: 'You know so well the difference between Mr. Ralph Lambton and me, that you will not expect much communications to pass between us—but it would be hard indeed on the children that because we are not on terms their Interests should suffer.' More than once he suggested that they should take the childrens' affairs altogether out of their mother's hands. It would indeed appear that he

27

took a much more rigid and conscientious view of his duties as a trustee than did his colleague, for Mr. Lambton, finding himself faced with some very heavy election expenses went so far as to suggest that the Trust should lend him the necessary money —a request which Mr. Wilkinson very properly and indignantly refused to countenance.

Between Lady Anne and the guardians, Dr. Beddoes must have had anything but an easy time of it and there is little reason to believe Ralph Lambton's suggestion that he wanted to keep the boys at Clifton for his own benefit rather than theirs. The voluminous correspondence between the three makes it clear that, while Wilkinson had selected Beddoes' school, the other two had never really liked the idea and were always anxious to remove the boys, either to another preparatory school or to Eton. Lady Anne must have been a perfect nuisance, for she was constantly hearing of schools which, she was certain, would be more suitable for the boys than Clifton. She writes of a school of Streatham: 'The terms are nearly £100 a year. The school is very highly spoken of. Sir Thomas Liddel's brother is there', and of 'Mitcham, where there is also a school of great repute'. Ralph Lambton counters with Dr. Maule's school, as being highly recommended by Lord George Cavendish: 'I really think if we take the Boys from Dr. Beddoes in Sept. we can't do better than send them to him till they are ready for the Upper School at Eton.' There is, too, in the correspondence, a letter from a Mr. Lloyd of Petersby House, who writes that 'The Terms of my Seminary are still, not withstanding the Times, £80 per Annum and five entrance. In these we include the Classics, French, Geography the Globes, Writing and Arithmetic, Reading; all but the first by really good masters residing in the House. The first taught by me and by a genteel young man who is my Usher.' It must be held greatly to Dr. Beddoes' credit that he stoutly and successfully resisted these attempts to remove the boys from his care in favour of whatever happened to be their mother's fancy of the moment; still more that he resisted the suggestion that they should go early to Eton, in direct opposition to their father's often expressed wish.

In 1801 Mr. Ralph, probably incited by Lady Anne, made a more than usually determined attempt to get the boys away from Clifton. Once more Beddoes fought for them and won. 'You will do right,' he wrote, 'to send *both* boys to a public school. Set that point down as settled—But I would intreat their guardians in the name of the boys to consider one question— whether a year's delay can produce any disadvantage to be set in competition with *an improvement in their constitution.*'

The boys were not removed earlier than had been planned and they owed their escape partly to Beddoes' determination and partly to Wilkinson's invariable support of him. Wilkinson had been William Lambton's friend and spoke with the authority of a man who fully understood his wishes for his sons. A close study of the correspondence leaves little doubt that he had the right on his side and was genuinely anxious to carry out the father's wishes. It leaves none at all that Ralph Lambton's suspicions of Beddoes were unjustified and that Lady Anne was nothing but a nuisance, whose preoccupation with the fees of other schools was not unconnected with her own financial vagaries. Perhaps only Dr. Beddoes realized what a harmful effect the disturbed home atmosphere had on the boys and especially on the elder.

CHAPTER IV

Thomas Wilkinson's confidence in his old friend was abundantly justified and all credit is due to Dr. Beddoes for his devotion to the boys and for his stout resistance to their mother's attempts to interfere. He knew all about these attempts and mentioned in a letter to Wilkinson in 1801 that 'Some time ago Lady Anne dropped in a letter to John her design of taking them from this place next September'. Lady Anne's indiscretion in mentioning her intention to the children must have been very unsettling for them and was obviously most unfair to Beddoes, who was doing all that he could to prepare them for the responsibilities which would one day be theirs. This thought was always in his mind especially about John, who would have to cope with the problems of a flourishing coal business as well as of a large landed estate. It is evident that, as soon as the boys went to him, he recognized the difference in their temperaments and that, at first the elder boy caused him a good deal of anxiety. In that year—almost as soon as he had got to know them—he wrote: 'Although John is less prepossessing than Billy, yet I think him not at all inferior in talents or disposition and very little in quickness.' Beddoes had a knowledge of child psychology which was astonishingly in advance of his time and, from his careful and regular reports to the guardians, we can get a clear picture of the child John Lambton throughout the seven years which he spent at Clifton.

He was not prepossessing at first—we have Beddoes word for it. He had been outrageously spoilt at home and he tyrannized over his younger brother. Yet towards the end of that year, Beddoes had already perceived the real goodness that was always in his nature and had realized that the usual harsh treatment then dealt out to troublesome children would irretrievably damage him. 'If the boy had been abused or beaten as obstinate,' he wrote to Wilkinson, 'he would turn out as malicious a tyrant as any the North of England is blessed with.' He soon found that John responded to his humane methods and that he could admit and try to correct his own faults. In that year, he took the boys to visit a Lady Holte, 'who is here—old and jaundiced. That day she was of a blackish yellow and her deshabille did not set her off to any advantage. John turned short round and would not be persuaded to go near her . . . next day he apologized.' It is very like the man who quarrelled with Cam Hobhouse over politics and then took the first steps towards renewing the friendship; who, after the débâcle of Canada, refused to meet any member of the Cabinet and yet, at the end, dined with Melbourne and did not refuse to shake hands with Brougham. The boy was impulsive and, at that age, under the sway of his emotions, and both distaste and enthusiasm were easily aroused in him. In the same letter Beddoes wrote: 'We must only take care that his propensity to enthusiasm does not take the turns of debauchery at school and college or of gambling in after life.' As it turned out, in a time and a society which was greatly given to both, Lord Durham showed no interest in either, and it may be that some credit for his abstention is due to Beddoes' insight. The boy began to expand and to relax in the liberal atmosphere of that household and to show a taste for learning and a proud delight in his own progress. 'It is astonishing,' Beddoes wrote in 1801, 'what a happy effect his success in learning has had upon his temper— He used to tyrannize over Billy when vexed—now he generally treats him with great kindness.'

The freedom of the curriculum appealed to all that was eager and inquiring in John's nature and its effects are clearly to be seen in his intellectual alertness when he became a man. He was never a classical scholar in the sense that Fox and Melbourne were, but he was a competent Latinist with a taste for verse. In 1801 a translation which he had made of a Horace ode was thought good enough to be sent to his mother for her admiration—perhaps too for her encouragement, for it was at that time that Beddoes was writing almost despairingly to Wilkinson asking him 'to give me credit with your banker's for the boys' stay with me from the first week of September 1798 to do. of March 1801. the balance of John's account. Having received nothing on the first account and made advances, I find myself almost aground.'

Next year Beddoes suggested 'the idea of a scientific tutor for John and William, that is of a person who understands mathematics chemistry etc—I know this is an extraordinary measure. The spirit of reflection is so strong in John that I am sure it will never be quelled though it may hereafter serve but to torment him.' At the same time he was forced to plead yet once more that the boys should not be taken away from him. In April he wrote: 'I wish most sincerely to keep them till May 1803 as I cannot finish my plan in less time. . . . I will challenge Eton and Westminster to produce me two such boys of their age who have so much insight into the persons about them or who could go through the world like John and William Lambton.'

Beddoes was a persistent man and, with Wilkinson's help, he carried his point, for the boys stayed until 1805. He may fairly have claimed to have fulfilled his boast of their accomplishments since he wrote of John: 'He can never forget that at ten and a half he could write Latin and Greek, both prose and verse, and that he was advanced in arithmetic, algebra and Euclid and that he was beginning to have information in chemistry and some other subjects.' Among the other things which John Lambton owed to this strangely advanced system of education was his unvarying ability in public life to express himself both in speech and writing in crisp and lucid prose. He was always economical with words and his Parliamentary speeches were remarkable for their brevity at a time when it was not one of the virtues required of an orator. They were also, it is worthy of note, free from any suggestion of pedantry and it is extremely rare to find in them any quotation from a language other than his own. Certainly they were always free from the wearisome affectation of the Latin tag which is a blemish on much of the contemporary oratory.

If, as it would appear, Beddoes' oddly named subject, 'Moral Relations' included what would now be called 'Current Affairs', both boys must have been aware of the shadow which was growing and darkening over all Europe as the names of Rivoli, Castiglione, Arcola, and Marengo were blazoned on the French colours and France which had opened the gates to Liberty turned to the task of destroying it. Pitt and the Tories made their contribution to the work in 1799 when they passed the Combination Laws, which made it a penal offence for two or more workmen to join together in any association to seek higher wages or shorter hours. They were not repealed until 1824, for the spirit of reaction and repression was growing in England. The fight against it was to be one of John Lambton's first and most consistent tasks from the beginning of his public life.

It is easy to see in the boy who left Clifton in 1805, the year of Trafalgar and Austerlitz, a foreshadowing of the man that he would be, in his fierce aversions and enthusiasms, his emotional instability, his dawning intellectual power, and in his readiness to repair wrong that he had done and his thirst for praise and encouragement. When he left he owed a great debt to Dr. Beddoes, to whom his mother owed by this time the best part of a thousand pounds.

There is very little recorded about his life at Eton. He seldom spoke of it in after life and we do not know whether he was happy there or not. He made no great stir in that little world and almost the only reference to him is a remark in Creasey's *Reminiscences of an Old Etonian* that 'Lambton was inclined to the popular rather than the oligarchical system of government'. It sounds rather like something written in the light of later knowledge but probably only means—if it means anything at all—that he was not one of the oligarchy of the college. He was not distinguished as a scholar, and perhaps Dr. Beddoes' rather advanced curriculum was not the best preparation for the severely classical learning of Eton. It is not surprising that he made little mark there. His talents were such as to need a wider sphere and a more free scope than those of the playing field or the sixth form room. Conventionality is the best way to distinction at a public school and he was never a notable conformer. There is, in the possession of the Lambton family, an exquisite miniature of him in the costume which he wore at the summer festival of 'Montem', but the only other interest in his schooldays lies in the names of some of the boys who were there at the same time—Percy Bysshe Shelley, Charles Greville, Stratford Canning, whose appointment as Ambassador to Russia was to be a source of trouble to him, and Thomas Turton, the future source of more than embarrassment in Canada.

Lambton's guardians had intended that he should go on from Eton to Edinburgh University, but he had ideas of his own and they were brought to realize the strength of his will when he had set his heart on any course. In 1808 he told them that he had decided to go into the Army. Wilkinson was distressed, though it was a very natural desire for any young man of spirit in that year which was to see the French armies pouring into Spain and Wellington taking his first steps at Roliça and Vimeiro towards that victory which he was only to achieve after seven years of hard fighting. There had been other soldiers in the family and in his own blood was the fighting strain of Lyon. Wilkinson's objection was that the Army was no fit career for a man whose first duty was to his own estates and industry. Soldiering, he felt, might be all very well for a year or two, but it could only postpone the day when the heir would have to assume his proper responsibilities.

He wrote: 'What is to become of your extensive concerns and how can the attention necessary for the management of your property be given if you are drawn off by other occupations. . . . Feeling as I do on this subject, I am bound to give you my sentiments upon it. They are short but, such as they are, I heartily wish that they may divert you from your purpose.' He added a warning that, 'If this profession be not seriously and diligently followed up it becomes a life of idleness and dissipation, in either of which views, I trust, you would abhor it from the bottom of your heart . . . if it is pursued as it should be, then it is of so laborious a nature that, in my opinion it will be more than your constitution is equal to.' Wilkinson's unfailing goodness of heart comes out in the final assurance, 'If you are at last to be a soldier, nothing shall be omitted on my part to promote your happiness and honour in your profession and by every means in my power to further your interest and advancement.'

Since Lambton was resolute there was nothing that his guardians could do but find a suitable regiment for him. There was talk of the Coldstream Guards, his grandfather's regiment, or of the county regiment, the 68th, but he wanted the cavalry. Ralph Lambton was on friendly terms with the Prince Regent and arranged for his nephew to have a commission in the Prince's regiment, the Tenth Light Dragoons, later the Tenth Hussars.

There are few records of his service with the Tenth and he only spent two years with them. The Army List shows that he was promoted to Lieutenant—presumably by purchase—in 1809, and letters which passed between him and his guardians that his allowance was, at Mr. Ralph's suggestion, raised then to £800 a year. It was an adequate but not an excessive allowance for a subaltern in the most fashionable cavalry regiment of the day, in which an officer's outfit cost not less than £400 and might at any moment be completely changed at the whim of the Prince Regent, the regiment's Colonel-in-Chief.

The only other mention of his soldiering days is found in the reminiscences of Harriet Wilson, the most eminent prostitute in London, whose clientele was almost exclusively noble and included, if her word can be accepted, the Dukes of Argyll and Wellington, the Marquesses of Hertford and Worcester, and the Earl of Craven. It certainly did not include Lambton who had neither then nor at any time, a taste for such dissipations. It was probably for that reason that she disliked him and wrote: 'I do not know what these young Lambtons are good for except sulkiness. I remember the officers of the 10th Dragoons, to which regiment the eldest Lambton formerly belonged, declare that he had contrived so to prejudice the whole regiment against him that there was no rest for himself or his brother officers till he left it.' There is no confirmation of this spiteful comment, nor need Miss Wilson's animosity be considered as anything but a compliment, but it would be interesting to know the reason for Lambton's sudden decision to resign his commission. It may be that he had thought over Wilkinson's advice. It seems more likely that the real reason was that he had just met the lady whom he hoped to make his wife.

While he was still serving, he got into his first financial scrape and caused Mr. Wilkinson some anxiety by asking for £500 to pay 'a poor painter' who had painted two portraits of him. The painter's name was Strachling and he seems to have been a shifty and unpleasant rogue as well as an incompetent artist. In 1809 the Tenth were under orders to join Sir John Moore's army in the Peninsular, though in the end only one squadron went and Lambton was not among its officers. Most subalterns nowadays, in such circumstances, have their photographs taken. Lambton ordered from Strachling the two portraits, one for his mother and the other for his sister Fanny. With his usual carelessness about money he had not made proper inquiries about the artist's price and, not having enough cash to pay it, gave bonds payable when he should come of age, adding that, should he be killed in action, his guardians would see that the 'poor artist' did not suffer.

Wilkinson had no intention of confirming what was obviously an unfair bargain and, with the help of Mr. Ralph and an art expert, disposed of Strachling's claim. He wrote in friendly reproach to Lambton: 'I trust that you will not engage in these bargains in any shape. I would almost as soon hear of you throwing yourself into the hands of the Jews, for both lead much to the same end.' With characteristic kindness his letter ends with the words: 'As you seem to be short of cash, I send you a note for £20.'

Lambton's reply was equally characteristic in its frank admission of folly:

'My dear Sir,
I am much obliged to you for your letter and hope you

35

will never think I have any idea to slight your advice. . . .
When I first desired him to undertake the pictures, I give
you my honour I thought they would be at the utmost £50
apiece. You may then conceive my astonishment when, *after*
they were sent home, he informed me his constant price was
£500 apiece. . . . He then continually annoyed me with the
most vulgar letters, to induce me to sign an acknowledge-
ment, which at last I was obliged to do, knowing that I was
utterly unable to pay that sum at present. This is the account
of that transaction into which I have fallen through my own
inadvertence in not making him fix his price at first. This I
have related to you, as well as to my uncle, that you may
not think I wish to conceal anything from you. . . .'

Strachling's letters confirmed this account of the transaction
in their insolence and shiftiness, but Wilkinson had dealt with
his sort before and there the matter ended. Lambton's next
activity was to be much more serious and to give his guardians
cause for more anxiety.

CHAPTER V

Lambton had fallen in love with Miss Henrietta Cholmondeley,
the natural daughter of Lord Cholmondeley by Madame St.
Alban, a French actress on the English stage. Kirkpatrick
Sharpe, a family friend, wrote that she was a beauty and so
much more charming than Lady Charlotte, the legitimate
daughter, that 'it made Lady Cholmondeley very glad to get
rid of her'. She had been brought up with the legitimate
children and it cannot have been an easy situation for her.
Probably her invidious position appealed to Lambton's
chivalry as much as her charm to his heart, but he seems to
have realized that his own family might be less enthusiastic.
He was only nineteen and, as he doubted whether he would get
their consent, he refrained from asking for it and carried her off
to Gretna Green, where they were married on 1 January 1812.
It was not a very gracious way in which to treat his mother
and the guardians who had always dealt fairly with him, but

even a suspicion of opposition would always be enough to arouse all the obstinacy that was in him.

The pair went straight from Gretna Green to Cholmondeley Castle and from there, at the earnest entreaty of both families, they went a few weeks later to Malpas Church, in Cheshire, where they were formally married again. Lambton Castle was ready to receive them though it was not quite finished. It had been built to the design of the elder Bonomi, a well-known Durham architect and the original design for a Hall was being converted into a Castle with turrets and battlements.

If it was a fake, it was a lovely one. Bonomi had chosen a stone of a mellow biscuit colour and the towers rose above the steep wooded slope that runs down to the River Wear and the Lamb Bridge. There were acres of garden with glass houses, and a lawn running from the side of the house to the battlemented wall on top of the bluff where the trees begin. On the other side of the river, the land rises again steeply and a long sweep of parkland runs past the old site of Lambton Hall, where now only the lovely Brewery Cottages remain, to the flat pastures in which, a year or two later a race-course was laid out. At first this was only used for private matches between Lambton's horses and those of his friends, but later there were public meetings at which horses from all over the North competed. (Thomas Slingsby Duncombe, who became a great friend of Lambton and who was one of the best gentleman riders in England, first met him when he came to ride in a meeting there.) The last meeting was held in 1825, and there is a pathetic entry in Lady Durham's diary about her husband and son—the 'Master Lambton' of Lawrence's famous portrait, who had so few years to live. 'At the last Lambton races,' she wrote, 'he rode on the course with his papa and it was beautiful to see him cantering down past all the carriages and horses.'

There were sixty couple of hounds in the kennels. William Lambton had bought them from the Sudbury (now the Meynell) country and when he died, his brother Ralph had taken charge of them and continued to hunt four or five days a week with them and with his own pack. Later, as the collieries began to encroach on their country, he concentrated both packs near his own home. In 1838 a severe fall put an end to his hunting and the Lambton pack was sold to Lord Suffield, the master of the Quorn, but, a few years later, they were sold again to Sir Matthew White Ridley and returned to the North. There are accounts of runs with them in Nimrod's *Northern Tours* and Robert Surtees of Hamsterley, the author of the Handley Cross novels, left a warm appreciation of Ralph Lambton as a man and as a master of hounds. Lambton and his wife were only to have a few years of life together, but they were happy years. There were lights and music in the great house and carriages bearing guests toiled up the steep hill beneath the trees and wheeled on the gravelled sweep before the battlemented porch. At night on days of festival the house could be seen from many miles away when all its windows were golden with the new gaslight which Lambton had installed; Beddoes' teaching had had its effect in his unending interest in scientific experiment, and it was among the first—if not the first—of the great country houses to be entirely lit by gas. Later, Sydney Smith wrote to his friend Lady Mary Bennett, 'What use of wealth so luxurious and delightful as to light your house with gas? The splendour and glory of Lambton makes all other houses mean.'

In summer there was cricket and the score-book for the year 1812—the year of Borodino and Salamanca and of the storming of Badajoz—has been preserved. The record even for that year is incomplete but there is enough to show that Lambton was something more than an averagely good club cricketer. During July and August—the only months for which complete figures remain—he took sixty-one wickets and his batting average was:

Runs	Innings	Time not out	Highest score	Average
612	24	I	99 (not out)	22.26

He always went in first and, if he maintained that standard through the rest of the season, he probably made over a thousand runs, no mean achievement in any club cricket, especially in those days of natural grass wickets. His brother William was a regular player, though not apparently as good, and the list includes many names well known in the North—Fenwick, Riddell, Beckwith and the like. Bonomi appears once, when he made a duck.

On the last pages of the book there is an intriguing list headed 'Fines' and every player, except Lambton himself, apparently incurred a fine of five shillings nearly every time. No explanation is given and it would be interesting to know for what offence the fines were incurred. Were they penalties for dropped catches? If so, the standard of fielding must have been desperately poor and it is hard to believe that Lambton never missed a chance. Perhaps they were for late arrival at matches —as he lived next door to the ground, he would be most likely to be there when the game was due to start.

In 1812 it was all very peaceful and remote from the endless steppes of Russia and the smoking breaches of Badajoz and Ciudad Roderigo, and, behind the white sails of her fleet, England went on her old peaceful ways. In April of the following year Lambton came of age and took possession of his estate, his vast colliery business, and an income which was little short of £80,000 a year.

But already there was a shadow over Lambton Castle and, as the greater shadow dwindled at Bautzen and Dresden and Leipzig, it steadily grew bigger. At the end of 1812 the doctors were seriously concerned about Henrietta's health and next year it was plain that she was wasting away in consumption. She bore three children, all girls, but the taint passed on to all of them and none were to live beyond their early twenties. Frances Charlotte, the eldest, who married The Hon. J. G. Ponsonby, afterwards Earl of Bessborough, in 1835 died on Christmas Eve of the same year. Georgina Elizabeth died, unmarried, in 1832 and Harriet Caroline, also unmarried, in 1833.

In 1813 and 1814, too, the doctors had reason for concern about Lambton. They knew that Beddoes had suspected him of a liability to consumption and themselves feared that his diagnosis had been true. They watched with growing anxiety the first onset of those terrible neuralgic pains which were to attack him at intervals throughout his life. The doctors called them the migraine or neuralgia but were uncertain of their cause and unable to find any effective treatment. They also noticed what they called, a little vaguely, 'a disorder of the liver' which was also to trouble him later in life.

The neuralgic pains were his greatest curse and their effect on him was always devastating. They came, the doctors who watched him noticed, whenever he became excited or angry—

and he was often both—and after strenuous exertion. A long day with the hounds or an especially thrilling finish to a race would often prostrate him and there seemed to be no treatment other than to lie in a darkened room until the agony burned itself out. They urged him to take life more quietly, to give up his hunting and racing, to restrict his diet and to take little or no wine, but he would not listen to them. He would not give up his sport, especially his racing, which, until later in life he took to yachting, was always his favourite sport. He loved entertaining his friends and loved and understood good wine and food, though, in a hard-drinking age, he was never given to excess. He had not come to his estate to live the life of a premature invalid and even those hours and days of pain were not too high a price to pay for living as he chose, but they had a grave effect on his temper, which had never been easy and became increasingly violent as he grew older. There was nothing but common sense to support the medical advice and that never weighed much with him against his own will, so the doctors could only hope that he might grow out of his troubles or that continued pain might discipline him.

For Henrietta they dared not hope; it could only be a question of how many more months they could prolong her life. There was a suggestion that she might benefit from a warmer climate and talk of moving to Italy, but the Member of Parliament for County Durham, Sir Henry Vane Tempest, died suddenly and Lambton, as a matter of course, was asked to take his place. He was reluctant because of his wife's health but at least it would mean long periods in the south of England and some escape from the hard northern winters and family tradition was strong in him. Ralph Lambton was member for the City of Durham, but resigned within a few months, feeling that it would not be fair that the two Durham seats should be held by members of the same family.

Lambton made his first speech in the Commons in a debate on foreign affairs. At Vienna the statesmen of Europe were trying to make plans for a durable peace and it was inevitable that, even in an atmosphere of high intentions, there should be some sordid bargaining at the expense of weaker powers. It was appropriate that Lambton, who was to spend so much of his life in the defence of the oppressed, should have begun his career in the cause of the unfortunate Norwegians, whom Alexander of Russia and Castlereagh proposed to hand over to Sweden as a reward to Crown Prince Bernadotte for turning traitor to the Emperor Napoleon. The big Powers ignored Norway's plea for her liberty and threatened her with invasion by Sweden, backed by the further threat of British troops.

Lambton spoke forcibly and, as ever, briefly against the dishonest bargain, acknowledging that 'I view with horror a free people delivered up at the barrier of diplomatic convenience and I confess I see with deepest sympathy their rights bartered away and their feelings outraged by being consigned to the power of their most inveterate enemies'. It was the first of many such pleas for liberty that he was to make and as ineffective as most of them as long as Europe was dominated by Russia's combination of lofty thoughts and selfish actions and Castlereagh's cold pragmatism. His speech made a good impression in the House, where many members had heard his father pleading for liberty, and he was modest enough not to spoil the impression by trying to make himself heard too often. He did not speak again on any serious matter until the following year, 1815, when he opposed the retention of the Corn Laws. As a large landowner, he stood to gain by the inflated price of corn and land, but he knew what distress rising prices were causing in his own North Country. A few thousand pounds more or less to him were a small matter beside a halfpenny in the cost of a loaf to a labourer or a miner who had little but bread to live on.

It was only very reluctantly that he had come up to London to take part in the debate. Henrietta was not well enough to be moved from the North and every report that he had about her told him of her failing strength and of the futility of hope. Towards the end of the year the reports seemed to give up all hope and he went home to be with her for the little time that she had left. There could be no thought of Italy now or even of a move to London and, all through that winter and into the spring of 1815, he watched helplessly as she grew weaker and relinquished her hold on life. All England was waiting for news from Belgium where Wellington and the Emperor faced each other for the first time in their lives and among the killed at Waterloo was Major Howard who had married Frances Lambton, John's sister. In the same week Henrietta died.

Soon the mail coaches were travelling up and down the countryside bearing the news of Waterloo. Their horses had flowers in their headstalls and streamers and laurels covered box and boot. The beacons sprang into light round all the hills in Durham and all night the great houses were lit up, but there was no glow in the windows of Lambton where Henrietta lay waiting for her burial and her husband mourned for her and for his sister's loss. The double blow was shattering to him. His grief, as it was always to be at any family loss, was extravagant. It was perhaps the first time that those who had known him as a man realized the intensity of his emotions and his complete abandonment to them. For a while he seemed to have lost his interest in everything, his courage, even his desire to live. He abandoned himself wholly to his grief, refusing to go out or to admit anyone who came to the House, rejecting the least word of sympathy or comfort. He swore that he had finished with the world, that he would never go to London again, that he would throw away his care of the estate, his seat in Parliament. As ever, suffering of mind brought on his neuralgic pains and the everlasting agony in his head prostrated him, till those about him feared that he would soon follow Henrietta to the grave. He had friends in the county and he had made more friends in London, but he would have none of them. But he could not stop them from writing to him and among those who wrote was Henry Brougham, with whom he had become friendly at Westminster. They were both stout opponents of Tory repression and supporters of Parliamentary Reform. It had been the beginning of that odd relationship which was to pass from friendship to suspicion and from that to open enmity. The two had much in common for, beside their goodwill and compassion, they shared a certain domineering habit which was bound sooner or later to bring them into collision.

Now Brougham wrote to him:

'I believe that mental exertion and the forced effort to engage in old occupations are amongst the best means for the recovery of tranquillity of the mind. You have advantages over most men in the possession of a strong and vigorous understanding, and a laudable ambition to employ it in the best way. You have youth and an exterior so agreeable as to prepossess all who see you in your favour. You have gained a good name and the reputation of a zealous, honest public man. . . . I beseech you do not for a moment retire from that contest of public men and public affairs in which you are formed to shine and in which you are already so distinguished.'

In one of Lady Holland's letters to Lady Mary Bennett, there is a pathetic description of Lambton at this time in which she speaks of the house in which there was so much splendour and so much misery and of its owner finding his only comfort in the nursery with his children. With that admirable good sense which always distinguished her, she expresses a hope that he will soon marry again and provide himself with an heir.

Such an orgy of self-pity could not last for ever, or even, with a man of Lambton's courage and intelligence, for very long. He was young and mentally alert and, though he had sworn to withdraw from all public business, he had tasted the drug and could not do without it. He could not indefinitely ignore his friends or that inner voice which accused him of cowardice and urged him to go out and fight for his causes. Perhaps the very violence of his grief exhausted it and left him empty and ready for a more worthy life. He decided to leave his home for a while and to travel, first in Scotland and then on the Continent. All the world was in Paris that winter and he was drawn to it in the resurgence of his eager youth. He could have done nothing better, for, if he had ever really thought of retiring from politics, Paris in the winter of 1815 killed the idea for good.

'The worst of all revolutions,' Fox had once said, 'is a restoration', and what Lambton saw during those weeks was the naked tyranny of a Bourbon restoration. He never forgot it, for he saw what weakness and cruelty can achieve when they are hoisted into power. He wrote to Wilson:

'Nothing can exceed the distress which pervades the whole country. . . . Such are the blessed fruits of a war carried on for the purpose of seating such scoundrels as the Bourbons on the thrones of France and Spain.'

In Paris he was much in the company of General Sir Robert Wilson, who had served on the Russian staff as an observer for Britain during the campaign of 1812 and who was soon to enter Parliament. Wilson was strongly suspected of helping La

Valette to escape from a Paris prison and Lambton no doubt sympathized, but there is no reason to believe that he was involved.

His visit to France did all that his friends had hoped for him and more. It had been impossible to hold aloof from that vivid bustling life. Paris was so crowded, so gay and unrepentant, so willing to let bygone Emperors be bygone. It was impossible, too, to give up political work when there was such a need in the world for men who had the courage and the inclination to stand up for liberty. Lambton had seen tyranny at its worst in France, as the returned royalists hunted down their enemies and men who had never seen a shot fired took high command in the army, while marshals and generals who had fought in every country in Europe starved in disgrace. He knew enough of his own country's affairs by this time to know that there would be no relaxing of the repression there unless every act, every attempt were doggedly and obstinately opposed. It was the beginning of the task to which he was to devote his life. In those whirling months in Paris, in its gaiety and cruelty, its refusal to recognize the facts of history and its revival of a faded farce of royalty, Radical Jack was born.

CHAPTER VI

When Mr. William Lambton was in France in the year 1785, he met the Count Scepaux, who was then commanding a regiment in garrison at Libourne. They became friends and when, after the Revolution, Scepaux had to leave France he came to England where Mr. Lambton befriended him. He seems to have been a voluminous letter-writer and such of his letters as survive in the Lambton MSS. give valuable information about the details of life there during the next twenty years. There are unfortunately many gaps in the correspondence and no copies of the Lambton family's letters to him are to be found, but his own correspondence goes on intermittently until 1834. Plainly he was not only a friend but also a pensioner of William Lambton who gave him, during his exile, enough money at more or less regular intervals to keep him in modest comfort.

The first of Scepaux's surviving letters is dated from London, 15 July 1798. It is an immensely long document, in which for the benefit of the Lambton trustees, he recalls the history of his friendship and anxiously asks, in his rather eccentric style, 'if I understood well that you as executors you and Mr. Ralph had come to a decision to afford me assistance as fulfilling the intention of my generous friend'. John Lambton was then only six and poor Scepaux obviously felt anxious about his chance of getting any help in later years. He writes, 'It is impossible to foresee what will be the disposition of the child, coming to the estate', although, he adds hopefully, 'being born of such father and such mother, if he is not liberal and kind to misfortune, he will hold very little of them'.

The trustees were sympathetic and Lambton, when he came of age, showed his willingness to carry out his father's wishes, but, for the first few years of his ownership, the estate was often short of income—there being, in Scepaux's phrase in describing Mr. Lambton's will, 'no personals'. The capital of the estate was nearly all in land and collieries and, for a few years, the income could not keep pace with the owner's ideas of expenditure. The family had always, apparently, been indulgent landlords and it was not until Henry Morton became the agent for the estate that a serious effort was made to collect the arrears of rent and to ensure prompt payment in the future. The collieries were immensely valuable but they needed constant expenditure on repairs and on the installing of pumping gear and engines, so that there were years when they only showed a nominal profit. There was a regular drain on income, too, in the list of pensions and annuities which Mr. Lambton had left in his will to various dependents, as well as the trust for the children's education with which Lady Anne took such liberties. But the chief drain was John Lambton's ineradicable habit of living beyond his income. He did not waste money, as so many of his fellow landowners did, on gambling and women, but he shared their taste for grandiose building and, as the tall towers began to rise over the woods above the Wear and gardens and terraces were laid out with scrupulous care for anything except economy, the estate began to feel its first embarrassments. It is here that Scepaux's letters are so informative, for he seems to have interested himself in every detail of the estate, partly no doubt, because it was his sole means of survival, but also, on the evidence of his letters, out of genuine gratitude and affection for Lambton himself. He even seems to have held some indefinite and probably self-elected position as courier abroad and financial adviser at home, and to have been willing to do a lot more than he was allowed. In France he charged himself with such matters as arranging journeys for the family, booking rooms at hotels and looking after some small and mysterious piece of property in Paris, which William Lambton must have acquired and which his son offered to make over to Scepaux if he could wrest it from the French Crown, which had, by some device, got hold of it. (Scepaux's last letter, dated 1834, shows that he had not so far had any success.)

In England, Scepaux took it upon himself to try to check the wild spending, and his one ambition, which he mentions many times, was to establish himself at Lambton and to take charge of the finances. 'You will write so I will instantly come to Lambton', he writes in an undated letter, and again, 'that I may form my plan I have the most earnest wish to go to Lambton'. There was an interlude in 1814, when Napoleon had gone to Elba and Scepaux left for Paris to pester the restored government for a pension with the magnificent valediction: 'The Count leaves London this evening for Dover it is all what he can say to Mr. Lambton as 22 years of dayly obligation can'nt come under any expression of thanks, that the blessing of God be upon Mr. Lambton's house. Farewell!'

But Elba could not hold the Emperor and next year Scepaux was back in England again and ready to resume his watch over the Lambton finances. In 1816 he offered yet again to take charge of the estate office for at least six months—'I should not flinch a farthing (daresay Master Stobart would not like my presence)'. Stobart was the agent before Morton and there is every reason to think that he would have resented this un-solicited supervision. He seems to have been both honest and competent and it is one of Scepaux's least endearing charac-teristics that he regularly tried to ingratiate himself by suggest-ing that various servants of the estate were robbing it.

This letter of 1816, however, does really show, if the facts are correct, that the finances of Lambton were strained. Scepaux writes that Lambton had sold land worth £2,100, thereby decreasing his income by £1,083 a year—an improbable figure as it would mean a return of something like 50 per cent.—and had bought more colliery land on which the coal was not being worked so that it would be some time before the transaction would show a profit. In another letter, undated but obviously written about the same time, he speaks of a mortgage on part of the land and of loans at 8 per cent. interest.

In both letters he suggests a scheme for restoring prosperity including 'a *firm* determination to live *within* your income . . . you must borrow first to pay your debts which debts cannot be paid out of income, that the sum you want is only upon your honour till you can sell detached property about Darlington'.

Scepaux's further suggestions for economy are generally directed at Lambton's expenditure on sport, especially on hunting and on his racing stables: 'I have since thought that it is this giving that the subscription to the hounds . . . it was very inconvenient to pay 600 sovns. and more you will merely those good friends will toady you as much as you will permit, remember how from 500 guas they brought you to 600 with Kennels . . . for God's sake hear your friend—300 guineas and nothing else; as for your stud . . . the sale of every head—the profit will be immense two grooms less plenty of oats which must be paid for. . . .' It would seem that Lambton did show the gratitude which Scepaux expected, for Scepaux writes: 'I had to-day yours of the 8th, who in the name of God is to present to your eyes the truth if it is not the man who wishes to be taken for your friend?' and, again and more pathetically, 'You speak if you had a letter from me every day you would shoot yourself, never do that . . . once you begin (to borrow at 8%) you are a man lost. . . .'

Lambton was saved at last from any such suicidal ideas—and a prolonged wrestling with Scepaux's literary style induces some sympathy with them—by the firm restoration of royal power in France and Scepaux's consequent departure to see what he could get out of the government there. The correspondence dwindled—though there is a lively interlude with Mr. Erard, 'the piano and harp man', about an unpaid debt—till at last in 1834 it ceased with Scepaux's death.

On the whole Lambton seems to have treated Scepaux generously about money, which is not surprising, and also with a quite astonishing patience, apart from a few protests. One thing is quite certain—he adopted none of Scepaux's suggestions and made little real attempt to restore his finances. The theme will occur again and again during the next ten years and more until the growing demand for coal and the better management of the lands by Morton increased Lambton's income to a figure which even he had to work really hard to outstrip in his expenditure. There is a world of difference between Scepaux's estimate of £9,378 7s. 8d. and Mr. Creevey's admittedly loose assessment of £90,000. No doubt the figure fluctuated greatly with the ups and downs of the coal trade. The owner's expenditure was a more progressive figure.

CHAPTER VII

The death roll in the Northumberland and Durham coalfields had long been a scandal and disgrace. In the first thirty-six years of the nineteenth century there were almost 1,000 recorded deaths, nearly all of which were caused by explosions of gas in the pits. One of the worst happened on 25 May 1812, at Felling Pit, where ninety-two were killed.

No such disaster had happened even in that district within living memory. Mining was a rough and hazardous trade, but for a year or two there had been no more than the normal amount of fatal accidents and the Felling explosion shocked the county into an awareness that such a thing must not be allowed to happen again. But, before much could be done, there followed a series of lesser though dreadful enough explosions. In October in Harrington Mill Pit twenty boys and four men were killed, in July eight at Fatfield. In December there was another explosion at Felling and twenty-three were killed and twenty-one seriously injured.

The disasters seemed all the worse for the time of comparative safety which had preceded them and the shocking rapidity with which they followed each other. The coal-owners of

Durham were not unfeeling men, nor is it fair to judge them
by the standards of a later and more compassionate day. The
death of a few miners at every pit every year was only to be
expected and, as few records were kept not many people knew
how often the accidents happened. It was not until 1815 that
a Judge of Assize, on being told that no inquest had been held
on a certain case because 'it was only the body of a collier'
protested in such vigorous terms that the public were aroused
and began to ask what was wrong with the mines. Several of
the owners, especially John Budley, who had some scientific
knowledge, had already been trying to find the cause of the
accidents and to suggest a remedy. In October 1813 the
owners met in conference at Sunderland and formed an
Association for the Prevention of Accidents in the Mines. The
Duke of Northumberland was president and Lambton was
among the vice-presidents, who also included the Marquis of
Londonderry, Robert Surtees of Mainsforth, the historian, and
Sir Matthew Ridley. One obvious cause was the lack of ventila-
tion in the pits, many of which had as yet no shaft other than
that which the men used for going to work and leaving, so that
noxious gases collected and hung about in the galleries where
the men carried naked lights. Many collieries had recently
introduced steam engines which meant that coal could be
worked at a lower level and that the pits would become hotter
and more dangerous every year.

A Dr. Clanning had invented an early form of safety lamp
which was tried in some of the pits, but it was a primitive
device and most of the men were characteristically chary of
any new method even though it might add to their safety.
George Stephenson was then working on a model of his own,
but Mr. Buddle, a Durham coal-owner, begged the Association
to apply to the man who was, in his opinion, the leading figure
in that field of scientific research and Lambton learned with
pleasure that it was his old acquaintance, the usher at Dr.
Beddoes' Institute in Clifton, now Sir Humphry Davy. Davy
came north in 1814 to investigate the state of many of the pits
and returned to London, feeling hopeful that he had found an
answer to their problem. He wasted no time in starting to
produce the first model of the Davy Safety Lamp, and brought
it up for test within a few months. Lambton was one of the pits

selected and Buddle wrote afterwards about what was done there. They were trying to see what effect a jet of burning gas would have on the lamp and among the watchers in the pit-bottom was Lambton. It was not a particularly dangerous experiment, as far as they knew, though Buddle had the whole of his coat scorched by the nearness of the flame, but there was a certain risk in any handling of a naked flame in that charged atmosphere. It need not be credited to Lambton as a special act of courage that he was there, but it is typical of the way in which he was always to deal with his mining problems. It was not enough for him to know that other people had them in hand. That inquiring mind which Beddoes had noticed was fully awake. Dr. Beddoes was dead but he would have been proud to know that his usher and his pupil were justifying his care and teaching.

The greatest effect must have been on the minds of Lambton's own colliers who saw their owner sharing in the experiments and, to some degree, in their risks. They did not speak of it outside the district—they were a homekeeping people from necessity and a silent people by habit—but its results began to be seen some years later when there was trouble in the coal-fields over wages and hours and when the men had learned to combine. In the Lambton papers there are records of several occasions when the men there stayed at work while the rest were on strike and once he went so far as to send for troops to protect them as long as they wanted to remain at work. To the end of his life he was never to give up that personal care of his people which he knew to be his duty. If he was an autocrat he had in him all that was good in the old feudal idea. As his men said when they looked at his body lying in the Castle hall, he cared about them. During the troubles Lord Londonderry announced, a trifle optimistically, that his men looked on him as their father and protector but, though Lambton made no such boast, it was much more true of his men, who saw that so early in his life as a coal-owner he was personally taking care of them.

After various adjustments the Davy Lamp was considered satisfactory and the first lot were ordered for use in the pits. Contrary to hope there was no immediate drop in the number of casualties by explosion. The whole lay-out underground was too hopelessly primitive and unsafe for any one device to remove the danger and, at first, the men did not understand the lamps or even like them. It took a few years for the benefit to have much real effect, but it was a beginning and it gave a chance to more men. The coal-owners, at any rate, were so well satisfied after a period of working, that they invited Davy to a banquet in Sunderland, where Lambton presided and, on behalf of all of them, presented Davy with a service of gold plate valued at £2,500.

The danger to life in the mines was not the only grievance of these men who had good reason to complain of the system under which they were engaged and paid. It had for many years been the custom of the trade in that district to 'bind' the miners for a period, usually of one year. It was a hard and unfair bargain which was entirely in the masters' favour. There was no agreement about rates of pay or guarantee of employment. A man might be bound and yet find himself out of work for weeks at a time with no compensation and no chance of a change of job, since the masters insisted that every man who left their employment must take with him a certificate from them to say that he had worked in their pits. The result was that if he produced the certificate at any other pit he would be refused work, because the masters had an agreement among themselves not to employ each others' men. The masters' obligation under the bond was slight and involved nothing more than employing a man, when they had work for him, at whatever rate they chose to fix. Should they not employ a man at all during his bond or for months, while part of the pit was closed for repairs or after an accident, it cost them nothing. There was no penalty clause for the masters, though the men were bound under a penalty, which was commonly £18, some or all of which they would forfeit if they committed any breach of quite arbitrary regulations, such as absenting themselves for a few days, not properly filling their tubs or filling inferior coal. As a hewer commonly earned 2s. 3d. or 2s. 6d. a shift it was a crippling penalty. Any man who incurred it would have to see his wife and children go hungry for many months. It was easy, too, in some pits, to incur the penalty for light-weight trucks, since some of them paid their 'keeker' or weighman on the monstrous principle of so many pence for every tub rejected.

The men had no choice but to accept the system or to starve

—literally to starve, for there was no unemployment pay and they were too poor to help each other in hard times. There was little hope of getting work in other coalfields, for the journey into Lancashire or Staffordshire was too costly for a man who wanted to take his family with him, and, in any case, the conditions there were not much better. The men had no organization. There had been attempts to form rudimentary trade unions in the late eighteenth century but the Combination Laws of 1799 had killed the movement. Sometimes, in desperation, they struck, but there were no funds to back them and their families went hungry and worse than hungry, for they were seldom much better in the best of times. The men soon gave up the attempt and went back to work, knowing that they had incurred the binding penalty if the masters chose to enforce it.

Yet, in some sort and at different times, they managed to achieve a loose form of combination which was called 'brothering'. It was necessarily secret, being illegal, and involved the taking of an oath to be 'brothers' to each other in any demand for improvement or refusal to work. Sometimes a man would take the oath and break it in sheer desperation because his children were crying for food, and would slink back to work while his 'brothers' were idle. A few days later his body, with throat cut or belly ripped up, would be found lying out on some desolate moor. They were a fierce, resentful race, these men of Durham, living hardly above the starvation line and often below it, racked by rheumatism and consumption, carrying their naked lights into a pit where at any moment a concentration of gas might blow them to bits, or where, in stormy weather, a rush of flood water might trap and drown them. They worked for ten hours at a stretch—the boys often for twelve, since they must start to clear the galleries, oil what little machinery there was, or grease the ropes before the men could begin their work and must stay to clear up when the shift was over. Women no longer worked underground but all of them in the villages, except the very young, could remember women as well as men being killed in explosions at the coal face.

Lambton began to know and to care for his men as soon as he was a man himself and his record as an employer is one of the most honourable things in his life. He did all that he personally could to improve conditions in his pits and even when he was in London or abroad on public business he kept in regular touch with his agent at Lambton, Henry Morton, as a mountain of correspondence remains to witness. He might be Lord Privy Seal or Ambassador, but he was always the Squire of Lambton, and he always managed to make time to read Morton's reports and to give his orders.

When, after the passing of the first Reform Bill, he was able to spare a little more time for his own affairs, he pressed on with the improvements which he thought the most urgent and gave coherence to his plans by the formation of the Lambton Collieries Association which included accident insurance and a rudimentary form of pension scheme to which he contributed largely out of his own pocket. He was never one of the employers who resented the existence of trade unions, though he always disliked and distrusted their leaders, not always without justice. When the repeal of the Combination Laws in 1824 allowed the unions to exist and most of the Durham coal-owners refused to bind men who were members of a union, the only pits where no objection to membership was raised were those belonging to the Marquess of Londonderry and Lord Durham.

In one of Morton's letters, there is a paragraph which is of interest because it shows the origin of the name by which Lord Durham came to be known to so many people in the North. Morton wrote that, on a visit to Sunderland, he had been at a public meeting and had heard 'Universal Suffrage' proposed by 'a person of the name of McCleod who has been exchequered about a dozen times for defrauding the Excise'. He was, he added, 'better known as Radical Jack'.

CHAPTER VIII

Lambton's grief at Henrietta's death had been so intense that it is surprising to learn that, only a year later he was married again. Yet old Lady Holland had thought it the obvious thing for him to do. His baby daughters needed a mother; he had no heir. The extravagance of his grief had perhaps made it burn out in a fierce flame instead of smouldering into grey ash, and he was young and life was strong in him. He had fallen in love with Lady Louisa Grey, daughter of Earl Grey of Howick, and on 9 December 1816 they were married.

Lady Louisa had had little contact with the great world before her marriage and very little education in the formal sense. She was brought up as were all that family in freedom of body and mind, running wild in the fields at Howick, untroubled by almost any discipline except the one sort which her husband had lacked, that of loving parents and outspoken brothers and sisters. (In that happy home their father was never anything but 'Car' to his children and they all argued freely about everything.) In all her letters to her mother, there is the same feeling of freedom and in her occasional comments, loving but critical, on her father, there appears a hint of those qualities in him which were to contribute more than most people realized to his difficulties with his son-in-law. She came to her marriage with her own dower of gaiety, wit, and shrewd observation, her delight in the sayings and doings of everyone with whom she came into contact. These were to stay with her unimpaired, surviving courts and salons, triumphs and humiliations, happiness and sorrow. Whether she were with her children at Lambton or in the rigid formality of the Russian court, sustaining her husband in grief and defeat, or excitedly watching a Canadian guest trying to eat jelly with a knife and fork, she was always the same brave and loving woman, with eagerness to welcome any new experience and courage to surmount any disaster.

The relationship between Lambton and Grey was a complex one, made up of love and misunderstanding, beginning in mutual confidence and ending in one-sided suspicion—for Lambton never ceased to trust and respect Grey. Once again, history has relied too much upon the detractors, Creevey and Greville, especially about the one extremely painful incident, related by Althorp and joyfully relayed by both of them, of Lambton's brutal attack on Grey at a Cabinet dinner, at the time of the First Reform Bill.

Mr. G. M. Trevelyan, with characteristic fairness, writes: 'The relation of the dignified Whig patrician . . . to the hot tempered Radical of ancient lineage whom his daughter Louisa had

JOHN GEORGE LAMBTON, aged 25
From a portrait by Thomas Phillips

married, forms a political and domestic comedy of many acts and scenes. If Lambton was Grey's gadfly, the need for it was apparent.' The relationship started off wrong from the very beginning because Lambton tried to find in it something which it was not natural to expect. When he was betrothed to Lady Louisa, he wrote to her father:

'I have never felt the blessing of a father's care or advice and I fear I have suffered from it. It is therefore more gratifying to me than I am able to express to be able to look upon you in that sacred light; upon you whom I have always venerated as the first of men in public life and, since I have been admitted to your society, as the most exemplary in private life.'

It was hard on both of them—on Lambton because he was doomed to disappointment, and on Grey, who already had a numerous family of his own and was unlikely to welcome this self-elected and turbulent addition to it. He gave much to Lambton—confidence, affection, example, counsel—but it was not enough and what Lambton wanted he could not in nature give. Lambton needed not only, as he said, the care and advice of a father, but even more, though he probably did not realize it himself, the restraint and discipline of a father. Grey could repay aggression with patience, rudeness with civility, outrageous demands with calm explanation, but what Lambton often wanted was a fight and Grey was no fighter in private life.

Had their relationship not been thus strained they might have been all their lives, as they were for a time, very good friends. They had much in common. Both were north-country aristocrats, devoted to their homes and estates, both were Whigs and enthusiasts for Parliamentary Reform. It is true that at times Lambton talked as if he had invented Reform while Grey had been working for it with William Lambton before the boy was born, in the days when they founded the Friends of the People. Yet to every problem their approach was different. There was of course the obvious difference between age and youth, but that was not the half of it. Grey's approach was intellectual, Lambton's mainly emotional. Grey could realize that something must be done and that a way must eventually be found of doing it. Lambton's feeling was that something must be done at once and that it must be done in his way.

Grey was a sincere reformer and infinitely patient, but without urgency or passion. It was commonly said of him that 'he loved the people but he loved them at a distance'. Sir Francis Burdett, himself a Reformer, once said that 'Grey ought never to have been a Reformer. He ought to have remained a minister. That was his line.' It must have been very galling to Lambton, in his generous urgency, to be told, 'Reform will come, but not in my time and probably not in yours.' Hot youth can put up with a snub or a blow rather than with a tolerant smile. It was probably less disconcerting to Lambton when Grey, sorely tried and for once out of patience, broke out with: 'Oh, damn Reform! I wish I had never heard of it!' That was in 1832 at the height of the battle, and probably many of them said it or thought it at moments. It was the sort of thing that Lambton might have said himself and regretted a moment later.

Yet Grey fought magnificently for Reform, when once he was committed to the battle. His leadership of his party during the last agonizing weeks which preceded the passing of the Bill was a miracle of tact and persistence. Yet, again, the gadfly was needed. Sir J. R. M. Butler says that the Bill was a triumph for 'Grey's statesmanlike conviction of the need for an extensive measure . . . the wisdom of Russell and the will of Durham'. Had that will not been there, Reform might not have come in Grey's time, for his finer feelings were all against driving the poor puzzled King too remorselessly. Lambton, with his Lyon blood, left his finer feelings at home when he went to a fight.

Grey had two fatal failings as a leader of a Parliamentary party. His heart was always at Howick and never at Westminster, which would not have mattered had it not been that his body also was too often absent. Many of his colleagues, like Althorp and Lambton himself, would far rather have been at home, but none of them hung up their harps and wept for their north-country Zions as often or as audibly as did Grey. Trevelyan describes his unwillingness to leave Howick as 'the plague of successive generations of his colleagues', and quotes an earlier instance of 1792 when the Whig party nearly split over the differences between Fox and the Duke of Portland. 'It was characteristic,' he writes, 'of the Grey we know so well in later life thus to absent himself in his beloved Northumberland while his fate was being decided in the South.' In 1805 Fox wrote to him, 'God knows that when you are in town without her [his wife] you are unfit for anything with all your thoughts at Howick', and, eight years later, Tierney, the leader of the Whigs in the Commons, protested, 'I do not know which of your ancestors it was who purchased or seized an estate in Northumberland, but I wish with all my heart he had been knocked on the head . . . no good can be done unless you come to town.' Lambton must not bear the blame for everything. Any side may be disconcerted on the eve of a Test Match when they suddenly learn that their captain is shooting grouse 300 miles away.

Grey's other weakness was a fastidiousness which made him revolt from the irritating and sometimes sordid manœuvres which party leadership often demands and a tendency to believe that all men were as honourable as he. He could never really bring himself to believe that another man would go back on his word or fail to keep a bargain made in good faith and this delusion was to lead him into some trouble in his dealings with William IV. It is in reading of those days of May in 1831 when Grey, from pure decency forbore to press the King too far for his comfort, that we understand the meaning of Trevelyan's phrase of the need for Lambton the gadfly. Gadflies, however necessary, are rarely popular and not seldom their reward is Socrates' hemlock.

The relationship between the two men began most happily both in private and politically. 'The nearness to Northumberland,' Trevelyan writes, 'of Lambton Castle in Durham, the happy intimacy which sprang up between the Howick swarm and their vivacious brother-in-law and the real affection that at once bound Lambton to Lord Grey brought modern democracy into the heart of the Whig counsels.' When Lambton had first entered Parliament, Grey had written him a charming letter of welcome and congratulation and Lambton's first speeches marked him as a man who might well become of importance to his party. Grey had led the Whigs in the Commons until he succeeded to the title in 1807 and, as Lord Holland wrote ten years later, 'his place has never been supplied'. The Duke of Wellington told Creevey that, 'As leader in the House of Commons Grey's manner and speech were quite perfect. But he is lost by being in the Lords. Nobody cares a damn for the House of Lords.' George Ponsonby, who led the party afterwards, had been, Trevelyan says, chosen on the principle 'of taking not the ablest but the least objectionable person'. Ponsonby was still nominally leader in 1817, till his death later in the year, and the normal thing would have been for Tierney to follow him, though he was not very effective and his commercial background was a handicap to him in a party which was almost wholly aristocratic and territorial. It seemed to Grey that his son-in-law would have the personal qualities, as he undoubtedly had the standing, to make an ideal leader after he had acquired some Parliamentary experience.

During the next few years Lambton's influence in the House rapidly increased. He did not speak often, but he was always effective when he did, and he had decided ideas about party management. He was one of the first members to appreciate the value of the Press as an ally and in 1818 set up a public relations office for the Whigs, arranging for the hire of a room in Westminster where journalists could gather to get first-hand reports from the members. Another useful innovation of his was the idea of a monthly party dinner while the House was sitting.

When he did speak in the House, it was nearly always a threat to or an assault on the liberties of the people that brought him to his feet. The brief burst of exhilaration which had followed the defeat of Napoleon had died away and Peace had not brought happiness or prosperity to England—only low wages and dear food, unemployment and unrest, and a renewal of Tory oppression.

The year 1818 must have been for Lambton one of those rare years in which a man can look forward and see a happy prospect unrolling itself before him. On 16 January, the bells of St. Mary's Church at Gateshead rang for the birth of an heir to Lambton, as they were to ring again every year until 1831. The child, who was christened Charles William, is familiar to most people through reproductions of Lawrence's famous portrait, 'Master Lambton'. It is not only fancy that can see in the face a look which does not belong to childhood, as though the eyes were looking out over a great distance of unknown country. When the boy was eight, his father took him to

Westminster and Lord Lansdowne, seeing him for the first time, said afterwards to a friend that the child had a look as though he were gazing into futurity.

Lambton had passionately longed for a son, to whom he could give all that his own childhood had lacked, and his delight and pride in the boy were almost excessive. Dearly as he loved his daughters and the children who were later to be born to him, Charles was always set in his heart a little apart from and above the rest. Grey was hardly less delighted and their common joy strengthened the bond between Howick and Lambton and their fellowship at Westminster. Nothing that happened afterwards could quite break that bond of affection, though in little more than a year the first signs of strain were to show themselves.

In that golden year of 1818, they were completely at one in their unending fight against the Government's oppression and its continual threat to liberty. Much of the actual work of fighting fell on Lambton, since Grey was in the Lords and, in the Commons, Tierney was a nonentity. Whitbread was dead and Romilly died in that year, so that Lambton and Brougham had to be always in readiness, though Brougham had to give much of his time to his growing practice at the bar, not only for selfish motives. He was always ready to undertake the defence of any man who had offended against the growing number of laws which forbade free speech and writing. Whatever was said afterwards against Brougham—and there was good reason for much of it—his unfailing courage in defence of these men did him infinite credit.

In January the Government brought to an end the suspension of Habeas Corpus and, in March, introduced a Bill to indemnify any of their servants who had made arrests under it—a Bill which Lambton described as irrelevant since what was required was 'a full, fair, and impartial investigation as to the conduct of ministers for the last twelve years, in order to ascertain whether they deserved indemnity or impeachment', the latter being, in his opinion, what they deserved, since they had 'used it to prop their tottering power, to secure their jobs and their places and to gag the mouths of the people'. The Attorney-General, who was in charge of the Bill, had paid an eloquent tribute to the humanity in private life of Lord

Sidmouth, the Home Secretary, seeking by it to show that such a man would never have allowed oppression or injustice. Lambton dealt with this rather naïve argument, saying that, 'To the private character of the Noble Lord a great deal of benevolence was attributed. That might be so or might not be so, but he must say that his public conduct bore no such stamp. But, whatever might be the feelings of the Noble Lord, history had shown that such feelings on the part of individuals were no guarantee against inhumanity in the administration of power.'

His speech had no effect on the voting and the bill passed. The Tories had too big a majority to be beaten by individual efforts, however heroic, but it added to his reputation, which he increased still more a few weeks later when he crossed swords with Canning in the debate about the Government's use of spies and *agents provocateurs*, especially the notorious Oliver. It was said of Canning that he never made a speech without making an enemy and he made the mistake of showing a certain levity and superciliousness towards Lambton, who met him with shrewdness and good temper and compelled him to withdraw some of the expressions that he had used. The Whigs fought stoutly at every point but they were always beaten by numbers and, when 1819 came in, the Government tightened the screw by passing the 'Gagging Acts' which virtually forbade free speech in public or free expression in writing on any subject of public concern. They did not resort to their well-worn expedient of suspending Habeas Corpus but the new Acts gave unprecedented powers of arrest and detention and were designed to entrap particularly such democratic leaders as Cobbett, Place, and Orator Hunt. Hunt had become such a danger in their eyes, that dragoons followed him as he moved about the country and the Government were only waiting for an opportunity to arrest and lock him up out of harm's way.

They found their opportunity, but they displayed a lamentable lack of elementary common sense in the way in which they took it. If they wanted him they could have taken him at any time, since he moved about not only openly but ostentatiously. There was something of the showman mixed with his undoubted courage, and he made rather theatrical progresses between the meetings, attended by a slightly ridiculous retinue, some of whom wore French caps of liberty and carried pikes. If all that the Government wanted was a simple arrest, the dragoons could have made it when they liked, but they wanted to make an example of him and to give the arrest all the publicity that was possible. They chose to do it at a meeting which he was to address in the North of England in August. Major Cartwright, one of the oldest supporters of Reform, had advocated the holding of a series of meetings in the big towns such as Birmingham, Leeds, and Manchester, which were not represented in Parliament, to send petitions to Parliament. Birmingham took up the idea and Manchester followed. It was there that Hunt was to be arrested and the Manchester magistrates were instructed to call out the Yeomanry who were reinforced by a squadron of the 15th Hussars, a wing of the 88th Foot, and a section of Horse Artillery. The date chosen for the meeting was 16 August and the place was a field on the outskirts of the town. It was called Peterloo.

CHAPTER IX

Samuel Bamford gives a full description of that day, which was to be known ever afterwards as the Peterloo Massacre. For several weeks before it, there had been drilling and marching at night by the mill-hands and labourers of Lancashire. Their leaders protested that the only object of these manoeuvres was to ensure the orderly arrival of the crowd at the meeting and their arrangement on the ground. Government spies, who watched them, saw preparation for military action, though none of the men were armed. Certainly the columns, when the day came, wheeled and marched on to the field with the precision of trained troops, but there were many old soldiers in the country so soon after the close of the French War, and some of those who ordered this parade of workmen had stormed the breach at Badajoz or stood in the squares at Waterloo.

The meeting was perfectly legal. The magistrates had not

forbidden it and the only object of summoning the troops and turning out the Yeomanry was to arrest Orator Hunt.

Hunt arrived late, surrounded by his usual escort and saw a field packed with people and a platform in the middle of it, on which was Bamford who was to act as chairman. Round the edge of the field were the Manchester Yeomanry, mounted and with swords drawn. In the lanes behind them waited the Cheshire Yeomanry, the Hussars and the infantry, with the horse-artillery in rear. One tenth part of that force could have taken Hunt without difficulty before ever he came near the field, but the magistrates, in their folly, let him reach the platform before they moved. To that folly there were no bounds. They had chosen a time and a place which gave no hope of making an arrest without involving hundreds of innocent people in trouble, and they added to it by detailing the Yeomanry and not the Hussars to ride into the crowd and fetch Hunt out. It was well known, all over the country, and was to be proved again and again that assemblies—even riotous assemblies, which this was not—would behave docilely when regular troops opposed them, but were bitterly resentful of any action by Yeomanry. Regulars were professionals, doing their proper job without discrimination or feeling, while the Yeomanry were mostly officered by the sons of employers or landowners so that on both sides there was rancour. Moreover, dealing with large and hostile crowds is a task which needs skill, discipline, and tact, and also, if it should come to a fight, promptness and restraint in action. The Yeomanry, raw men, on raw horses had none of these qualities. It was no blame to them, but nearly all the casualties at Peterloo were their work. The Hussars, when they came on after the Yeomanry had blundered, rode in a solid wedge, knee to knee, and their pace and weight split the crowd before them as an axe splits wood. Bamford admits that only the front rank used their sabres at all, and that they used only the flat. The Yeomanry, who began the attack, charged in line at an unsteady canter, lost their dressing and scattered into small groups, none of which could penetrate the crowd, who were now close-packed as those on the edge tried to move forward out of the way of the horses.

The horses got out of control—more men were ridden down and trampled on than sabred—and the men, inexperienced and ill-led, lost their heads and their tempers and laid about them with the edge of the sabre. When the crowd broke and fled, the Cheshire Yeomanry rode them down and the 88th, who arrived late, used their bayonets on a few stragglers. Mercifully the guns did not come until it was all over, but by that time, eleven dead lay on the ground and there were between 400 and 500 wounded.

The Manchester magistrates had shown both cruelty and folly, but the blame lies mostly with the Government who had encouraged them and who now publicly congratulated them. The crowning insult of a congratulatory message from the Prince Regent caused an outburst of indignation which flamed up all over the country.

One after another the Counties began to make their voices heard in angry protest and condemnation. In Yorkshire, the first to move, Earl Fitzwilliam organized a giant meeting of protest and paid for his presumption with the loss of his Lord Lieutenancy. Durham was not far behind and inevitably it was Lambton who assumed the responsibility of arranging their protest. Grey was as indignant as Lambton, but was always a little doubtful of the value or the propriety of public meetings, which, he said, 'might be justified if they confined themselves to demands for an inquiry'. It is significant that this seems to be the first instance when Lambton felt obliged to take a stronger line than his father-in-law cared for. He was too honestly angry to confine his protest within any bounds and too shrewd not to guess what would be the result of any inquiry which a Tory government might set on foot. He had already begun to organize a public meeting to be held in the city of Durham, when he learned that he had been forestalled by the other faction in the county. The Durham clergy, under the leadership of Prebendary Philpott, were strongly reactionary and had called a meeting in Sunderland to pass a vote of thanks to and confidence in the magistrates of Manchester for their courageous stand against the threat of revolution. It is a melancholy fact that in almost all the struggles for liberty, justice or mercy that happened in this early part of the century, the clergy of the Church of England, as represented by their bishops and dignitaries, were solidly on the side of reaction. Had it not been for the Bishops' vote in the Lords, the First

Reform Bill would have become law at its first presentation, and even such crying needs as the abolition of slavery and factory reform found no friends among the hierarchy of the Church.

Philpott was a typical reactionary, a man of violent speech and a furious pamphleteer. Even the Tory Greville had no good word for him, describing his countenance as 'fearful' and saying that 'he was the man he looked'. It was immediately clear to Lambton that before he could hold his own meeting he must first dispose of the opposition, and the action which he took was characteristically prompt and vigorous. Messengers galloped from Lambton all over the county to his friends and allies to summon them to Sunderland on the day appointed for Philpott's meeting. Time was short and some of them had to travel long distances and it was urgent that enough of them should arrive in time to interfere with Philpott's assembly, so Lambton undertook the task of holding up proceedings until he could hope for a majority to vote against the resolutions. It is impossible not to feel that he looked forward to the prospect with something very like delight. There was enough Lyon in him to relish the idea of a personally led raid on an enemy stronghold.

The hall in Sunderland was filling up. Church dignitaries, junior clergy who were afraid of Philpott, and Tory laymen were crowding in at the doors, and Philpott himself was on the platform, when the Lambton coach with its outriders and liveried footmen rattled over the cobbles of the street and the owner of Lambton dismounted and stalked into the hall. He was almost alone and would be until more of his supporters could arrive but he had not the least hesitation in taking charge of the proceedings, though the resolution had already been read to the meeting. It affirmed that 'This assembly views with concern the attempts of misguided men to bring the laws of the country into contempt' and also that its members 'affirmed their loyalty towards their Sovereign and an attachment towards the laws and Constitution of the Land'. Lambton at once began to speak against the resolution, and continued to speak with some eloquence and at, for him, unusual length, in spite of all clerical efforts to stop him, while all the time the sound of hoofs and the clatter of coaches from outside told him that his party were gathering. He denounced the arrangements made for calling the meeting as 'underhand' and the meeting itself as 'hypocritical', and went on denouncing them until there were enough of his friends present to support him. One of them moved an impromptu resolution that 'Mr. Lambton do now take the chair'.

Among considerable uproar, Mr. Lambton took the chair, from which he at once proposed the adjournment, *sine die*, of the meeting, a motion which he declared to have been carried. His supporters were now numerous and formidable enough to dissipate any opposition, and the Sunderland meeting ended without further discussion. Its chief legacy was the lasting enmity between Lambton and Philpott which was later to culminate in a rousing fight in the House of Lords between the Earl of Durham and the Bishop of Exeter.

Lambton's own meeting was held on 22 September and, since he was in the chair from the start, was a much better conducted affair. He spoke in strong condemnation of the folly of the Manchester magistrates and of the brutality of the Yeomanry. 'Some slave,' he said 'had brought forward the words on the banners of the meeting that day, "Liberty or Death", as a proof of the traitorous nature of the meeting. When the time came that the coupling of these words should be deemed the harbinger of rebellion, he would be glad to disown the country which had given him birth.' He described the Cabinet's complimentary message to Manchester as 'an insult to the people' and the Sunderland meeting as 'contrived in some obscure corner of a vestry and the address intended to be proposed would probably have been moved by the Rector, seconded by a curate and perhaps signed on behalf of the meeting by a sexton'. 'I know,' he added, 'by experience that resolutions and addresses proposed in such a manner have been palmed on the country as the opinion of Sunderland.'

It was not to be expected that a man of Philpott's temper should tamely accept such an arbitrary dismissal of his meeting and he replied to Lambton in a series of pamphlets in which he quoted the more inflammatory passages of Lambton's speech together with some further quotations which are not to be found in any written record of it. He was the most formidable enemy whom Lambton had yet made, but among the more

65

Tory landowners of the county there began to grow a feeling that, intolerable as Philpott was, Lambton was displaying alarmingly radical tendencies. Their leader was Sir Thomas Liddell of Ravensworth, an old family friend, who was coming to the conclusion that it was time to look for a more temperate candidate for the party. Lambton was used to opposition at Westminster but it was a new experience for him to be distrusted in his own county and by men of his own standing, even personal friends and associates in the hunting field and on the cricket ground. The number of his adherents in the county grew rapidly, but most of them were among the class who had no votes and it must have given him something of a shock to realize that the day was not far off when he might have to fight hard to retain the seat which his family had enjoyed almost as a right for so many years.

There was not yet enough opposition to him to be dangerous, but in the following year, 1819, he threw himself into a hotly contested election at Westminster, where a vacancy had been caused by the death of Romilly. Lambton was inspired to do this solely by his loyalty to Earl Grey and found himself in the rather odd position of opposing the official Whig candidate, Cam Hobhouse. The other candidates were Frederick Lamb, brother of the future Lord Melbourne, and Major Cartwright. Lambton would gladly have supported Hobhouse, who was very much of his own way of thinking and was a friend to Parliamentary Reform, but Hobhouse's election address, which was drafted by another Reformer, Sir Francis Burdett, committed the blunder of making a fierce attack on Grey for his half-hearted leadership of the party and his luke-warm attitude towards Reform. Lambton might have—indeed did have—his own opinion about this, but it was intolerable to him that anyone should attack Grey and, when Hobhouse went out of his way to endorse the attack in an early election speech, Lambton threw all his weight on to Lamb's side. He wrote to Lady Grey: 'I have been roused by the infamous attacks on Lord Grey to take a very active part in the election and to carry it through. I feel sure my conduct in warmly resenting such calumnies is right.' Lamb headed the poll and Lambton reported to Grey that 'Two hundred persons at least must be wounded on both sides; one they say is killed. All this is to be attributed to Burdett's violent language. I trust we shall not forget it.' Grey answered: 'I can only repeat that it is impossible I ever should forget the affectionate zeal with which you have resented the insulting and injurious attacks made on me.' Such promises are easily made in the first flush of gratitude and as easily forgotten, but Grey never forgot his.

England's misery deepened through this year of 1819 under the rule of what came to be known as the 'Savage Parliament'. George III lingered on at Windsor, an old, blind madman, and the country viewed without enthusiasm the near prospect of his succession by the Prince Regent. The Whigs had something to hope from the change since the Prince had always affected friendship with them, though less out of regard for their principles than from a desire to annoy his father. Meanwhile the Tories held the country in their harsh grip and the peoples' misery and anger broke out in rioting and destruction of property in the West and South of England. The Special Commission who were sent from London to try the arrested did their duty as thoroughly as Jeffreys had done after Monmouth's rebellion. No lives had been lost during the trouble and there had been no serious damage to property, but the Commissioners condemned nine men to death and over 500 to transportation. Perhaps Lambton took this lesson to heart as he had taken that of the Bourbons and remembered it later in Canada, when, after a rebellion which had caused loss of life and much destruction, he exacted no life in retribution and showed generous clemency in lesser punishments. Brougham and he were hard at work throughout the year in protesting against acts of tyranny and maintaining the cause of individual liberty which seemed almost to have died out in England. At the end of the year it was known that the King could hardly live for more than a month or two and the Whigs took heart from the belief that the Prince Regent, when he became King, might dismiss the Tories and call them into power. Even the country as a whole, disillusioned as it was by his extravagance and his flagrant immorality, dared to hope that there might be some change for the better in the new year, which could hardly be worse than the old. Especially the people hoped for Parliamentary Reform, believing that when it came and they were able to elect their own men to represent them, they would see a renewal of justice and government in their interests rather than in those of an aristocratic clique. Reform was the mirage—a gleaming prospect which few men understood but many demanded and, since the Whigs were pledged to it, in theory at any rate, a Whig government was their only hope.

Yet the Whigs and the Reformers who were not Whigs, sincere as they were, were too hopelessly divided among themselves to offer any very sure prospect of immediate reform. The official Whig leaders were far from united and so much did they differ on the scope and immediacy of the measures which they recommended that it seemed that they would have difficulty in forming a government or a policy. Their leaders in the Lords, Holland and Grey, were men of experience and caution, sincere in their determination to achieve Reform but without illusions as to the difficulty of the task and content to advance step by slow step. The younger men in the Commons, Lambton and Brougham and their friends, were growing impatient and beginning to resent what seemed to them an excess of caution in their elders. Indeed, both inside and outside Parliament, the greatest danger to the cause was its superfluity of prophets, each of whom was convinced that he and only he had the true revelation and that all others were misguided, if not charlatans. The abuse which they poured on the tyrannical Tories was mild in comparison with their freely expressed opinions of each other. Orator Hunt was in prison, without benefit of trial, and Lambton, while loyally fighting in Parliament for his release, privately described him and his party as 'damned, mischievous, brawling quacks'. Hunt called Cobbett 'an impudent mountebank' and an 'unprincipled cowardly bully' and Cobbett returned the compliment by habitually referring publicly to Hunt as 'The Liar'. Jeremy Bentham accused Cobbett of 'malevolence and lying' and proclaimed that he was 'universally known for a rascal'. Cobbett borrowed £3,000 from Burdett and made no effort to repay it with anything except abuse, and later, when Cobbett died and a fund was raised for a memorial, Burdett sent Cobbett's bond to the organizers and told them to take his subscription out of it. Even Lord Grey was not spared and, when he publicly deplored the 'introduction of American methods into English politics' Francis Place described his speech as 'apostasy and nonsense'. England at the moment was like a vast market place in which vendors of patent cure-alls and infallible elixirs stood at every corner proclaiming their own virtues and damning each other for quacks. It is little wonder that Grey, in a mood of depression, wrote to Holland: 'I will desire you to look at the men themselves who lead this cause. Is there one among them with whom you would trust yourself in the dark?'

That black year ended at last and a few weeks later the reign ended with it. On 29 January 1820 the King died. The Prince Regent became George IV and the Whigs waited with declining hope for the invitation which was strangely late in coming. The new King was in no hurry to call on his old friends until he had seen what their enemies could do for him and the reforms for which his country pleaded were of less importance to him than his pressing need to get rid of his wife. The country was distracted from contemplation of its own troubles by the eccentric comedy of the Bill of Pains and Penalties, which Creevey so aptly called 'a bill to declare the Queen a whore and to settle her on the King for life'. Public opinion was for the most part against the King, if not whole-heartedly for his wife, since most people felt that whatever she had done, her husband had no right to complain of it. Lambton took no part in the proceedings since they never reached the Commons, but Brougham's advocacy of the Queen and a magnificent speech by Grey had much to do with the withdrawal of the Bill and had drastic effects on the Whig prospects. The King was furious with the many Whig leaders who had supported the Queen's cause and was determined to cling to the Tories who had been on his side. Many of them had supported him less from conviction than from party policy and had feared that the only result of the Bill could be to hold his own promiscuity up to derision and they were only partially consoled by the Duke of Wellington's assurance that 'the King is already degraded as low as he can be'.

So the Whigs foresaw more years in the wilderness and Grey assured his son-in-law that 'Reform will come, but not in my time and perhaps not in yours'. But Lambton was not to be content with such tame acceptance of delay. He intended Reform to come in his time and within Grey's as well and, since the official wheels seemed to be bogged down, he decided to drive his own carriage at his own pace.

CHAPTER X

The last two or three years had been a period of fruitless effort, for, however hard Lambton fought for his causes, he could never command a majority in Parliament, so that, every time he rose, he knew that it was to face defeat. Nothing could conquer his courage, but his health began to suffer and the pains in his head became worse and more frequent. He found, too, that the social life in London was exhausting with its endless round of receptions and parties. The hours of standing tired him and his liver suffered from the food and wine of those interminable dinners. Unhappily his temper began to show signs of fraying and his petulant outbursts earned him from Creevey the nickname of 'The Angry Boy'. (Creevey also called him 'King Jog' because he had made the foolish remark that '£80,000 a year was the sort of income that a man could jog along on'.)

Few politicians go through life without making enemies, and a man so outspoken and pugnacious as Lambton could hardly expect not to do the same, but he was beginning to antagonize not only his opponents but members of his own party. He was sharply made aware of this in the election which followed the accession of the new King, as the Parliamentary procedure of those days demanded. There were only 4,000 electors in the county constituency of Durham and he held his seat by a majority of 600—a comfortable win, but the smallest margin which he had yet known. He was a well-known and popular figure among the working men and the smaller tradesmen of the North, but they were not voters and his fellow-aristocrats were beginning to look doubtfully at him. His summary method of dealing with Philpott's meeting had alarmed them and they began to wonder whether he were not a traitor to his class. Just before polling opened, he received a plain warning from Sir Thomas Liddell of Ravensworth, an old friend of his father, who wrote to him:

'Dear Lambton,
    These are not times to suffer private feelings to interfere with what I consider a public duty; and I will formally tell you that your conduct, both in Parliament and in the County of Durham, has appeared to me so dangerous and likely to

do such incalculable mischief that, even if you were my own brother, I should oppose you by all the means in my power. I cannot conclude without assuring you that it is with extreme regret that I return you this answer.'

Lambton replied at once,

'Dear Sir Thomas,
    In answer to yours I beg to say that I feel gratitude for your frankness, compassion for your fears, little dread of your opposition and no want of your support.'

It was excellent repartee but it did not increase his popularity among the gentlemen of the county.

It was a lively election since his Tory opponent, a Mr. Richard Wharton, had started a scare about '100,000 armed Radicals, all ready to rise in open rebellion'. Political comment in those days was pleasantly uninhibited and the *Black Dwarf*, a Whig paper, 'Published by T. J. Wooler at No. 76 Fleet Street, price 6*d*.', said of Mr. Wharton:

'This slanderer of Reform, thus detected and dismissed, had the further stupidity to attempt to canvass Sunderland and the Wearmouths! This, it will be remembered, was the very centre of the rendezvous of the *100,000 armed Radicals* whom this Wharton helped to vouch for as ready to rise in armed rebellion. His presence there is a good conviction of his own falsity; for, had there been twenty children, armed with birch-rods disposed to attack the government, this Wharton would have kept out of the way and left the Yeomanry to defend it if they would.'

Lambton was back at Westminster in fighting mood and it was unfortunate that he came into conflict with the official leaders of his own party and especially with Lord Holland. Holland House was the traditional home of the Grand Whiggery and from thence came the pure milk of the Gospel of Charles James Fox, dispensed after its author's death with a rigidity which he would never have tolerated in his lifetime. Holland shared with Grey the belief that Reform was desirable, but that the time to press for it had not yet come and was still very far off. Lambton had no patience with such pusillanimity and, since no one else would take the necessary step, announced that he would himself introduce a Bill to

Parliament. He gave an outline of it to his leaders who were appalled to find that it went far beyond their wildest imaginations in its proposals, especially in its suggestion of household suffrage. They met to talk it over in Grey's rooms in Hertford Street and Holland remarked that the proposal of household suffrage was 'as bad as a revolution'. Lambton took violent exception to the comment and declined to have anything more to do with Holland. Grey, who had been almost as startled as his old friend, took upon himself—by no means for the last time—the duty of trying to induce his impetuous son-in-law to see reason. He wrote to him a letter in which, while he admitted that he thought it 'highly desirable to raise the character of the House of Commons in the opinion of the public, by uniting the representative more closely with the constituent body', he would not agree that Reform ought to be part of the official Whig policy. He thought that it would be better to 'have that object pursued individually by those who are favourable to it, in such a manner as may neither divide the Whig party nor pledge them to it in such a way as may make their acceptance of office—if anything so improbable as it being offered to them should occur—a reproach to them without it'.

Even a distant prospect of power has a strangely sobering effect on some men's intentions, but Lambton was not one of them. To him a conviction or a principle was everything and he had neither the temperament nor, as yet, the experience to know the importance of timing and the futility of anticipating the favourable moment. Nor did the danger of dividing the party distress him. He was, in fact, never what might be called a good party man, since he looked on his party solely as an organization for supporting his measures and never learned to assess a measure by its value in gaining or keeping power for the party. Also he was still very much annoyed with Lord Holland.

His answer to Grey shows how far he already felt himself to be estranged from the official Whigs, and yet how strong was still his personal affection for Grey.

'As for Lord Holland,' he wrote, '. . . it is right that his great friendship for you and his commanding talents should produce a corresponding influence over your mind, but, when it is exerted to the bane of the most important question that ever existed—on which you have acquired the greatest reputation—I must deeply lament that its power neutralizes your efforts. As for myself, his language respecting my motion in your room in Hertford Street was such that I will never forgive it. Doubtless all this will end in my complete separation from the Party. I should not care if you were not at the head of it. From any of the others I never received a particle of consideration.'

This rather unhappy correspondence, parts of which are in both the Howick and Lambton MSS., continued on the same lines and shows both men at their weakest, as they so often were when they disagreed. Grey is sweetly reasonable, almost intolerably patient; Lambton varies between defiance and self-pity. Grey refers with conscious pathos to his age and, inevitably, to his probable retirement; Lambton harks back to his forlorn youth and his need for counsel, though he seems to prefer counsel when it agrees with his own opinion. 'Deserted as I have been through life, left entirely to my own guidance and resources, such as they are, having no one to fall back upon in any emergency for advice and instruction'—it is his familiar complaint, containing some truth, but suggesting a foundling on a doorstep rather than the heir to Lambton. Again it is reasonable to feel that if only Grey had shown less patience and more authority—if even he had lost his temper and let himself go—Lambton would have been more satisfied. But that Grey could never do and other correspondence at this time shows that he knew that Lambton was in very bad health and suffering from constant pain. It was the first of their serious disagreements, and it is easy to see the way in which their temperaments and their close association were bound to lead to the really distressing letters and scenes of a few years later. Lambton remained obstinate and would not be dissuaded from his intention of introducing his own scheme of Reform, though he had to postpone it till the end of the year. The House of Lords was fully occupied with the wretched affair of the King and his wife and, as Lambton himself said, Parliament would not have listened to an announcement of the coming of the Messiah. At the end of the year, he gave notice of his intention to introduce a motion, but it was not until 17 April 1821, that he thought the time opportune.

He never had a chance of succeeding and, as it happened, by sheer ill luck he met with the most decisive defeat of his career up to date and with just the sort of personal humiliation which he was least able to endure. His proposals, which had so much shocked Lord Holland, had suffered no diminution since their ill reception in Hertford Street and were even more far-reaching than those which finally composed the First Reform Bill ten years later. He was supported by his friend Sir Robert Wilson and by Cam Hobhouse, whom he had opposed in the Westminster election. His chief opponent was the Leader of the House, George Canning. He had sparred with Canning before and was not afraid of him in debate, but he was still inexperienced and few living men knew more about Parliamentary tactics than Canning. Hobhouse, who hated Canning, did not make matters easier by indulging in some riotous and personal fun at his expense, though he should have known that few men had ever got the better of him in the end, however long Canning might have to wait for his riposte.

This time it came very soon. When Hobhouse had finished, Lord Nugent said to him: 'Either you or Canning will this night have had the damnedest dressing ever a man received in Parliament.' But, to everyone's surprise, Canning did not speak that night. Lambton and his friends thought that he was reserving himself for the next day, but the Army Estimates were to be taken first and their own debate could hardly be resumed until much later in the evening. Lambton was exhausted after his long speech in favour of his proposals and left the House during the debate on the estimates to get some food and to lie down for a short time. And his supporters, seeing him leave, thought that they might as well go too and return with him. When the Army Estimates were concluded, there were only 100 members in the House. It was too good a chance for so astute and unscrupulous a tactician as Canning to miss. Without making any speech, he divided the House on Lambton's motion which was defeated. Lambton, coming refreshed into the chamber a few minutes later, was greeted by a roar of derisive laughter.

It was not a situation which any man could have carried off easily, least of all one of his inordinate pride and violent temper, and he made a stupid and undignified scene, storming at the

Speaker and challenging members who were laughing at him
to stand up and do it to his face. The Speaker, with more
ingenuity than truth, ruled that, though members were undoubtedly laughing at someone or something, he could not
see sufficient evidence that they were laughing at Lambton.
Lambton named two members, Huskisson and Dawson, who
solemnly assured the House that the cause of their mirth had
been something quite unconnected with the debate or with
Mr. Lambton, an explanation which the Speaker declared to
be satisfactory. Canning's move had been astute but not very
honourable and, had Lambton had the sense not to make a
fuss, he would have met with a good deal of sympathy. As it
was he lost his head completely and was hardly restrained by
Brougham and Hobhouse and induced to leave the House.
The whole business was silly and not worth remembering, but
it served to increase the suspicion with which some members
looked on Lambton and to embitter his relations with his own
party, since he felt that his leaders had condemned him to this
humiliation by leaving him to speak for Reform without their
sanction and help. He had written to Grey that 'all this will
end in my complete separation from the party', and it looked
as if the date of that separation could not now be very far off.

The circumstances of Lambton's defeat were unimportant—
many men have survived worse humiliations—and the defeat
itself was not a disaster since not even he could have foreseen
any other result against a Tory majority without full support from his own party. On Lambton himself the effect was
grave. For the first time he had openly defied his leaders and
opposed his father-in-law. From that day onward there could
be no disguising the split in the Whig party. The incident left
him sore and resentful and the difference between his leaders
and himself spread to other matters than Reform. It was
characteristic that the next person with whom he fell out
was Hobhouse who had supported him in his battle with
Canning.

The Whigs, as the traditional defenders of liberty and of all
the oppressed, had for some time announced their intention of
trying to do something to help the Irish Catholics and of revis-
ing the suffrage in Ireland. They viewed the task without
enthusiasm, knowing that whatever they proposed would be

defeated in the House and would almost certainly be displeasing to the Irish whom it was supposed to benefit. They had no settled plan or policy and had not advanced beyond the stage of pious platitudes. The younger members of the party were no more interested than their leaders, though Burdett brought forward a moderate measure for the emancipation of Irish Catholics, which passed the Commons and was lost in the Lords. The Whigs then seemed to feel that they had done all that could be expected of them and were disposed to assent to some even more moderate improvements which the Tories were about to introduce. The Tories were indifferent to the plight of the Irish, but thought that a measure which endowed the Catholic Church in Ireland and gave a few votes to Catholic laity would serve to content the country and to put off any more drastic action.

Lambton was almost alone among the Whigs in objecting to this compromise, which even Brougham and Hobhouse supported. He believed profoundly in freedom of worship for all religions and denominations and his growing spirit of obstinacy drove him once more into disagreement with the rest of the Whigs, who were growing rather tired of his enthusiasm for uncomfortable causes. Brougham, Hobhouse, and Althorp were ready to vote for the Tory proposals. Could not this young Lambton for once be guided by wiser heads than his own? Must he be for ever wasting the time of the House with his quixotry? When the debate came on, Brougham took it on himself to administer a stern rebuke to this restless and self-opiniated colleague. In Lambton's present temper, nothing more was needed to harden his determination and to confirm him in his obstinacy. He spoke strongly against the measure and declared that he would never vote for it, 'though it should cost him every friend that he had in the world'. It did not then cost him Brougham's friendship—that was to come later—but it led to a coolness between Lambton and Hobhouse. Both of them regretted their difference, and Hobhouse, who later became Lord Broughton, under which title he published his entertaining *Recollections of a Long Life*, left an account of the way in which their breach was healed.

'On May 15th,' he wrote, 'I saw Lambton at Brooks'.

There had been a coldness between us since our squabble but he came up and shook hands with me. He said he was willing to do anything to show that the difference between Burdett, me and him had not affected his regard for us. I answered that he could do that very easily if he would come to our annual Westminster on May 23rd. He replied that he had always intended to come to the dinner and that he would do or say anything that might be considered advisable on the occasion. I told him that he was a good fellow and I was very glad at this renewal of friendship with him. He had many excellent qualities, obscured a little by a hasty temper and too much home indulgence.'

Much has been written of Lambton's temper, but little of his readiness to make amends and to renew an interrupted friendship. Fierce as he could be when any principle was involved or when his personal pride was touched, he was never anxious to prolong a quarrel; nor could he, as Brougham could, nurse resentment until he could find a chance of gratifying it. Beneath all his pride and combativeness there lay a deeply affectionate and loyal nature. His political activities sometimes obscured it and gave him the reputation which was fostered by those critics who, like Croker and Greville, saw him mainly in public life and were opposed to him in party warfare. But that was only one side of him.

CHAPTER XI

People who heard Lord Durham speaking in public often remarked that allusions to his home and family were frequent. It is easy to see why this should have been so, for the family to him was everything and home the true reality. It was the centre of his life, the well-spring of his immense compassion, the touchstone of his judgement. In all his dealings with the problems of governors and governed he unconsciously kept in mind the relation between father and child. Perhaps it was partly for that reason that, though men called him Radical Jack, he had little sympathy with popular demagogues and a proper respect for constituted authority, unless it happened to conflict with his own impulse of the moment. His flashes of arrogance and defiance were always over personal matters and were most often displayed towards men who held some sort of authority over him such as Grey and Melbourne.

Life at Lambton was not quite as informal as at Howick, but all the evidence which we have from inside the home—and there is much—shows that they were in every way a happy family and that the children were allowed a good deal of liberty of thought and speech towards their father and mother. Their wholly delightful letters, which still survive, letters written during his frequent absences in London, are spontaneous and obviously written in the confidence that their thoughts and lives are as important to him as to themselves. They are full of what they are reading, of their expeditions and their achievements with gun or pony and, almost invariably, of pleas for his return as soon as possible. Some of the letters are more formal in tone and the copper-plate writing between ruled lines shows evidence of supervision, but there are many, written sometimes in untidy scrawls, which plainly come from the children's love and confidence rather than from duty. There is a typical example in the letter from George, the second son, written when he was seven or eight from the seaside—possibly from Scarborough—to his father in London.

'Dear Papa,
    I wish you would come back again God bless my dear Papa Good morning Papa. Tom caught me a very pretty fish but it was all dead so I kept it for my dinner today. Papa, will you bring me a funny Cosack [sic]? I went into the sea and bathed so nicely and I was very naughty. I am going to have a goat what Charles is going to give me when I am good. This day I am good. I wish you many happy returns for your birthday to-morrow and I am very sorry you are away. I want you to come back.'

That longing for their father's presence—'I want you to come back'—runs through all their letters as do the loving messages—'Alice sends you millions trillions of kisses'—from whichever children were not writing that day. Such letters could only come from a home in which there was love and confidence. In the same way Lady Louisa writes of her loneliness at Lambton when he has left her for his Parliamentary duties.

> 'Now, my dearest Lambton, I must tell you a little how sorry I have been to lose you, I don't think I ever felt so much at parting with you in my life, you have been so good to me, it makes me feel as if I loved you more than I ever did tho' I did not think that that was possible. . . . I cannot say how much I miss you, how very melancholy yesterday afternoon and this morning have seemed to me from not seeing you come into my room as usual. . . . I watched your carriage going away till it was through the gate at the top of the hill the other side of the bridge. I should rather have said the grey horses for had it not been for them I should not have been able to distinguish the carriage after it got among the trees. . . .' 'Good-bye, my dearest, I have nothing to tell you and nothing to answer, I must bid you good-bye. . . .'

Lady Louisa was a wholly adorable person, but life must sometimes have been difficult for her when her husband and her father had quarrelled, since she loved and was loyal to them both. In her letters to her mother there are indications that she was quite aware of her father's idiosyncrasies and no doubt, knowing them both so well, she realized better than anyone else that not all the blame for their disagreements ought to lie with her husband. Certainly she knew all about Grey's aversion from leaving Howick, which was such a trial to his colleagues —'Papa is very bad about it and grumbles extremely as he says he cannot see the reason for it'. She writes too of his habit of making the worst of his small ailments—'I am very sorry to hear that Papa suffers but I don't mind his colds nor do I think they can last long'—and her mother writes with equal freedom and understanding—'He complains occasionally of his stomach but, after all, we cannot reasonably expect him to be exempted from all uncomfortable feelings—after all, who is?' There is a glimpse there and in other letters of the Grey who was always a little bit obsessed with the minor troubles of his life and a trifle querulous when he had to do something that he did not like—most of all when he had to leave his home.

There were four younger children of the marriage, another boy and three girls and, though the heir inevitably held a special place in his father's heart it was never at the expense of the others. There are correspondence with George and Alice, messages from Mary, kisses from Emily; mention always of the book which Mamma is reading aloud and eager inquiries as to who is Papa's favourite person in it; excited comment on the tiny excitement of the moment, like George's fish or the lark which Charles shot, or the way in which the daughters are doing their hair—all the minutiae of a truly happy family and all of it valuable as testimony to that deep goodness which was in the father's heart. None of it contradicts, though all of it must be weighed against all that his enemies said of him, for he cannot be understood unless it is realized that he had all these strains in him—that, as he was Lambton, Villiers, and Lyon, he was also Radical Jack, King Jog, The Dictator, The Lord High Seditioner; and always Dearest Papa and My dearest Lambton. Perhaps acceptance of the seeming contrast may help to an approach to his real nature in the essential truth that what he was in his own home he was in the greater world, and that his conception of the family was the guiding light of his whole life.

There was, too, that side of him at Lambton when the two worlds touched and his friends from his public life saw him at home. There were often guests at Lambton and many of them have written of what they found there. They were of all sorts—political colleagues like Hobhouse and Brougham, sporting friends like Tommy Duncombe, inquirers into social conditions like Harriet Martineau, Royalty in the person of the Duke of Sussex and professional guests like Mr. Creevey. All of them have something to contribute from their own observation, from Brougham who was bored there, as he generally was in country houses, to Miss Martineau who found the conversation so good, from Sydney Smith who admired the gas light to Mr. Creevey who could not get any fish at dinner. Creevey's acquaintance with Lambton began in 1821—'I dined at Lambton's yesterday, en famille', is his record of their first meal together. Thereafter he became a regular guest both in London and at Lambton and as regularly reviled the hospitality which he so readily accepted. Of all Lambton's contemporaries, Creevey tells us most about him, and his diary is such good reading and has been so deservedly popular that he did more than anyone to create the generally unfavourable opinion of him. It would be tedious to examine every incident, but the story of the fish is typical. On 24 October 1825, Creevey, who was a guest at Lambton, wrote to his friend, Miss Ord:

'. . . Soup was handed round—from where God knows; but before Lambton stood a dish with one small haddock and three small whitings in it, which he instantly ordered off the table, to avoid the trouble of helping. Mrs. Grey and myself were at least ten minutes without any prospect of getting any servant to attend to us, altho' I made repeated application to Lambton, who was all this time eating his own fish as comfortably as could be. So, my blood beginning to boil, I said: "Lambton, I wish you would tell me what quarter I am to apply to for some fish." To which he replied in the most impertinent manner: "The servant, I suppose." I turned to Mills and said pretty loud, "Now, if it were not for the fuss and the jaw of the thing, I would leave the room and the house this instant"; and I dwelt on the damned outrage. Mills said: "He hears every word you say"; to which I said: "I hope he does." It was a regular scene.'

No doubt it was and no doubt Lambton behaved badly. Yet it is a strange guest who makes a 'damned outrage' out of a hitch in the service of dinner and perhaps there was more behind the incident than Creevey cared to tell. He had been a guest at Lambton in the previous year, when he records: 'A very large division of us have got together to quiz the whole concern of dinner, so that we really have a very jolly time.' He also mentions on an earlier visit that King Jog was in a fury because his guest had been making fun of his pedigree. It may not be possible to excuse Lambton's failure as a host but quite easy to understand it. Deprivation of fish is not a severe penalty for a guest whose idea of amusement is to quiz his host's dinners and to make fun of his pedigree. We can accept Creevey as an accurate reporter with the mental reservation that he probably asked for all the trouble that he got. It should be added that even Creevey was not proof against Lady Louisa's charm. When he had left Lambton after the episode of the fish, he wrote: 'Nothing could be better than Lady Louisa, in her quiet way to everybody. In every respect and upon all occasions she is a very sensible and discreet person.'

Lord Broughton, who was several times a fellow-guest at Lambton, remarked that though Creevey was a man of good education and of some talent he had the unfortunate habit of seizing every opportunity to raise a laugh at someone else's expense. But Creevey is valuable because he shows us more of the private life at Lambton than do the other adverse critics like Croker and Greville, whose accounts are mostly concerned with politics and who were of the opposite party.

CHAPTER XII

Lord Durham's whole nature was dominated until he approached middle age by a deep and destructive feeling of insecurity which dated from his very earliest years and which he only overcame after a fierce struggle and at the very end of his life. Superficially it may seem absurd to talk of insecurity when he had almost every material advantage that a man can have—wealth, position, personal beauty, a full and interesting life, and a clear-cut tradition. In such things he was favoured as few men are. Yet we believe that through most of his life he was dominated by this feeling to such an extent that it might be said that he lived always in fear.

For many years he lived in fear, not for himself but for all those whom he loved and over whose lives there seemed to hang a doom, a recurring curse of sickness and premature death. The man is lucky who reaches maturity without experiencing the grief caused by a family loss or the death of a great friend. If we consider the life of Lord Durham and of those who were closest and dearest to him, a 'doom' does not seem too dramatic a word to describe the succession of losses and sorrows which is their history.

When he was barely five, his father died of consumption, and five years later the seeds of the same disease were found in him. His first wife died of it only three years after their marriage when he was twenty-three, and, since his doom never dealt its blows separately, his brother-in-law was killed in the same year. Of the three daughters of his first marriage one died at the age of twenty-three and both of the others before they were twenty. Consumption was again the cause of all three deaths. It is hardly possible that he can have failed to realize that the disease had passed from his father to him and from him on to his children, and it may well be that that realization gave him a sense of guilt, quite irrational but none the less intolerable. He may well have asked himself whether he were not to blame for having married and for begetting children. He never spoke of it—it is not such a feeling as men admit even to those who are nearest to them—but his consciousness of the doom, if not of his own guilt, comes out in his occasional and uncontrollable outcries of pain as in his dreadful letters to Grey at the time of his son's death and his despairing cry to his brother Hedworth at the same time or very near it: 'Are all that I love to be taken from me, wife, daughters, mother, son? Is there to be nothing left?'

The deaths of his daughters by his first marriage fell in the years between 1832 and 1835, immediately after his son's death at the age of eleven in 1831 and in 1832 his mother died. It is little wonder that he saw himself as dogged by some destroying fate and that this belief took hold of him at an early age, since for many of those whom he loved he could see the approach of death long before it came. It is only necessary to read Lady Durham's memoir of her son, Charles, to understand what years of apprehension they both endured on his account, for as early as the year 1825, when the boy was only seven, his parents were warned about his danger and they had to endure six years of fruitless effort and diminishing hope.

The first entries in the book are all of pride and delight in the boy's tiny accomplishments when he began to reveal his character. When he was 'quite a little child' he suffered some slight accident and had to have his arm in a sling which he begged to have removed 'for fear I should be frightened'. There are his earliest speculations about God and about worship. He had been told of people who worship idols and asked, 'Do they say, "Our Beasts, which art in Heaven"?' About the same time he remarked: 'They tell me that God made me, but I don't understand how that can be, for I'm not made yet, I shall not be quite made till I'm a man and I do not feel Him making me.' In 1822, when the boy was four, they were at Howick and it was his greatest joy to listen while his mother played the harp and sang to him. There was an English air which 'made his heart feel like velvet and gold' and his favourite tunes were 'Silent, Oh Moyle,' an Irish air, and 'Zitti, Zitti' from *Il Barbiere*, arranged as a duet for harp and pianoforte. Later, at election times, he was a fierce Whig partisan and 'could not bear to hear the Liddells mentioned', and, at the election of 1825, when his father was involved in the only duel which he ever fought, the mother remembered 'the only time in my life, I believe, I could not bear to see him playing about and sent him out of the room to his Aunt Bess'.

In 1824, when he was six, the family were at Scarborough—'He used to look so well, so beautiful by the seaside and enjoyed his bathing so much,' and in the following year, when they had their first warning about his danger, there is the account of his riding by his father's side on the Lambton racecourse. Lawrence painted the famous portrait, *Master Lambton*, in 1825 and it hung ever afterwards in Lord Durham's dressing room, but Master Lambton 'wished it had never been painted' because so many people used to crowd round him and admire him.

That is almost the last of the happy entries and thereafter the record is one of declining hope and of flashes of false recovery. It is clear that all the doctors whom they consulted, though they diagnosed consumption, had very little idea what was wrong and even less how to treat it. The family physician was Dr. Eden who seems to have given up all his other practice and travelled with the family wherever they went, for in the search for a healthy neighbourhood they left Lambton for long periods and took houses in London, at Norwood and Putney and at Brighton, where finally the child died. There are in the Lambton MSS. two receipted bills from Dr. Eden, formally made out to the Lord Privy Seal, which show that in one year his fees amounted to £1,116 17s. 8d. and in another £1,472 10s. 6d.

This record properly belongs to later periods in Lord Durham's life. It is worth mentioning because the devastating effect on him of Charles's death was not a sudden thing, but the culmination of a long period of hope and despair extending over the years when he was busiest with the first of his great works, the Reform Bill and torn between his duty and his longing for his boy. It can only deepen the impression that through those years Lord Durham became so increasingly distraught with his private anxiety and the ill health which resulted from it that his judgement was impaired and that, at the most critical moment of the Reform Bill, he only managed to take part in the negotiations at terrible cost to himself, at great inconvenience to his colleagues and to the permanent damage of his career.

The next stage of his life will bring him to that time of his great political triumph and of his deepest sorrow. These few years began inauspiciously, for during 1825 his health was worse than ever and the anxiety about Charles was becoming grave. Lady Louisa, for all her courage, was affected by the double task of looking after them and was herself far from well. At Christmas of that year, Lambton wrote to his brother George, that the pain which he suffered from his 'nervous rheumatism'—it was the doctors' latest name for it—was almost unbearable. 'The tortures which I have suffered in my head, I cannot describe to you.' The doctors recommended a warmer climate for the whole family and they took a house near Naples, where Lady Louisa and the children spent most of the next two years. Lambton was with them until the late spring of the following year, but he was restless and unhappy without his familiar occupations and travelled often to England and back during the sitting of Parliament. In the summer he went North to attend to the winding up of his racing establishment at Lambton, since he was now convinced that he lacked the strength to look after it properly as well as the time to attend race-meetings. Lady Louisa went with him this time, bringing the children, but the visit was not a success. In any case he had to make it since another election was due and he had to defend his seat, which he did without difficulty, with, in fact, so much ease that he was able to spare time to go into Northumberland to help his brother-in-law, Lord Howick, whose opponent was the Hon. H. T. Liddell, son of Lord Ravensworth. It was, in those days, an uncommon thing for one member to help in another's constituency and, though the Lambtons were landowners in Northumberland, there was much unfavourable comment on his incursion. The unfortunate result was his involvement in a personal quarrel with a Mr. Thomas Beaumont, a supporter of Lord Howick.

On 30 June, Howick was speaking at Alnwick. Lambton was on the hustings with him and Lady Louisa was watching from a window near by. As soon as Howick had finished, Beaumont sprang to his feet and accused Lambton of having prompted him throughout. Lambton hotly denied it and there was an unpleasant scene during which Beaumont called Lambton a liar. Lambton, naturally, demanded an apology which was not forthcoming, and after that there could be only one course of action possible for either of them. Lady Louisa waited in terror at Lambton while Grey, to whom she had appealed, rode unattended and distracted about the country looking for the place of meeting. It is little wonder that he did not find it, for it had to be changed twice because of the threat of interruption by law officers since duelling was illegal. The two men met at last on the sands of Bamburgh Castle and exchanged shots, happily without damage to either.

Howick was not elected and all over the country the elections went badly for the Whigs since the Tories had fought largely on their principle of opposition to Catholic relief and there has seldom been a time when England has failed to rally to the cry of 'No Popery'. Characteristically, Lambton himself favoured relief and made no secret of his opinions during his election speeches, but his personal popularity was enough to return him, though many of his friends among the younger Whigs were less fortunate. Lord John Russell lost his seat in Huntingdonshire and Brougham, who had boldly attacked the traditionally Tory stronghold of Westmorland was heavily defeated. It looked as though the country could settle down to an almost indefinite extension of Tory government, and, after spending a few months in London, Lady Louisa and the family returned to Italy. It was during those months that Lawrence painted the portrait of 'Master Lambton'. Lambton would not go to the studio until it was finished. When at last he went he stood, so Lawrence told a friend, silent for a long time in front of it and then said, almost inaudibly: 'Most beautiful.' And again: 'Most beautiful.' Later he wrote to his wife who was at Naples: 'Did I tell you that I have got Charles's picture here? It is over the chimney-piece in my bedroom. I therefore see his angelic face the last thing before I go to sleep and the first when I awake.'

MASTER LAMBTON
From a portrait by Sir Thomas Lawrence

PART TWO

'Nothing but the Bill'

1826–1832

D

The virtue, spirit, and essence of a House of Commons consists in its being the express image of the feelings of the nation. It was not instituted to be a control *upon* the people, as of late it has been taught by a doctrine of the most pernicious tendency. It was designed as a control *for* the people.

EDMUND BURKE. *Thoughts on the
Causes of the Present Discontent.* 1770.

Certainly kings that have able men of their nobility shall find ease in employing them, and a better slide into their business; for people naturally bend to them as born in some sort of command.

FRANCIS BACON. *Of Nobility.*

CHAPTER I

Those pessimists among the Whigs who, in 1826, predicted a long period of Tory dominance, had failed to take into account the growing dissensions among their opponents. Divided as the Whigs themselves were, they were hardly more unhappy than the Tories, who were by now almost split into two factions—the older men like Wellington and Eldon, who were not prepared to concede any measure of reform, Parliamentary or otherwise, and the more liberal Canning who was hankering after a coalition. In 1826 Lord Liverpool died and Canning formed an administration in which he found places for three Whigs, Lord Lansdowne, Tierney and Brougham. Grey refused to have anything to do with it and wrote to Russell of 'the fatal mistake of joining Canning at the expense of the importance of the Whig Party'. Lambton was sympathetic to many of Canning's ideas but, in loyalty to Grey, he held aloof from the coalition, and in any case he was spending so much time abroad because of his health, that he was not in a position to take a very active part in politics for months at a time.

Canning's death in the autumn of 1826 put an end to the experiment and he was succeeded by the melancholy Lord Goderich, known to Mr. Creevey as 'Goody' or 'The Domestic Goderich'. His government lasted only for five months, but during that time it achieved the rare distinction of being the sole administration of modern times which never faced Parliament.

One other and minor distinction of theirs was that, in 1827, they offered a barony to Lambton, who had just returned from Italy. Characteristically he was furious and did not hesitate to say so, writing to Goderich that 'it is no promotion for the first commoner in England to become the last of her barons', and fuming to Grey about 'the earldom which has for too long been denied to my family'. Everything connected with that promotion was unfortunate. The Tory Press at once stated without concealment that Lord Durham had been bribed with a barony to support the coalition—and not only to support it but to induce Grey to do the same. Lambton had not yet learned to ignore such commonplace abuse and his clamorous complaints about the earldom which he ought to have had added to the unpopularity which the slanders caused. He protested as loudly against the suggestion of a bribe and made a public statement in which he wrote:

'Lord Goderich communicated to me the King's intention to raise me to the Peerage on my return from the Continent. In the month of December, before there was any notion of the Government being broke, after the patents were prepared . . . the King ordered the Peerages of which there were several to go on . . . but I went to Lord Goderich and told him that—advanced as was the business—*if the Duke of Wellington had anything to do with my peerage, I could not and would not receive it.*'

He described the story as 'an infamous lie' and in this he was supported by Brougham, who publicly said: 'Lord Durham is wholly incapable of making any sacrifice of his principles to obtain a peerage.' Probably few people really believed the story, but it was a godsend to the more scurrilous Tory papers and one of them printed a set of verses which were remarkable for their viciousness even in those days of uninhibited controversy:

> *Who is this new-born Peer whose hue*
> *Is turmeric dissolved in custard?*
> *In face of party Buff or Blue?*
> *Lord Mustard.*
>
> *Who boldly 'neath his lady's eye,*
> *Flew at Tom Beaumont like a bustard,*
> *Sure to be bound if she were nigh?*
> *Lord Mustard?*
>
> *Who sent to Mr. Canning word,*
> *When Grey's unsparing speech he'd just heard,*
> *He'd rat if he were dubbed a Lord?*
> *Lord Mustard.*
>
> *Who boasts that all the Lambton blood*
> *Wit, fame and worth in him are clustered?*
> *(Fit scion for those men of mud.)*
> *Lord Mustard.*

If only Lambton had managed to ignore that and other scurrilities of the same sort the trivial storm would have passed in a week, but he had an unfortunate taste for making trouble about things which other men would have treated with silent contempt. He made some fuss about the title of Baron Durham, which had been suggested for him but which he did not like. He was anxious to have a title which would display his long and honourable pedigree and demanded to be made Lord d'Arcy, to which the King refused to agree. This fuss caused some derision among the Tory and the older Whig peers, who were not anxious to welcome him to their House, and the Duke of Bedford wrote caustically to Lord Holland:

> 'So Mr. Lambton, the great commoner, has fallen into the ranks of the mushroom aristocracy of yesterday. He certainly has not changed for the better and was far more respectable as Mr. Lambton of Lambton Castle than as my lord anything. I think it is quite immaterial whether his title is Durham, Wearmouth or Wallsend; though as the former is a principality, he may consider himself a make-believe prince and, having been King Cole, is now Prince Durham.'

There was, of course, no ground for the suggestion that Lord Durham had given or promised any return for his peerage. The offer had been made during Canning's lifetime and he had made it clear in writing to Canning that he would continue to oppose the Tories as heartily in the Lords as he had in the Commons. His integrity was so absolute and so well known that he could have afforded to ignore the mean attacks and the whole incident is only important in the story of his life because his behaviour is typical of him at this time. It shows that childish love of display, and that unfortunate knack of irritating other men by clamouring for recognition of the importance of his family, an established fact which no one questioned and which was of considerably less public interest than he thought it to be.

At the end of the year Goderich's administration perished from sheer inanition and the King turned to the one man whom he knew that he could always trust to do his best for him. Early in 1828 Wellington began to form a Cabinet. There would be no more talk of coalitions and, as everyone who knew the Duke realized, very little hope of any concessions in the direction of Reform.

Lord Durham was not displeased. After the nebulous days of coalition the situation had returned to the rigour of directly opposing parties which suited his temper. 'My great consolation in a Tory government,' he wrote to Grey, 'is that I shall find myself by your side.' He described the new government as 'this most imbecile administration', and added, 'If any skirmishing takes place, I shall find my way to the advanced positions. I am sick of all this temporizing.'

The Whigs had counted on some favour from George IV when he had come to the throne, but every succeeding year had shown them how misplaced had been their hopes. Their opposition to his wishes in the matter of his attempt to divorce his wife had ruined their chances and the Tories were still in power when, in 1830, he died.

William IV was hardly the man whom anyone would have chosen to preside over a country which was in a state of political ferment especially when Reform was certain to become the main subject of debate in the near future. He lacked ability, judgement, and dignity, but he had one great advantage over his predecessor. He was completely honest and he genuinely loved his country and meant to do his duty. Yet he was at heart a Tory and hated the idea of Parliamentary Reform, which, to his muddled way of thinking, involved a reduction of his Civil List and the incursion into Parliament of a whole horde of workmen and revolutionaries. Queen Adelaide was an even stronger supporter of the Tories and it was hard for both of them that his reign should become the period of the growth of Radicalism and the beginning of the decline of aristocratic government.

Yet no sane or unprejudiced person who looked at the state of representation in England at that time, could doubt the need for a drastic change. There were 513 English and Welsh members of the Commons, of whom only eighty-two represented counties, while 403 came from cities, boroughs, and the Cinque Ports. By far the greatest proportion of these were 'rotten boroughs' which were as much the private possessions of their patrons as their houses or estates. The distribution of seats was farcical, for Cornwall, with one of the lowest county populations in England, had forty-two boroughs and returned more members than the whole of Scotland. Wiltshire had thirty-two,

Yorkshire and Sussex twenty-six each, Devon and Hampshire twenty-four. Essex had the unique distinction of boasting that no election had been held there between 1774 and 1810.

Nearly all of these boroughs were represented by two members or by the same number as the counties, so that Rye, with fourteen voters had the same representation as the County of Durham with 6,000. Two members represented the seven voters of Winchelsea, two the 16,000 of Yorkshire. In all, the close boroughs with a total electorate of 90,000 returned nearly 400 members.

It was a system which had worked passably and had even been reasonable 100 years earlier before the great towns had begun to grow and while the country was almost exclusively agricultural. But industry had grown and the towns with it, while the franchise remained as it had been since the Revolution of 1688. Between the years 1760 and 1801 Oldham's population increased from 4,000 to 12,000, Leeds' from 17,000 to 53,000, Manchester from 27,000 to 53,000, yet none of them returned a single member.

In every constituency, whether it were borough, city or county, an election always meant a riot of bribery, drunkenness, and chicanery. Durham County was not a closed constituency and the Lambton interest was strong there, but Lambton had calculated that the last election had cost him all of £30,000. Most of this huge expense was accounted for by hospitality at the local inns, since it was expected of the candidate that he should entertain all his supporters throughout the fortnight or three weeks during which polling went on. In many districts it was considered correct for him to make all his supporters drunk enough to keep them in a good humour and as many as possible of his opponents' too drunk to vote. It was not thought at all unfair to collect a number of opposing voters, to make them paralytically drunk and to keep them in that condition and safely locked up until polling was over. No candidate who was not a rich man or who could not command the support of rich men had any hope of success. To begin with he had to pay for his seat in hard cash, and its patron usually demanded payment long before the election was due. In the previous century, Wilkes had paid £7,000 for the right to contest Aylesbury and the average price of Hastings was £6,000. At Grampound, in

Cornwall, each of the two seats cost £2,931 4s. 8d. The cheapest seat in England was probably Abingdon whose modest price was only £300 down and £100 a year as long as that Parliament lasted, while almost certainly the most businesslike was Sudbury in Suffolk where the electors used to meet before polling day and fix a tariff for the sale of every vote. (In 1801 the price was £10 a vote plus as much free liquor as the voter could drink while polling lasted—no mean addition to the cost when the period was seldom less than a fortnight.)

Polling was open and it was a common thing for a voter to record his vote and go straight to his candidate's agent to draw his bribe in cash. If he failed to vote or voted against his man— and some of them were in a condition when they could hardly tell who was their man—there was no hiding their lapse and they could expect prompt punishment. On all the Duke of Newcastle's vast estates it was an accepted rule that anyone who did not vote for his nominees could expect to be turned out of his house on the day after the poll. In this way the great landlords could control the results of elections in which those of them who were peers were not allowed to take part; in fact, members of the Lords owned 300 boroughs which returned members to the lower House.

CHAPTER II

The mounting political excitement of the times—times when Reform was the chief topic in London clubs and country houses —is reflected in Lord Durham's letters to his wife, written when he had left her at Lambton with the children and gone to London for the opening of the session. He went there by a leisurely route, staying at various country houses on the way for a day's shooting or a race meeting, and arrived in Cleveland Row at the end of October.

At once he was in the thick of it. In November 1830 he wrote the first of a series of letters in which he kept her up to date with the daily excitements of the political world. All the talk was that the Government were on their last legs and that not even

Wellington's enormous prestige could save them. The Whigs' great fear was that Wellington would be shrewd enough to realize that he could only save his party by conceding at least some measure of Reform—enough, at any rate to show the country that the Tories were in touch with modern needs. The Whigs knew that, when the first Parliament of William IV met, the Prime Minister would have to make some sort of allusion to Reform, if not to announce a definite policy. They believed that, bitter though it would be for him to give even the shadow of a concession, Wellington would realize that he must make at least a gesture and would outline some vague idea which would give an appearance of yielding to popular demand without making any real improvement. There were certain boroughs where the scandal was so blatant that he could afford to throw them to the Reformers as a token of his goodwill—Gatton with its one voter and two members, Shoreham, which the Duke of Richmond called 'a whore who is anyone's for their money', or, the most notorious of all, Old Sarum, Cobbett's 'accursed hill' which consisted of 'three fields and one thorn-bush'. Some years before, Lord John Russell had made out a case for the disenfranchisement of Grampound for more than usually scandalous corruption and Castlereagh, for the Tories, had agreed to it. Surely the Duke would have the political wit to make some small sacrifice of the same sort. Had he forgotten Edmund Burke's words about 'Old Sarum, where the representatives, more in number than the constituents, only serve to inform us that this was once a place of trade and sounding with the busy hum of men, though now you can trace the streets only by the colour of the corn and its sole manufacture is members of Parliament'? In that case the Tories might manage to hang on to their power for a few months longer—hardly for more, since any concessions that Wellington might make would be unlikely to satisfy any but the most modest demands.

In the meantime, the Whigs had their own troubles. They were determined to bring in a drastic Reform Bill as soon as they should have the chance, to treat it as a Government measure and to back it with all their power and prestige. But as soon as Lord Durham arrived in London he found that their project was endangered by a threat from his old friend Henry Brougham.

Brougham was a true friend of Reform, but he was too impatient to wait for the right time or wanted the personal prestige of introducing the proposals as his own idea and not as the official policy of his party. Before the session opened, he informed Lord Grey that he was ready with his own proposals which he meant to lay before the House at once, even though the Tories were still in power.

On 2 November Durham wrote: 'We had been all day in trouble respecting Brougham, who had intended giving a notice on the first day about Reform, which might have frightened a number of people unless it was understood clearly that it came from himself and not from the Whigs as a body.' The difficulty, as Durham wrote, was to get Brougham to give up this idea without letting him think that the Whigs were disowning him or going back on their promises. The attempt would be premature, and not only premature but misleading, as there were certain important points on which Brougham differed from the official Whig policy, the most vital of which was the disenfranchisement of the close boroughs which he was known not to favour. Durham, as an old friend was begged to dissuade him and, after some trouble, succeeded. 'However, last night,' he wrote, 'I hope I accomplished it. He was very reasonable and all will, I trust, go on right. But it gave me a great deal of trouble and cost you a letter.' In the same letter, he mentions that the Government were having trouble with Palmerston, who was always too liberal-minded a man to follow Wellington indiscriminately, and who had the political insight to realize that nothing could stop Reform.

On 2 November 1830, Earl Grey rose in the House of Lords and regretted that the gracious speech from the Throne made no reference to Parliamentary Reform. The Duke of Wellington replied with an explicit declaration of his entire faith in the present system and the impossibility of improving it. After this panegyric, he ended by saying:

'Under these circumstances, I am not prepared to bring forward any measure of the description alluded to by the Noble Lord. And I am not only not prepared to bring forward any measure of this nature, but I will at once declare that, as far as I am concerned, as long as I hold any station in the government of the country, I shall always feel it my duty to resist such measures when proposed by others.'

The Duke was not normally responsive to an emotional atmosphere, but, as he resumed his seat among the stricken silence of his supporters and the barely concealed delight of the Opposition, even he seemed to guess that he had committed a blunder. He turned to Lord Aberdeen, who was sitting beside him, and asked: 'I haven't said too much, have I?' Aberdeen replied grimly: 'You'll hear of it.' Another peer, coming late into the House sat down behind Aberdeen and asked him what the Duke had said. Even more grimly Aberdeen answered: 'He said, we're going out.'

The next few days were enough to prove the accuracy of Aberdeen's prophecy. There was an outburst of popular fury all over the country and especially in London, where threatening crowds gathered before Apsley House and were only deterred from violence by the sight of the gunners who stood, with lighted portfires, by the Waterloo cannons beside the front door.

The Tories were dismayed and the Whigs were jubilant. There were Tory peers who hated the idea of Reform as heartily as did the Duke, but who had the sense to see that an appearance of concession would, for a time at least, have contented the country and saved the Government. Lord Durham wrote exultantly to his wife:

'The Duke, or rather "Dick" was worse than ever. I never heard such wretched, vulgar slip-slop. . . . The current of public feeling is setting strongly against the Dictator. His declaration against all Reform has done him serious injury and last night Lord Winchelsea told him he was much mistaken if he thought he could conciliate the Tories by it, he could as soon "storm Heaven", and that they saw the necessity of Reform as well as others. . . . Nothing can exceed the "Dick's" unpopularity—They say the doors of his carriage are always locked for fear of his being dragged out by the mob.'

Letters from Mr. Morton, the agent at Lambton, showed that opinion in the North was as hot as in London. 'The King's speech has disappointed many persons at Newcastle, etc., but the worst indignation is openly expressed at the Duke of Wellington's observations on Parliamentary Reform and the immaculate system of the present representation of the people in the commons. Those who have previously supported him are now outrageous at him.' He added, with apparent pleasure, that the Rector of Walsingham had had his windows broken though—'a disposition on his part to be too officious in shutting up the alehouses at a certain hour' was more to blame than popular feeling about politics.

The least disturbed man in the country was the Duke, who remarked to his friend Lady Jersey at a party: 'Lord, I shall not go out. You will see, we shall go on very well.'

But he had lived for too much of his life in a world where popular clamour could be disregarded and within a few days he realized that his party could not cling any longer to office. He made a spirited, rather than a skilful effort to explain away his words, but equivocation was not in his line and Grey easily made him look foolish. Durham wrote to his wife on 9 November.

'We had an explanation from the Duke of the cause of the most extraordinary step taken yesterday and never did a mouse produce such a mountain.—Lord Grey, as you will see, exposed it very well—and it is impossible to say how much the ministers and especially the Duke have been damaged by the whole proceeding. The *Sun*, I see, said that Lord Lansdowne had been sent for—not a word of it is true; but how they can go on much longer I cannot conceive. All about the King are furious with them. After all he must dislike being involved in their unpopularity.'

The Tories were still in, but it could not be for more than a few days and the Whigs were confident. 'It was decided,' Durham writes, 'at a meeting at Althorp's on Saturday to have no amendments on the address but stoutly to oppose all measures in detail. This is the true policy.' In the same letter he refers to the difficulty which the Tories were having with Palmerston and says: 'The Duke as I said before, has made another offer to Pam of 3 seats—without telling one of his colleagues until it was over.' Palmerston, it would seem, was already moving away from the Tories and it is no surprise to find him a little later at the Foreign Office in a Whig administration.

Lord Durham's next letter is triumphant—a hurried scrawl, undated except for a scribbled '1/2 past 5' at the top:

'The King has sent for Lord Grey—he says nothing could be more satisfactory than his conduct and he has entrusted Lord Grey with the formation of a new administration.'

On 17 November his letter is full of Cabinet-making and we come to the first reference to Lord Melbourne who was afterwards to play so large and important a part in his life: 'In the evening Ld. Palmerston came and had an interview with Ld. G. of considerable duration. He was to consult his two friends, Melbourne and C. Grant this morning. However there is no doubt of their junction. The D. of Richmond also will join the new Govt.—of which I am very glad because he is an excellent straightforward person. None of the places are yet settled—but the King has given Ld. G. carte blanche. . . .' Brougham was again the difficulty—'He has frightened so many people (the King among the rest) by his wild speeches that it would be hard to place him in a situation which would please him and at the same time not offend others.'

Lord Durham would have been less than human if he had not begun to speculate about his own chance of office and apparently he hoped for the Foreign Office, which Grey was tempted to take for himself, 'except that he feels that he must take the Treasury as Prime Minister which he does not like'. 'You will naturally ask,' Durham writes, 'something of myself. Ld. G. asked me my views—which I explained to him in the same terms that I had often done before of which you are not ignorant—but told him that I would sacrifice all my own inclinations to assist him in the most arduous task which he has undertaken. . . . I trust Sir J. Graham will have a post. . . .' The letter ends with an urgent plea to Lady Durham to bring the whole family up to London at once and with instructions for the despatch of the coach horses and hacks, the cabriolet and curricle groom—also 'a small barrel of strong small beer sent up by sea directed to Mrs. Taylor, Whitehall—the same sort that I drink. There should also be one sent up for my own use.'

In a letter to Princess Lieven, written in the first flush of success, Lord Grey expounded his principles of Cabinet-making. It was, he said, his intention 'to show that in these days of democracy and jacobinism, it is possible to find real capacity in the high aristocracy—not,' he concludes magnificently, 'that I wish to exclude merit if I should meet it in the commonalty.'

Grey was in little danger of meeting any quality in a commonalty which he had never had anything to do with, and his Cabinet consisted exclusively of aristocrats and land-owners, except for Brougham who was neither, but it was to show that he had among his many good qualities the outstanding one of being able to set the right man to the right task. His administration included five men who were afterwards to become Prime Ministers and, in Palmerston, one who was to make a great name at the Foreign Office. He did not subscribe to the view which was later to be expressed by Thomas Jefferson when he thanked God that he could find men of ability for every position without having to employ his own relations. Grey was happy to find room for six of his connections, which led to his administration being derisively known to enemies as 'The Grey List'. They included his son, Lord Howick, two sons-in-law, Lord Durham and Edward Ellice, and Lord Duncannon who was later to marry Lady Frances Charlotte Lambton, Lord Durham's daughter.

Lord Durham may have been disappointed at being only Lord Privy Seal—in that informal and closely-knit political society it does not seem to have occurred to Grey to tell him why he had been selected for an office of minor importance—but he was delighted to be in office and characteristically showed his delight in a less inhibited way than would most men. Cam Hobhouse, who was not at that time included, though later he joined the ministry, and may have been a little sour on that account, wrote in his diary: 'My Lord is acting the Cabinet Minister already and has already taken on two new footmen and ordered his Windsor uniform.' It is easy to believe him. Lord Durham never lost or hid his love of the trappings of office nor was he ashamed to show a feeling which many men shared while affecting to despise it.

Once more Grey showed his shrewd judgement of men in choosing Durham for the task which he regarded as his first and most important obligation, but the news was only casually imparted to him one evening when they left the House of Lords together and Grey said: 'Oh, by the way, Lambton, I wish you would take our Reform Bill in hand.' Durham willingly agreed and Grey then asked him whether he had any objection to consulting John Russell. Durham was more than willing since few men had made a closer study of all the problems connected with Reform or had more decided ideas about how to deal with them. Durham then added Sir James Graham and Lord Duncannon to his advisers and the Committee of Four came into being. They held their first meeting at Lord Durham's house in Cleveland Row, where they continued to meet through December and the first months of 1831. The speed with which they drafted their suggestions was astonishing. In a little over two months the Committee had finished their final draft proposals and were ready to lay them before the Cabinet. The original draft of their report is among the Lambton MSS. and is dated 14 January 1831.

They worked not only fast but silently, for Lord Durham had, from the beginning, insisted on strict security so that no hint of their proposals should leak out before the Cabinet had heard them. He took the chair at every meeting and also acted as secretary, making notes of the discussions and recording them as minutes. For greater secrecy Lady Durham and her daughter were persuaded to act as copyists and there was hardly any consultation with anyone outside that little group, though Thomas Turton, who had been at Eton with Lord Durham, gave them some legal advice. (It was the same Turton who was to cause so much trouble later in Canada, though through no fault of his own.)

CHAPTER III

Historians have often debated the question of how much Lord Durham himself contributed to the Reform Bill. A few years after its passing, when it was the fashion to decry him in every possible way, it was said of him that he did none of the work and claimed all the credit. (His enemies were to take the same line over the Durham Report.) For this he had to some extent himself to blame since he loudly and constantly proclaimed that the Bill was his own and abrogated to himself all the credit which was his due and a good deal more. He was also in the habit of saying, with much truth, that the Bill would have been a much better one if he had had all his own way about it, but that was his attitude towards most things and it was not until many years afterwards that the gradual extension of the franchise proved that he had been more shrewd and far-seeing than most of his contemporaries, even his colleagues on the committee. It would be as absurd to give him the whole credit as to deny him a fair share of it and undoubtedly the one serious fault in the Bill was its omission of his proposal for voting by ballot. Probably it was inevitable at the time, since it was difficult enough to get the King to stomach Reform at all and might have been impossible had balloting been a part of it. It was over this point and, to a less degree over the franchise qualification, that he and his colleagues disagreed. Lord Durham was ill when the draft was presented to the Cabinet and, in his absence, they unanimously agreed to abandon the idea.

It is impossible not to think that he was right, if not tactically at any rate in principle. When voting was open and public there could be no end to both bribery and intimidation nor was there any protection for an elector who felt obliged to vote against the will of his landlord or his patron. Lord Durham would have killed this evil with one stroke by the introduction of the ballot box, but his colleagues were appalled at the idea that any man should pay good money for a constituency and yet put himself in a position where electors might take his bribes and vote for his opponent. Reformers they were, but there was a limit to their altruism, and, in fact, the election which followed the passing of the Bill was the most corrupt and Dionysian revel which the electors of England had shared for many years.

A good deal of light is shed on this and on the whole question of how much credit each member of the Committee could justly claim by the correspondence of 1834 between Lord Durham and Lord John Russell. Grey had suggested the addition of Russell to the Committee not only because of his great knowledge of the subject, but also because it was to fall to him to present the Bill in the Commons. Normally this would have been done by Althorp as Leader of the House, but he was such a wretched speaker that his introduction might have proved fatal to its chances. As it was he nearly caused the fall of the Government a few days before the Bill was due by his glaringly inept presentation of his budget.

Russell was one of the few men with whom Lord Durham remained friendly throughout his career and it was to Russell that he entrusted the work of preparing the first draft. In his letter of 19 October 1834, Russell wrote: 'In the latter end of November or the beginning of December 1830, I went by your desire to your house in Cleveland Row, where you informed me that you had received a commission from Lord Grey to ask for my assistance in forming a committee to prepare a plan of Reform.' This was the first draft which was afterwards kept among Lord Durham's papers, endorsed in his writing, 'Lord John Russell's plan of Reform'. Russell did not claim any originality for his scheme since, as he wrote in the same letter: 'Lord Grey and other Reformers had repeated since the year 1780 the great outline of Reform.' Russell, as he goes on to explain, embodied in his draft those general principles and suggested the disenfranchisement of fifty boroughs and the reduction of fifty more to one member each. He was writing from memory, four years afterwards, and mentioned that the franchise qualification was to be '£10 in the old boroughs and (I think) £15 in the new'. He was quite certain in his memory that Lord Durham insisted on the ballot, that Graham and Duncannon did not like it, and that he himself only agreed reluctantly on condition that the franchise should be raised to £20. Graham proposed a scheme of registration to which the Committee agreed after a few alterations had been made and they all wished Parliaments to be limited to a life of five years.

So far it is clear that, with the exception of the ballot, the whole committee were in agreement and that on that point alone Lord Durham was obdurate. His illness when the draft went forward to the Cabinet gave the committee an opportunity of dropping the idea. The Cabinet, the King, and ultimately Parliament accepted the rest of the provisions, but, in the absence of the ballot, bribery and bullying continued to thrive at every election until the Ballot Act became law in 1872. It ought not to be forgotten that Lord Durham, not for the only time, saw clearly the need of a reform long before any of his contemporaries, since it was his unhappy fate often to propose some good and novel idea for which other men later got the credit. The difference between him and them was that they took a more practical and common-sense view of ideas than he. In this case Russell and the others and later the Cabinet knew that the suggestion of the ballot would kill the Reform Bill at once. They may not have been opposed to it in theory, but they knew that it was tactically impossible. No such mundane doubts ever troubled Lord Durham's aristocratic aloofness. If a certain course seemed to him to be right it was a matter of no importance whether it were practicable or not. It was generally attributed to his pride that he would not consider details, but there was more than pride in his contemptuous refusal to consider immediate convenience or consequences. He had absolute integrity and he was never to be moved from a chosen course by the thought of personal or party advantage. If a policy was right, it was right, and if the Government could not carry it, they must go. (Less high-minded men reflected that if a policy was right it would be of little use if its only result was to let the other side in.) Perhaps he had, too, a feeling that any policy was right if he supported it, for that unflinching champion of the people was always sure that he knew what was best for them.

In this case he was right, though it took forty years to prove it; yet his colleagues were no less right because they were determined to take what they could get at the moment and leave the rest for another time. From a purely political point of view it was as well that Lord Durham was unable to present his own report to the Cabinet. He would surely have fought strenuously for his ballot and would possibly have wrecked his Bill or split his party, but it was the beginning of embittered relations within the Whig Cabinet and there could hardly have been a worse time for it, when they needed all their strength and unity to carry their reforms into law.

It is possible now, after a lapse of more than 100 years and after passions have cooled, to come near to an assessment of the credit to which he is entitled for the Bill. Russell did much of the practical work of drafting and supplied the hard political common sense which made it at last acceptable. Graham and Duncannon did their share particularly in the preparation of the Bills for Scotland and Ireland, of which they had special knowledge. Lord Durham applied the grand design and the driving force which set all in motion. Sir T. R. M. Butler sums up the position in his *Passing of the Great Reform Bill*.

'On this occasion Radical Jack . . . played no small part in the production of a winning strategy. . . . Durham and Brougham alone may be said to have really understood the middle-class point of view by sympathy and connection and both were in correspondence with Lord Grey; it is probable that they were the main channels by which he became aware of the rising enthusiasm of the people. . . . It would appear that Lord Grey's statesmanlike conviction of the need and the advantage of an extensive measure was the prime source of the Reform Bill; that the wisdom of Russell and the will of Durham embodied this conviction in a bold and simple form.'

In spite of his failure to impose the ballot, the accomplishment of the draft Bill must be accounted one of the great moments of Lord Durham's life. The pity was that, in those frantic weeks of preparation, he had so much overtaxed his strength that his health gave way and, as soon as the strain was relaxed, he suffered a series of the most excruciating attacks of pain that he had yet known. He had presided at every meeting of the committee and had kept all the minutes in his own hand. It is little wonder that the end of the task found him exhausted and unable to take part in the Cabinet discussions which followed during the next few weeks. The committee kept him informed about the proceedings and still hoped that he might be well enough to take part in the debates when the Bill should reach the Lords. However much they may have differed about technical points they all realized that his absence from Parliament would deprive them of their strongest fighter. Graham especially wrote at intervals to tell him the latest news and his letters show how much he had come to admire him. Graham probably had not expected to be asked to serve on the committee—he was added because of his special knowledge of Scottish electoral problems—and was frankly delighted by the invitation. 'No honour,' he wrote in reply, 'which Lord Grey could have conferred on me would have gratified me more than being chosen by him as an associate with such colleagues in so noble an undertaking.' Durham had obviously made him welcome and put him at his ease, for he wrote on 19 November 1830, that, 'The kind expressions in your note gratify me extremely; on my first entrance into public life you received me with generous kindness and I hope to its close we shall act together as Friends and never cease to entertain that warm regard which is the true cement of official intercourse, and increase our power of serving the Public with efficiency.'

Lord Durham was ill at Cleveland Row when the discussions began in the Cabinet in January and Graham wrote to him on the 25th:

'My dear Lord,

I have been grieved to hear how ill you have been. I would have called on you long ago, but I feared that the excitement of discussion would do you harm. . . . *The Measure*, on the whole, was well received; Brougham alone dissentient and disposed to carp by raising little points when he could found no real objections and very much inclined to defend the Nomination Boroughs. We have another Cabinet today at four and I will call on you afterwards taking my chance of your being well enough to see me.'

Two days later, he wrote again: 'Pray come to the Cabinet tomorrow. Althorp and others wish to lower the Qualification; I am afraid and foresee difficulties.'

There could be no question of Lord Durham's attendance at the next or at many future meetings, and his forced inaction had grave effects on him, for he had nothing to do but lie in his darkened room and brood about his troubles, public and private. In his absence, the Cabinet, though they agreed to most of the provisions suggested for the Bill, resolutely refused to consider the ballot. To his mind this was a vital part of it, and their action came to loom in his sick fancy as deliberate insult. They also rejected his suggestion of triennial Parliaments, which he thought important, though less important than the ballot. These things preyed on his mind and were responsible for the growth of that bitterness against Grey which he was soon to reveal so blatantly. It was neither the first time nor the last when he was to reveal that fatal weakness of his of thinking that a measure or an action was necessary for the simple reason that he wanted to see it come about.

His private troubles alone would have been enough to torment him. He was receiving alarming reports from Morton, his agent, of the progress of the pitmens' strike in the Durham coalfields where, though the Lambton men were still working, most of the other men were idle and were threatening violence if they did not come out in sympathy. A strike would involve him in financial loss and worse still would endanger that good relationship on which he justly prided himself. Worst of all, it would cause suffering to his men for whom he felt such a personal responsibility. But there was worse still. His heir, the boy Charles William, was dying. It might be a matter of months or even of a year, but the doctors, who knew so little about the disease, knew at least that they could do no more. 16 January was Charles's eleventh birthday and on that day, as in past years, the bells of the churches of his county rang out their Triple Grandsires in greeting. They were never to ring for him again.

CHAPTER IV

The supporters of Reform throughout the country were well organized and determined to let their voices be heard. In the last few days of February, petitions poured into Westminster from every district of England and Scotland and were laid on the table of the House. Many of them went so far as to demand the ballot and popular suffrage—a proof that Radical Jack was, as usual, more in touch with popular feelings than were most of his colleagues. Althorp, as leader of the House, had to present over 100 petitions, including one from Manchester with 12,245 signatures and one from Edinburgh with nearly 22,000. The Cabinet, on the eve of their great enterprise, could take heart from this overwhelming display of the support which they enjoyed in the country. They had two other good reasons for feeling hopeful.

They had the advantage of complete surprise. Until Russell rose at six o'clock on that evening of 1 March 1831, to open the Bill, not one of the Opposition had any idea of the extent of its provisions—a disadvantage which was to prove very important when Peel came to make his much-criticized decision not to oppose the first reading.

The other, and perhaps the greater advantage which the Whigs had was that Radical Jack was back in the Cabinet and in the House. All the contemporary writers have laid great stress on his ruthless treatment of Grey but have not given him credit for the change which he worked in the mentality of the Cabinet. In his absence they had been divided and some of them were ready to desert the cause of Reform, if they could see an opportunity. Durham had not been back for more than a few days when he showed what can be achieved in a divided council by one man who knows exactly his own mind and does not care how unpleasant he has to make himself to get what he wants. There was no more talk of backsliding now that Grey's resolution was backed by Durham's strong will and singleness of purpose, and, when the Bill should reach the Lords, it would have no fiercer defender than the man who had presided over the Committee of Four and might fairly claim to be its chief author. Much as they feared his temper in council, they would be glad enough of his presence when Wellington's heavy batteries opened in debate.

All political London was astir that night, and the streets were filled with restless crowds who somehow expected that the gentlemen in Parliament were about to work a miracle before bedtime. In the great Whig houses, the windows were ablaze with light, where the curtains were drawn back to give a glimpse of rooms in which the friends of Reform sat at their dinner tables and were prepared to sit as long as the debate should last. At Westminster, messengers and servants hung round the taverns near to the House, ready to run with the latest news of what was going on inside and to earn a guinea and a bellyful of ale from the Whig hosts if the news were good.

Punctually at six, Russell rose in his place—'a little fellow not weighing eight stone', a Tory member remarked, 'and his head hardly reaching above the table'. There was absolute silence in the House and his first words, quietly as he spoke, carried into every corner of the crowded chamber:

'I rise, Sir, with feelings of the deepest anxiety, to bring forward a question which, unparalleled as it is in importance, is as unparalleled in points of difficulty. . . .'

Russell was no great orator, but he was master of his subject and of the art of lucid exposition. He had all the self-assurance which is sometimes found in very small men, and in that tiny body were compact enough courage and pugnacity to take on the whole of the Tory party—single handed if need be, as, according to Sydney Smith, he had declared that he would not hesitate to take command of the Fleet, if he thought it his duty to do so. He showed his courage and self-possession later that evening, when after detailing his proposals for the rotten boroughs he was interrupted by the Opposition with angry shouts of 'Names! Names!' As calmly as though he were reading a shopping list, Russell announced the names of the boroughs in Schedule A, all of which were to be disenfranchised, while the jeers and derisive laughter from the Opposition benches grew to an uproar. When he had finished, he paused, looked up smiling and added, without any change of voice, 'More yet', and went on to read Schedule B, the boroughs which were to lose half their members.

In a famous passage early in his speech, he made good use of the not very original image of the foreigner visiting England to learn her method of government and the reason for her prosperity and greatness:

'Would not such a foreigner be much astonished, if he were taken to a green mound and informed that it sent two members to the British Parliament; if he were shown a stone wall and told that it too sent two members to the British Parliament; or if he walked into a park without a vestige of a dwelling and was told that that too sent two members to the British Parliament?'

He ended with a significant note of warning:

'No half-measures will be sufficient. No trifling, no paltry reform can give stability to the Crown, strength to the Parliament or satisfaction to the Country.'

When he sat down again, he had spoken for two and a half hours.

There were many on both sides of the House who said that Peel should have risen as soon as Russell sat down and should straightway have moved the rejection of the motion for leave to bring in the Bill. With the temper of the House what it was at that moment, he might, they thought, have strangled the Bill at its birth. Croker, who strongly held that view, enlarged on it in a letter to Wellington which elicited the reply that the Opposition had agreed on their policy and had not had time to reconsider it. Peel had been in a very awkward position, since he did not like to risk a complete change of tactics without previous consultation with his chief and without even a hasty word with his colleagues in the Commons.

For the moment the Whigs had gained the advantage of surprise, but the Tories were full of fight, and for seven days the battle raged in the Commons. Day after day the dawn broke and in the House the candles paled as the first grey light stole in through the windows to find the members, rough-chinned, blear-eyed, and irritable, but still in their places. Night after night the heavy guns fired from each side, as Russell and Croker, Althorp and Weatherall, Peel and Macaulay unmasked their batteries, and the fortune of battle swayed so that no man could catch more than a fleeting hope of victory or a glimpse of defeat. Croker's speech was magnificent, hard-hitting and practical; Weatherall's was a full-blooded mixture of argument, invective, and characteristically genial vulgarity. Peel did much to restore his party's confidence and to annul the effect of his tactical blunder, if blunder it were; and, on the last night, when young Mr. Macaulay swept into his peroration, older members, light-headed from lack of sleep, fancied themselves carried back to the great days of Fox and Sheridan and seemed to catch, in the dim light of the candles, a glimpse of blue hair-powder and scarlet shoe-heels. It all ended on the eighth night, when leave was granted to bring in the Bill. There was no division. The Tories were standing by their original plan, even to assenting to the introduction of Bills for Scotland and Ireland.

On 21 March the Bill was read again and, after two days of debate, was carried by one vote. Macaulay, in a famous description of the scene, wrote:

'The tellers scarcely got through the crowd, for the House was thronged up to the table and all the floor was fluctuating with heads like the pit in a theatre. But you might have heard a pin drop as Duncannon read the numbers. Then again the shouts broke out and many of us shed tears. I could scarcely refrain. And the jaw of Peel fell and the face of Twiss was as the face of a damned soul; and Herries looked like Judas, taking his necktie off for the last operation. We shook hands and clapped each other on the back and went out, crying and huzzaing into the lobby. And no sooner were the doors opened, than another shout answered that within the House.'

Yet, when the shouting had died down, the Tories were well satisfied. Their plan was still working and they could still destroy the Bill in Committee. They were heartened by the knowledge that they had so nearly achieved their object at this early stage, and indeed they had come nearer to it than they had dared to hope and had only been defeated by a strange chance. Calcraft, who had been Paymaster in Wellington's last administration, had suffered a sudden and quite inexplicable change of heart and had voted against his party, though he had spoken against the Bill. So great was the issue, that he did not meet with the tolerance which, in those days, was usually extended to a member who went into the lobby against his party. So strongly was he made to feel the enormity of his offence, that he broke down under the strain and, a few days later, killed himself.

The Tories were left with the comfortable assurance of being able to find some technical point on which, in Committee, they could trip the Government and so defeat the Bill, while giving to the country, as they hoped, only the appearance of being careful about details, while preserving the principle. They still retained a rather vain hope that so the country might take them for friends, not enemies of Reform. The Whigs, were for all their victory, in a less happy position. The narrow margin of one vote—and that a pure chance—did not appear to them to be sufficient warrant for persisting with the Bill in the existing Parliament, and they knew that the King would take fright, especially as Grey had unintentionally left him under the impression that the Bill would pass both Houses without undue bother. The Cabinet reverted to their hesitation and even Grey lost heart and began to talk of retiring or of an appeal to the country. Palmerston and Melbourne renewed their pressure in favour of modifying the Bill to make it acceptable to waverers among the Opposition. Once again it was Radical Jack's scornful rejection of any compromise which kept the Whigs true to their course. He wrote at once to Grey insisting on a renewal of the fight without compromise or concession, and openly advised that this time the Government must be in a position to tell the House that they had the King's assurance that all necessary steps would be taken to pass the Bill through both Houses.

In face of this defiant courage, the Cabinet did not feel able to give in without another fight, but they earnestly begged Russell to go carefully through the Bill to see what alterations of detail could be made which would make it sound more attractive without impairing its main strength. Russell obligingly made one or two very slight amendments, which, in his opinion, made it even more effective, and, in the opinion of the rest of the Cabinet, left it exactly where it was, as far as its chances of success were affected. He moved five boroughs out of Schedule A into Schedule B, so that they would lose only one seat each instead of two, and took seven boroughs out of Schedule B. He also allotted, by way of balance, an equal number of extra seats to the counties and the large towns. It was obvious that Russell was only interested in making his Bill as technically perfect as possible and was not giving much thought to improving its chance of acceptance, but, as it happened, one of his alterations gave to the Tories their hoped-for chance of attacking it on a matter of detail. The original Bill had reduced the number of members by sixty-two. After Russell had amended it, this figure was altered to thirty-five.

On 12 April, before the House rose, Russell announced his new proposals and, as soon as the House went into Committee on the 18th, Wellington launched his counter-attack. Before there had been any discussion, General Gascoigne rose—and moved, as an 'Instruction' to the Committee:

'That, in the opinion of this House, the total number of knights, citizens and burgesses returned to Parliament by that part of the United Kingdom called England and Wales, ought not to be diminished.'

From a purely tactical point of view it was a shrewd move,

though, as far as any longer view was concerned, the suggestion could hardly have been more helpful to the Government or more harmful to the Opposition. *The Times* next morning called it 'Giving the Reformers more of a good thing than they wanted' and its effect would have been to throw more seats open to competition which would benefit the supporters of free elections. But the Tories were thinking only of the exigencies of the moment and the opportunity of posing as the champions of more extended suffrage was, however false, too good to miss. It took the Whigs completely by surprise, since the House had not yet gone into Committee and they had not expected the fight to begin before then. They fought it strenuously through the night, but at four o'clock in the morning the House divided and the Government, with 291 votes against 299, were in a minority of eight.

The Tories had gained a tactical victory, but once again they had been short-sighted and their strategy played into the Reformers' hands. The one thing which was bound to help the Whigs was an appeal to the country, and this they could now honourably claim. If, as they had good reason to believe, the country was solidly in favour of Reform, now was their chance to give an overwhelming demonstration of it, and return a party with a big enough majority to carry it in the Commons.

The Tories would plead that they had only upset the Bill on a technical point and for its own good, but no one would believe them. The Whigs could be relied on to expose the sham and hold them up to the execration of the people as the enemies of Reform.

At first Grey hesitated and at once Durham, Brougham, and Russell were at him, urging him not to let such a chance slip. Althorp lent his solid weight in support and Grey posted off to Windsor to ask the King to dissolve Parliament.

He met with a flat refusal. The King hated the idea of Reform, but he had consented to the terms of the Bill because he believed that it was the desire of Parliament and therefore his duty not to oppose it. He believed now that Grey had misled him and somehow or other he had got it into his poor, muddled head, that Grey had promised him that he should never become involved in a dissolution because of Reform. The Commons had rejected the Bill; he had done all that could be required or expected of him and he would do no more. The Whigs had made their bed and they must lie on it—and, he sincerely though privately hoped, die in it. His feelings found expression in literary composition and he wrote what Peel said was the only poem of his life.

I consider Dissolution,
Tantamount to Revolution.

It neatly expressed his feelings and those feelings were now to bring on a Constitutional crisis.

CHAPTER V

The next forty-eight hours passed for both Whigs and Tories in an atmosphere of mounting drama and frenzied activity, relieved by interludes of the purest farce. The Cabinet met next day, 20 April, and resolved to make another appeal to the King to grant a dissolution. Grey had already written to the King begging him to reconsider his refusal. Cam Hobhouse noted in his diary: 'Lord Grey employed Lord Durham to write his answer, which he showed me. It was very well done and bound the King to Reform in as civil and respectful terms as possible.' Lord Grey seems to have thought much of the letter, for in a note to Lord Durham, he calls it 'perfect'.

On the twentieth, while the Cabinet were at their meeting, the King set off from Windsor and drove up to London, so that he could be at St. James's Palace and readily available. As soon as they had finished their discussion, Grey went to St. James's, taking with him a copy of the minute which the Cabinet had passed, humbly praying His Majesty to reconsider his decision and to grant a dissolution. Once again Grey showed his unfailing ability to reassure and persuade his master and next day received from him a long and rather rambling letter, setting out his decision and the reasons which now led him to change it and to grant the Cabinet's request. The King was now, it said, of the opinion, that as there appeared to be no likelihood of anyone else being able to form a stable government, he regarded dissolution as 'the lesser of two evils'. Its tone was not cordial, but it gave the Cabinet what they wanted and their hopes were restored. They decided to postpone the appeal to the country for a few days, as they wished to carry certain money orders which were needed for the routine business of the country.

The Tories, knowing that these orders were necessary, thought that they saw a unique chance of discrediting the Whigs by keeping them in office for the simple pleasure of defeating them whenever they wanted. Their recent triumph had gone to their heads and for the moment they had lost all thought of the country's need, or, in fact, of anything but the enjoyment of kicking the Whigs when they were down. They had always professed to be the party which paid the greatest attention to the dignity and comfort of the King, but they did not consider the intolerable position in which they were placing him by leaving him with a government which could not even provide the day-to-day means of running the country. Knowing that they had a majority in the House, they resolved to pass a motion humbly praying His Majesty not to exercise his prerogative of dissolving Parliament. They were relying on the King's personal dislike of Reform and even more on the Queen's notorious preference for the Tories and her supposed influence over her husband in political matters.

On 21 April, Lord Wharncliffe, one of the leading Tory peers, fired the first shot in this new campaign, by giving notice in the House of Lords of his intention to move the address to the King on the following day. That night the Lords rose early and all those peers who were in the Cabinet went to dinner at Lord Durham's house leaving the Commons still in session. Althorp, of course, was in his place and, while the peers were at dinner, a frantic message from him warned them that the Tories were using every possible device to prolong debates on any trivial matter, so as to prevent the House from reaching the money orders. Althorp wrote that he thought that there would now be no chance of reaching these until midday on the 22nd, by which time Wharncliffe would have moved or would be in the process of moving his address to the King. If this ingenious plan succeeded, the Government would be in the miserable position of holding office at the pleasure of the Opposition, unable to move even a simple money order unless it pleased their enemies to allow them. It was hardly likely that the King would ignore the House's plea and persist in dissolution which would, ostensibly at any rate, be against the expressed wish of Parliament. Althorp urged Grey to leave the money vote to care for itself and ask the King for an immediate dissolution.

The Cabinet acted promptly on his advice. Grey sent a message, before they left Lord Durham's house, asking for an audience of the King, and begging that it might be as early as possible on the next day. The King answered at once that he would see Grey at half-past eleven. Even so there was little enough time to spare. Parliament met at two o'clock in the afternoon, which gave Grey exactly two and a half hours to persuade the King and to arrange all the necessary formalities which a dissolution required.

The Cabinet met again very early on the 22nd and decided to beg the King to come in person to dissolve Parliament. It was their only hope when time was so short, for, if the King were to send a Commission to dissolve it in his name, and if, when the Commission arrived, the Lords should still be debating Wharncliffe's motion, the Lords would be perfectly within their rights in keeping the Commission waiting until they had finished their debate. But not even the Tories, beside themselves as they were with elation at their imagined triumph, would have the insolence to keep the King waiting.

At last the Cabinet were united. Not even the waverers like Melbourne and Palmerston could stomach such defiance from the Tories, and now they were glad of men of swift action like Durham and Brougham. There have been many contemporary accounts written of the frenzied events of the next few days, among which the correspondence of Grey is probably the most reliable, closely followed by Brougham's memoirs, except that he allots to himself all the credit which was undoubtedly due to him and a good deal which was not. One or two of his statements, notably that he himself gave the order for the King's escort to parade, are open to grave suspicion, but he played a notable part in the affair and much of his story is borne out by the accounts of it given in Grey's letters to his wife. Lord Durham, who was the third chief actor, left no record of his share.

Grey took Brougham with him when he went to St. James's and the King received them punctually at half-past eleven. He was furious when he heard of Wharncliffe's threatened motion and roundly swore that he was not going to be dictated to by Lords or Commons, Whig or Tory, reinforcing his intention with a number of those sailorly expressions which time had not yet erased from his vocabulary. It is typical of the difficulty of getting a clear account of these hours of desperate haste that Brougham states that it was the Lords' impudence which moved the King to agree to come to Westminster in person, though Grey writes that he had agreed to it before Wharncliffe's motion had been mentioned. Whichever account is accurate—and it is a matter of no importance—William behaved like the man of action that he had been in simpler and happier days, and when Grey urged the need of haste, he replied genially that he 'always rode at single anchor'.

It was well that he did so, for less than two hours were left before two o'clock. The troops had not got their orders, nor were the royal coach and horses ready. Brougham, with little tact and perhaps less truth, told the King that he had already ordered out both coach and escort, and nearly turned the King against the whole thing by his presumption. But the King had given his word and would not go back on it. If, he said, the coach could not be ready, he would go in a hackney cab, and there is no doubt that if that had been necessary he would have done it. In such a crisis, Grey had need of another man of action and he summoned Lord Durham, with whom in a hasty conversation he arranged the necessary ceremonial for the King's arrival. Grey himself would carry the Sword and Durham the Cap of State, while Brougham was to hurry to the House of Lords and do all that he could to prolong their Lordships' deliberations until the King could arrive. Brougham had more experience of facing angry crowds and outfacing enemies than had most men even in those days, and did not doubt his ability to stir up such a storm in the Lords that it would be impossible for them to debate Wharncliffe's motion or anything else. The Commons would at the same time be busy in opposing the passage of the money votes, and the more time that they wasted in that way the better. Althorp would be there and though he had his faults, he was completely imperturbable at a time of crisis. The Commons could be safely left to him.

Durham undertook to see to the King's coach and horses and, running downstairs and into the court of the Palace, leaped into the first coach which he saw and shouted to the coachman to drive like the devil to Lord Albemarle's house. (The coach happened to be Brougham's, which was waiting to take him to Westminster.) Lord Albemarle, the Master of the Horse, was at a late breakfast, when Durham broke in upon him, loudly demanding all the King's horses, and Lord Albemarle was a man very conscious of his own dignity and not fond of hurrying. He had never before met Radical Jack in a tearing hurry and, though he agreed to give the orders, he proposed to finish his breakfast first, only to be told that there was no time for that. Albemarle asked, with ponderous sarcasm, whether there was a revolution beginning and met with the grim answer: 'There will be if you stop to finish your breakfast.' Few people could deny Radical Jack when he was in that mood and Lord Albemarle left his breakfast table and almost ran out to give his orders.

At the Tower of London, artillerymen in blue coats and plumed helmets had run out and loaded their guns and laid them with the muzzles pointing across the river towards the green hills beyond Greenwich and Blackheath. As the first gun boomed out in salute, the coach and escort were jingling down the Mall, between lines of Foot-guards.

The cheering swept like a wave from St. James's, through the Mall and Whitehall to Westminster where the waiting crowds heard it and cheered in answer, without an idea of what was happening. Word went round there that Sailor Billy, the People's King, was on his way to Westminster to do some great act for his people—what it was they had no idea, but it would certainly bring down the price of bread and send up wages and perhaps, since the golden age was dawning, it would include free beer and votes for everybody.

In stately Westminster, the Lords Spiritual and Tempora[l] were making so much noise themselves that they could hardly have heard the massed batteries below the ridge of Mont Sain[t] Jean. Yet, by some miracle, and in an unexpected pause i[n] their unseemly proceedings, the sound of a saluting gun pene[-]trated the walls and someone shouted that the King was on hi[s] way. Lord Shaftesbury had thankfully abandoned the Woolsac[k] to its rightful occupier and the Lord Chancellor was joyfully encouraging the storm which he should have been allaying. Few men would have liked to be in his place, but Brougham was for once in the happy position of being able to be as undignified, as offensive, and as belligerent as his heart desired. In courage and in ingenuity he was quite equal to one of the most difficult tasks which can ever have faced a Lord Chancellor.

Noble Lords had forgotten their dignity and were exuberantly behaving as though they were back in the Long Chamber at Eton in Dr. Keate's absence. Lord Wharncliffe was on his feet and was proposing his motion in a speech of extraordinary venom and most injudicious length, though little could be heard of it through the storm of jeers and abuse which came from the benches opposite and from Noble Lords who only lately had spoken gravely in disapproval of the rowdy behaviour of the common people at the hustings.

The Lord Chancellor, someone remarked, 'bounced up and down on the Woolsack like a pea on a drum', varying that exercise with a series of dashes to a side door to ask about the progress of the King's procession. It was coming down Whitehall now at a most unseemly trot, and, in the robing room of the House of Lords, harassed officials were frantically polishing the crown, which had just arrived from the Tower in a hackney coach—in the confusion, it had as yet struck no one that the Coronation had not yet taken place, so that His Majesty had no need of his crown.

At last Lord Wharncliffe, having by his verbosity done his own motion as much harm as his enemies could have desired, ran out of breath—the coach was wheeling at the bottom of Whitehall now, so fast that the outer ranks of the escort were cantering to keep their dressing—and the Lord Chancellor hurled himself into the gap, ignoring the subject before the House and bursting at the top of his very considerable voice, into a tirade against the malcontents 'in another place', who were even then refusing to His Majesty's Government the few miserable pounds needed for the use of His Majesty's subjects. It was highly irregular, but the Lord Chancellor was responsible for ensuring regularity and it was difficult to call him to order, though exciting to try to shout him down. Whig peers had been a little disconcerted by the sight of the empty seats which should have held their leader and the Lord Privy Seal, and none of them were alert enough to rise to fill the gap—and to keep talking about anything or nothing as long as it was not about the motion before the House. Even Tory Peers were so carried away by the ecstasy of hurling unchecked jeers at their opponents that they did not mark the passing of time or the steady booming of the Tower guns.

In the Commons an even happier state of chaos reigned. Manners Sutton, the Speaker, in his anxiety to be impartial without giving the Whigs a chance to speak, announced that Sir Francis Burdett had the ear of the House and, almost in the same breath, called on Sir Robert Peel to speak, so that three members were on their feet at once, Burdett and Peel speaking against each other, and Althorp rising to a point of order. He argued that Burdett had caught the Speaker's eye and that Peel was interfering with him. Sir Robert, for perhaps the first time in his Parliamentary life, lost his temper and went off into a long and angry tirade, during the course of which, he was understood by Mr. Le Marchant, Althorp's biographer, to say that the day was coming when it would be a disgrace to any man to serve the Crown. So Sir Robert went on and on and wasted more and more time, till his neighbour pulled him down by the tail of his coat, while Mr. Speaker's impartiality went to the winds and he called on Tory after Tory to speak; and they all spoke angrily and at length and wasted more time, and Althorp, who was tenacious of an idea, when once he had grasped it, continued to rise to points of order whenever he could make himself heard.

In the Upper House, their Lordships had gone back beyond Eton to the uninhibited days of the nursery and were coming to blows. His Grace the Duke of Richmond had noticed Lord Lyndhurst, a mere baron, sitting on the Dukes' bench and moved partly by a desire for Reform, partly by respect for his own Order, but mainly by party venom, abruptly demanded of Lyndhurst what the devil he thought he was doing there. Whereupon Lyndhurst shook his fist at the Duke and offered to fight him, and the Marquess of Londonderry joined in though he was so speechless with rage and excitement that no one knew on which side he had stationed himself. Momentary sanity returned to Wharncliffe and he perceived—it had eluded him while he was on his own feet—that his noble friends were wasting time, so that he turned to a Peer who was rising to support him saying: 'For God's sake don't put us in worse case than we are already.'

Outside the coach had slackened speed and the escort were turning inwards, their swords flashing in salute as it wheeled into the Yard. In the Lords there was a sudden lull and the silence was so surprising and so complete that they noticed that the guns had stopped firing. In the Painted Chamber, the officials were giving the crown a last rub, and in a corner of the room the Prime Minister and the Lord Privy Seal bowed low as the opposite door opened and the King came in. The Lord Chancellor, out of breath and with wig almost falling off his head, came forward to greet his master, who asked what all the noise inside was about, and, on hearing that the Lords were still debating, nearly caused the Chancellor's heart to stop by courteously suggesting that perhaps he had better wait till they had finished. But Grey and Durham were beside him now with the Sword and the Cap of State and suddenly someone asked whether it was in order for His Majesty to wear the crown since he had not yet had his coronation. For a moment everyone was nonplussed till the King solved the nice point by seizing the crown and putting it, slightly askew, on his own head, announcing, in unconscious imitation of the late Emperor of the French, that he was perfectly capable of crowning himself.

The Lord Chancellor did not stay to offer an opinion on this novel constitutional doctrine, but ran back into the House, where he arrived not a moment too soon. Noble Lords had noticed that the Woolsack was vacant, and one of them shouted that Black Rod had gone to summon the Commons. Wharncliffe tardily remembered his motion to beg the King not to exercise his prerogative of dissolving Parliament and realized that he had about two minutes in which to get it through. The Peers wasted those two minutes in debating who should take the Woolsack to put the motion and, as four or five candidates were pushed forward, there was some delay in selecting one, and they had come to no satisfactory decision when it was seen that the Lord Chancellor was in his place, mopping his streaming face and grinning like an amused Satan. Then, all at once the space below the bar was crowded by an inrush of members of the Commons; and behind the throne the great doors opened to admit the King.

There was silence now in the House, as the King, with his crown still a little crooked, came in behind Earl Grey who bore the Sword of State aloft, and in front of Lord Durham with the Cap of State. The Whigs had held out just long enough and help had come.

CHAPTER VI

The story of the next two years in Lord Durham's life is almost unbearable, but without full knowledge of it we cannot hope to understand the position in which he stood at the end of it. In 1830 he seemed assured of a brilliant political career and of succession to Grey as leader of the Whig party and possibly as Prime Minister. When those two years had passed, he was almost estranged from his party and at enmity with his father-in-law. It seemed certain that there would be no future employment for him under a Whig administration, especially any which contained Brougham, once a friend but now rapidly becoming an implacable enemy and Melbourne, who was increasing in power in his party and was the likeliest man now for the leadership. The course of these enmities and their consequences will be traced as Durham's political history develops. The most pressing question now is that of his relationship with Grey and the tragedy in his own home. He was entering on one of those periods, which some men know, when every form of trouble comes on them at once and threatens their health, their sanity, and even their existence.

Towards the end of 1830 the pressure of ills had already begun. He was at work on the Reform Bill with his committee and could not leave them until it was finished, yet his private life made insistent demands on him as his son grew steadily worse and at the same time trouble was abroad in all the North Country coalfields which involved his Lambton pits and his own fortune and—which was as important to him—the lives of his miners.

Perhaps the furious energy with which he worked at the Bill and the speed to which he urged the committee were evidence of the need which he had to finish with it and to be able to give his time to his family and his estate. Perhaps, too, he drove himself and his colleagues because it was better for him to wear himself out with work rather than to brood and fret about troubles which he could do little to avoid and not much to relieve. For, as he sat drafting and amending in Cleveland Row, the letters from Lady Durham told him that Charles was dying and that the doctors now admitted that they had done all that they could. The family trailed dismally from one place and one house to another in a vain hope that change of air or scene might give the boy a shadow of hope. He had seemed to be mending in October 1830, when Lady Durham's diary records that he was in 'great health and spirits', but it was a short-lived and cheating recovery and in the winter they moved to Norwood where they took a house for three months, and where, Lady Durham wrote, Charles was 'increasingly ill'. Dr. Eden, the family physician, was always with them and there were visiting specialists, but none of them could achieve a diagnosis. They spoke of a growth in his stomach, of consumption and pains in the legs, they hinted at dropsy and tried a variety of painful remedies, such as puncturing the soles of his feet and a succession of diets any one of which sounds to us today enough to kill him.

Norwood had proved useless and they moved in the spring to Sudbrook. There Dr. Eden reported hopefully that 'the enlargement in his stomach would be gone in ten days' but, in her diary of the same date in August Lady Durham reported 'violent cramp in his legs—feet and legs swelled'. Plainly Sudbrook was no better than Norwood and they looked wearily for another home. The doctors, after the fashion of the day, spoke of Italy but it was clear that the boy would never stand the journey and, as a last hope, they chose Brighton. Lady Durham writes that they went there in their carriage and that Charles was wrapped in blankets and had to be lifted into and out of it, and that even with the most careful handling he suffered great pain. At Brighton, they called in Sir Matthew Tierney, who pierced the soles of his feet because he was complaining of 'a soreness of the shins'. The draft Bill was by then out of the committee's hands and Lord Durham was a little stronger and managed to pay several visits to the house at Brighton. On 9 September Lady Durham wrote that 'I observed to Lambton that he looked like his picture and Lambton replied that he never saw him so beautiful'.

In desperation the doctors experimented wildly with dietary changes and ordered him to have no more ale, porter or wine, but to drink only brandy and water or asses' milk. Three days later, on 12 September, they were 'struck with the alteration for the worse' and recommended mutton chops. Lady Durham found that he could no longer endure the thought of the two eggs on which the doctors had insisted for his daily breakfast and noted that even the substitution of a beef sandwich for the mutton chops failed to revive his appetite. His feet and legs, which were tightly bound with flannel gave him intense pain and now he could take no solid food and was kept alive with sips of brandy and water. They knew that it could only be for a few weeks at the most, and Lord Durham stayed at Brighton until the day in September when Lady Durham made the last entry in her diary. 'Lambton tried to give him some brandy and water but it would not do—he looked at us both after we came down and once he shrank a little at my touching the bedclothes—but only a little. He tried to speak and we heard something like Papa—love—Papa, Mama—and then again, Papa, love. This was the last. He was lying with one hand on his pillow under his head—the other was between Lambton's but Lambton took one off and laid mine upon his so that his hand was between one of each of ours. I kissed his face once—he moaned no more—nine o'clock.'

The date was 24 September 1831. In a fortnight or less the Reform Bill which had passed the Commons in June was due to come before the House of Lords, and Durham was to have been, with Grey, its leading supporter. There could be no question of that now, for those desperate days had exhausted the last of his strength and he was too ill even to travel to Lambton with the body of his son for the burial in the collegiate church of Chester-le-Street. Grey had been at Brighton when the child died but was obliged to go to London for the opening of the debate in

the Lords on 3 October. The funeral party left Brighton on the
following day and Lady Durham went with it, leaving her
husband to the care of his brother, Hedworth. Durham was
almost out of his mind with grief and physical pain and it
took the combined efforts of Grey and Hedworth to restrain
him from trying to travel north. Later Lady Durham wrote
to Hedworth: 'There is no telling what we may have to
thank you for.' It really seemed for a time that his mind might
give way under the torment and he himself wrote to Grey, in
one of those dreadful letters which are preserved in the Howick
MSS.:

> 'One long dreary day succeeds another from the miseries of
> which, laudanum affords the only relief. . . . I never get any
> real sleep without laudanum. . . . I feel as if my head would
> burst.'

While Durham lay helpless in Brighton, Grey fought for the
Bill in the Lords and was defeated by a majority of forty-one,
among whom were twenty-one bishops. The force behind them
was the black-browed Philpott of Exeter with whom, when he
was Prebendary of Durham, Lambton had quarrelled at the
time of Peterloo and whom he was to encounter again when
next the Bill came before the Lords.

Lord Durham's physical and mental states at this time are
of vital importance because they dictated the conduct which,
during the next few months, was to cost him the regard of
almost all his colleagues and a good deal of his reputation in
politics and was to bring him into the most violent and distressing collision with his father-in-law.

The new Parliament elected in 1831 had shown so overwhelming a majority for Reform that the Bill had passed easily,
only to be thrown out by the Lords. That rebuff left the Reformers with only one course, since their Lordships were un-
affected by changing political temperatures and, however
often the Bill were to be presented to them, would certainly
reject it. If the Administration meant the Bill to pass they
must persuade the King to create enough new peers to make
sure of it.

They had had this in mind earlier, but had hoped that, if the
situation should arise, it would be necessary to ask for only a

few creations. The majority against the Bill now meant that at least forty new peers would have to be brought in, and to this the King would never agree. The Cabinet themselves were sharply divided about the number of peers for whom they ought to ask and a few of the most prominent members were even in favour of postponing the whole attempt. Palmerston was luke-warm and Melbourne somewhat less; Brougham who was a genuinely keen Reformer was not in love with the Bill and was personally unhappy as Lord Chancellor, nor could he fail to realize that in that intensely aristocratic assembly he was looked on as something of an outsider.

Their various opinions gave rise to strangely divided coun-sels. Grey had put aside all vacillation (and nearly all thought of Howick) and was for a straightforward appeal to the King to let it be known that he would create as many peers as were neces-sary even though it should be forty or more. Althorp thought that the Cabinet should resign unless the King would promise this, but Grey shrank from so open a threat, though Russell and Brougham supported it. Richmond was ready to drop the whole thing; Palmerston and Melbourne were negotiating with a group of Peers, who came to be known as 'The Waverers', for a compromise Bill, which might be introduced by a coalition or at least supported by such few Tories as would rather concede a little for the sake of saving more. Above all Grey was hampered by the delicacy of his feelings for the King who, much as he hated the idea of Reform, had made a great sacrifice of his feelings in accepting it in principle.

The King now saw his only hope in the Waverers and on 2 December General Taylor, his private secretary, wrote to Grey:

'Although the alterations or moderations which may result may not meet the views and expectations of Lords Wharncliffe and Harrowby [the leaders of the Waverers], they may, in His Majesty's conception, strike others as more important or they may afford a plea of which many may be glad to avail themselves for *discovering* differences between the old Bill and the new one, which shall, in their opinion, be sufficient to convert the previous dissent into assent.'

This attempt by the King to find a *via media* won some support in the Cabinet, when Grey, though he was not in

favour of it, felt it his duty to put it before them. The concessions which the Waverers demanded were not fundamental
and the Bill would not have been much impaired by them. All
that they asked was some alteration in Schedules A and B of
boroughs which were to be totally or partially disenfranchised
and an increase in the total number of members. The half-
hearted among the Cabinet were ready to agree and even
Russell and Brougham, though, like Grey, they hated the concessions, were not prepared to stand out against the rest of their
colleagues. After all, the Bill, even so truncated, would be an
enormous step in the right direction and would make a later
advance possible. It would gratify the King, to whom they were
indebted, and it would be drastic enough to satisfy public
feeling. None of them could disguise from themselves that,
unless some alternative could be found, the Bill would fail
again in the Lords and the country would be on the edge of
revolution. They had, too, to remember that if they were to
resign, the Tories would probably introduce an even more
temperate measure so that the Whigs would have sacrificed
their principles and lost office for nothing. The general feeling
was that the King's suggestion was worth trying, especially as
there was always the hope that Wellington's implacable hatred
for the whole principle of Reform might wreck the Tories'
attempts to find a compromise and his enormous prestige
might avail to frighten the King away from a wholesale
creation of Peers.

So the Cabinet were ready to try it, and, in this mood of
unusual agreement and cordiality, they met at dinner on 6
December at Althorp's London House.

The face of the Cabinet waters had been stilled, but a sudden
tempest shattered the calm with the return of Radical Jack.
Not the most sanguine member had hoped that he would
approve of the compromise. As soon as he was well enough to
travel he had gone to Brussels on a visit to King Leopold, with
whom he had been friendly when Leopold had been in England
as the husband of Princess Charlotte. From there he had made
it plain in his letters to Grey and the others that he expected
them to stand firm on the whole Bill and not to concede the
smallest of details. There was no self-pity in these letters, no
personal rancour, as there had been a few months ago, but

there was the old fighting language of Radical Jack, clear proof that, whatever he had suffered, his will and urgency were unimpaired. The best that they could hope for was that he would stay away from England while the new suggestions were being debated, and if possible until Parliament had had a chance of deciding on them. But it was not—it never had been—Radical Jack's way to keep out of a fight—there was too much Lyon in him for that—and he arrived in time for Althorp's dinner where he made the famous scene of which his enemies have ever since made such delighted capital and which his staunchest admirers can only deplore.

The occasion must have been painful in the extreme and Creevey and Greville—neither of whom was present—have described it in detail. There is no reason to question their accuracy though it came to them by a rather devious route through Richmond and George Bentinck, who told it to Greville who relaid it to Creevey. Fortunately there is a first-hand account in Althorp's memoirs, for 7 December.

'We had a dreadful scene at the Cabinet dinner yesterday. Durham made the most brutal attack on Lord Grey I ever heard in my life and, I conclude, will certainly resign. He will put this upon alterations in the Bill, unfairly, because there is no alteration of any consequence in the main principle. And I doubt whether he knows anything about the alterations as he will not allow anyone to tell him what they are. But if he resigns on this ground, he will break up the Government.'

There is never any reason to doubt Althorp's word about anything, and not only is his honesty evident but also his essential kindness of heart since he gives none of the details of the 'brutal attack' on Grey which the diarists relate with relish. Yet no doubt it happened as they said and Durham did hurl personal abuse at Grey and accuse him of having been the cause of his boy's death. It is impossible to feel anything but pain and shame for him, but it would be absurd to make too much of the incident. Lord Durham had been in great agony of mind and body and had dragged himself back to the political world to avert what he believed to be a betrayal of the cause for whose sake the Whigs had assumed office and to which their honour was pledged. Unhappily, while his will and fighting spirit were stronger than ever, his judgement was in eclipse and he refused even to listen to the arguments which had satisfied his colleagues. He did not care whether he upset the government or not or what the effect might be on him. He was for 'The Bill the whole Bill and nothing but the Bill', as the cant phrase ran in the country then. Being what he was and having endured as he had, he had lost all self-control and, as was not uncommon with him, confused a political demand with a personal wish. The whole Bill and nothing but the Bill because it was right and because it was his—to him it was as simple as that.

And yet—we may fairly ask the question—was Lord Durham's judgement so much impaired? His was a mind which saw, on occasion, a good way further than most men's and, if he had no distinct prevision of future dangers, he must have seen that, when once compromise had crept in, there could be no more certainty. He was for facing the King with a demand for a definite number of new creations, coupled with the threat of resignation as the alternative. It might be unpleasant for His Majesty but unpleasantness was unavoidable and Radical Jack was never the man to shirk it for himself or for anyone else. Perhaps he did not actually foresee what was to happen—that the King would go back on his pledged word and, having accepted the principle of unlimited creation, would suddenly jib when he learned of the exact number involved. But he was wary and determined enough to try to provide against any possible future obstacle. Perhaps too, because he knew Grey better than any of them, he saw the one weakness in his character which might endanger the cause. Grey was sensitive about the King's feelings and loth to press him further than he had to but he was also vain about his influence at Windsor and apt too soon to congratulate himself on his success in negotiations there. It was to his credit that he was so honourable himself that he did not doubt but that another man would keep his word as he would himself. Lord Durham took an altogether more realistic view of human nature and especially of royal nature.

Grey had long and earnest talks with the King and was rewarded with the promise that, 'The King will not deny to his ministers the power of acting at once up to the full exigency of the case'. That was on 15 January 1832 after the Bill had passed the Commons for the second time with a majority this time of 116. The Cabinet, responding to Durham's insistence, had made only a few changes in detail from the first Bill and it was their policy to present it without further alteration to the Lords, relying on the King's promise and on their lordships' fear of having their numbers increased and their prestige diminished. (Durham, unusually tender of their feelings, or recollecting that he himself was a peer as well as a Reformer, had suggested the sensible method of filling up the new vacancies first with the sons of existing peers.) There seemed to be a good prospect that the Bill might be forced through the House without the necessity of translating the threat into reality. But still Radical Jack was unsatisfied. There was still a loophole, since no number of creations had been agreed on and there was no threat of resignation. Russell, Brougham, and even the loyal Althorp were inclined to support him and there was another stormy meeting at which Grey, putting on for once all the imperious strength of his character and prestige, refused to make any further move until the Lords had been given their chance, and carried the Cabinet with him.

All but Radical Jack. He would listen to no reason and he was not to be swayed by Grey's persuasive powers or overawed by his authority. The rest gave in. Radical Jack flung out of the room and banged the door behind him. He banged it on more than a disgusted assembly of colleagues, who thereafter referred to him as 'The Dissenting Minister'. He shut out, as it seemed for ever, his hopes of future office, of honours and place, of friendship with his colleagues, and of happy relations with his father-in-law. He went out into the political wilderness. Lord Broughton, writing later of that scene, said that 'All condemned his conduct'. (After the scene at Althorp's dinner, Melbourne had remarked that if he had been Grey, he would have knocked Durham down.) The only thing left for him to do—so they all agreed—was to resign. But he did not resign. Probably he never considered it. Reform was still to be fought for and won and he would be needed in his place in the Lords.

CHAPTER VII

When the Bill came up for its second reading in the House of
Lords, Lord Durham met his old opponent Bishop Philpott of
Exeter. Philpott was just the opponent whom Radical Jack, in
his present mood, needed. He was a violent and unscrupulous
fighter with a gift of invective which he varied with loud
appeals to his God to support his arguments. (His enemies,
who were many, said that he regarded his Maker as the chairman of the Tory party.)

The debate began decorously on 10 April with a speech by
Earl Grey, which Greville called 'strikingly moderate'. It
lacked the fire and eloquence of his speech in the earlier debate,
but it was closely reasoned and temperate in tone. The
debate maintained the same moderate temperature throughout
the first two days, in spite of unkind suggestions from Wellington and Londonderry that the Reformers had shown undue
leniency to certain boroughs, notably Tavistock, and counties,
notably Durham, where their own interest was predominant.

On the fourth day, the aged Lord Wynford contributed a
rambling speech from which his colleagues gathered with some
difficulty that, on the whole, he rather thought that he was
against Reform.

When Bishop Philpott rose, the temperature rose with him.
Much of his speech was as irrelevant as had been Lord Wynford's, since it dealt with the topic of religion in Ireland, but
his hostility was never in doubt. With mounting violence—and
not without several appeals to his Maker for confirmation—
he attacked Grey and Durham and accused both of them,
and more especially Durham, of betraying Cabinet secrets to
the Press.

It was not until the following evening that Durham got a
chance of answering him. He began quietly with a reference
to his absence from the House when last the Bill had been
before it and apologized for intruding into the debate at so
early a stage, 'because, from the severe and painful indisposition
under which I have lately laboured and from which I am, in
fact, still suffering, I fear that, if I delay addressing your
Lordships till a later period of the night's debate, I shall not

have strength sufficient to avail myself of the indulgence of the House'.

He dealt briefly with Lord Wynford's speech, which, he said, 'had embraced many topics and related to many subjects, but some of these are entirely unconnected with the question itself and others with its present stage'. He congratulated him on the moderation of his speech unmarked as it was by 'that tone of party rancour and personal animosity towards His Majesty's Ministers, which has, in so marked a manner, distinguished the debates of the last two nights'.

At this point Lord Durham paused, and those who watched him saw him turn towards the benches where the white-sleeved bishops made a light patch in the subfusc colour of the House. When he spoke again, there was a note in his voice which had become all too familiar to his colleagues in the Cabinet.

'Very different,' he went on, 'was the tone and temper of the noble Lord's speech from that which proceeded from the reverend bench on the last night. Of that exhibition on the part of a reverend bishop, I shall only say that, if coarse and virulent invective—malignant and false insinuations—the grossest perversion of historical facts—decked out with all the choicest flowers of his pamphleteering slang——'

A shout of protest interrupted him and peers on both sides engaged in an angry debate about the propriety of his language. The Earl of Winchilsea, who had sat unmoved through Philpott's diatribe, asked whether it became noble Lords to sit patiently and hear such personalities. He had risen to a point of order but such was his excitement that he forgot the correct procedure and gave an opportunity to that experienced Parliamentarian, Lord Holland, who pointed out that he had proposed no motion: 'He trusted that the noble Earl would attend to the rule of the House, which was in such a case to move that the objectionable words be taken down.' Grey, loyal as ever, but not a little apprehensive, said that he saw nothing objectionable in the words and was followed by the Duke of Buckingham, who appealed to the noble Earl 'in the spirit of peace and goodwill and in a wish that their Lordships' discussions should be carried on without offence to anybody' to withdraw the offensive expressions.

Buckingham ended with the expression of a somewhat vain

hope that 'the noble Lord, in his calmer moments, would not persevere in such an imputation'. Lord Durham, ignoring his advice, then rose and persevered.

'My Lords, I was interrupted by the noble Earl in the course of a sentence which I was addressing to your Lordships, and it now seems to be his intention that the words which I uttered should be taken down. I have not the slightest objection to that course being adopted—but the contrary— and I now state to your Lordships the reasons which induced me to use those words. I shall not stop to inquire whether the words "pamphleteering slang" were the most elegant I could have used. They do not perhaps suit the noble Earl's taste, but they are the only words which I consider correctly describe the speech of the reverend Bishop.'

Having disposed, to his own satisfaction at any rate, of that particular expression, he turned to another which he had used: 'malignant and false insinuations', which he justified by fling- ing at Philpott a flat denial of the charge of revealing Cabinet secrets. He added: 'I will now repeat that declaration and pause for the purpose of allowing any noble Lord the opportunity of taking down my words.' No noble Lord availing himself of this generous offer, Lord Durham grandly remarked that, as it appeared no further interruption would be offered to him, he would dismiss the subject. The rest of his speech was devoted to refuting the charges made by Wellington and Londonderry and an eulogy of the middle classes whose enfranchisement was a main object of the Bill.

'As for intelligence, look at the great towns of the Empire— Leeds, Manchester, Birmingham, Sheffield, Liverpool, Newcastle, Edinbugh, Glasgow and many others; and by whom will you find the scientific institutions, the literary associations, the charities—in short, all the associations tending to the advancement of the Arts, literature and science—and to the amelioration of the human kind—by whom will you find them supported? By whose example and purse maintained? The Middle Classes.'

At the end of his speech, Lord Durham returned to the sub- ject of Philpott, who had suggested that, if the Tory view were accepted, the result might be left to Providence: 'When the consequences have been left to Providence, after the suggestion of the reverend Bishop, the course of events has always been uniform—in the first case, bigoted resistance to the claims of the people; in the second, bloody and protracted struggles; and finally, but invariably, unlimited, disgraceful but then useless concessions.'

In the debate which followed Philpott tried to retreat from his position on the plea that 'he had not said that he believed but only that it was believed', but he was sternly handled by Lord Goderich, and finally pulverized by one of Grey's most crushing rebukes. Greville wrote in his diary: 'Philpott got a terrific dressing from Lord Grey and was handled not too delicately by Goderich and Durham, though the latter was too coarse.' Greville was no admirer of the bishop, of whom he had already written: 'He has a desperate and dreadful countenance and looks the man he is.' Lord Durham's speech had its effect not only on Philpott but also on the Duke of Wellington and the Marquess of Londonderry, both of whom qualified their remarks about the representation of Tavistock and County Durham and disclaimed any suggestion of improper favour on the part of the framers of the Reform Bill.

Before the House had met, Grey had written to Althorp: 'According to the best information I can obtain, the majority on the second reading in the House of Lords appears to me to be nearly certain.' The House divided in broad daylight on 14 April, after an all-night sitting and the result justified Grey's optimism. The voting was 184 to 175, a majority of nine, and this time twelve Bishops had voted for the Bill and fifteen against. The Whigs were jubilant. Only the committee stage remained and, while they were sure to encounter criticism and some opposition, they had no reason to fear defeat. They felt secure in their possession of the King's promise that he would not deny to his ministers the power of acting at once up to the full exigencies of the case. But there were two dangers with which they had not reckoned. One was the Duke of Wellington's inability to recognize defeat. The second—which Lord Durham alone had suspected—was that the King might break his word.

Many of the Duke's opponents in the past had paid the penalty of thinking that they had him at their mercy. His strategy now, according to Trevelyan, was 'an attempt, not indeed to destroy the Bill or even perhaps seriously to cut down its provisions, but to reassert the power and prestige of the House of Lords by taking the conduct of the Bill out of the hands of ministers and handing it over to the leaders of the Opposition'. When the House went into committee on 7 May, Lyndhurst rose to propose a motion to postpone consideration of the disenfranchisement of the boroughs and to proceed straight to the enfranchising clauses of the Bill. It was a direct challenge to the Government since Grey had let it be known that they would not agree to that procedure. The destruction of the boroughs was a first principle of the Bill, because, until that was settled, there could be no discussion of the method of allotting the seats which would be freed. They must clear the rubbish from the site before they could begin to build. Creevey mentions that it was believed that the Whigs would not resign on what would appear to be a mere question of detail.

Lyndhurst provided some unintentional comedy during his speech by his claim to know as much as the Whigs about the feelings of the people, basing his claim on a recent walk down St. James's Street and a conversation with his bootmaker. With great subtlety, he had asked him what 'people of his class' thought of the Bill. The bootmaker was not perhaps a profound politician but he was a good man of business and promptly replied that 'he did not expect any more business if it was passed'. Fortified by this contact with the great heart of England, Lyndhurst opened his attack.

Wellington's strategy was successful. Wharncliffe and the Waverers, glad of an opportunity to reinstate themselves in their party's good graces, voted against the Government and the motion was carried. That night, before leaving Westminster, the Cabinet met and resolved that their only course now was to ask the King to create not less than fifty peers, or, failing that, to accept their resignation. It was the policy which Lord Durham had steadily advocated for the last three months, and had they listened to him at first, they would have saved themselves a lot of trouble. The only dissenting voice at this meeting was that of the Duke of Richmond; even the lukewarm Palmerston was ready for a fight. The Duke of Wellington had accomplished one thing at least. He had united the Whigs.

The minute which embodied their decision was dated 8 May, and, in the afternoon of the same day, Grey and Brougham drove to Windsor, where the King received them with embarrassment and without any show of cordiality. A long and unpleasant interview produced no decision, but left Grey with the impression that the King was running away. This impression was confirmed by the manner of their dismissal, for the King was patently anxious to be rid of them; 'he did not', Althorp writes, 'even offer the poor fellows any refreshment.' They stopped at an inn on their way back to London and dined off a dish of mutton chops, to which Brougham added some kidneys. 'Grey,' he wrote in his memoirs, 'cared not for kidneys, but he ate them when they came.' Grey was not perhaps in the mood to be particular about what he ate. For the second time within a discouragingly short space, he had to confess that his management of his master had been less skilful than he had claimed. Next day, a letter from the King put an end to any hopes which he might still have been harbouring.

'It is not,' he wrote, 'without the truest concern that the King acquaints his confidential servants that, after giving due consideration to the Minute of the Cabinet which was brought to him yesterday by Earl Grey and the Lord Chancellor, and to the consequences of the alteration which it offers for his decision of being deprived of their services, or of sanctioning the advancement to the Peerage of a sufficient number of Persons to insure the success of the Reform Bill, in all the principles which they consider essential, His Majesty has come to the painful resolution of accepting their resignations. . . .'

On the same day, the King, who was obviously ashamed of himself wrote a charming personal letter to Grey, thanking him for all his past services and offering, with some hazy idea of making amends, to make his brother Bishop of Hereford. Grey replied with a warmth of gratitude which only his known integrity saves from the suspicion of insincerity. He declined the bishopric for his brother on the score of having just presented him to the living of St. Botolph Bishopsgate. The King, rather after the manner of a small boy offering a larger piece of toffee, answered that the bishop-designate could retain his living as well, but, by the time that the letter reached Grey on the following day, the Government had resigned.

It is difficult to account for the King's desertion except by a sudden fit of cowardice, which was not one of his usual failings. The country unhesitatingly blamed Queen Adelaide, who was a pronounced Tory and was supposed to exercise political control over her husband. There was an outburst of popular fury directed against both of them. Pictures which hung in public places were torn down and inn-signs with the Royal Arms were burnt. Only a few weeks ago the King had been 'Billy the People's Friend' and now he was Tyrant and Oppressor. All the time, he was neither, but an honest, muddle-headed old man, trying to cope with a situation which was beyond him and to do his best for everybody.

The 'May Days' which followed, were as crazy as a dream. The Government had resigned but no successors had replaced them, nor were any likely to want to try. The King's solution, that the Government should continue to govern without holding office, commended itself to nobody but its author. His efforts to find an alternative government were unavailing; nor were they helped by the House of Commons, which, on the motion of Lord Elvington, declared their continued confidence in the present administration and prayed the King 'to call to his counsels only such persons as would carry into effect unimpaired the Reform Bill'.

CHAPTER VIII

The cause of Reform had triumphed, in spite of the Lords. Whatever administration might come into power could not last a week unless they could pass the Bill. Even Wellington realized that he could no longer withstand the will of the country, though he recommended Peel or Lyndhurst for the distasteful task of reversing the traditional Tory policy. Lyndhurst would have tried, but his following in the country was confined to his bootmaker, and Peel refused to have anything to do with such a betrayal. In the Commons, men on both sides admitted that the only proper men to carry the Bill were those who had framed it. If the Tories were to take office on that condition no one would trust them, since they would plainly be doing it for the sake of a party success. In all this tumult, Grey kept his head and his temper, writing to the King in terms of exquisite courtesy without a hint of concession and, in the House, maintaining an appearance of waiting while someone formed an administration. The King, almost distracted, turned to the one man who, he knew, would never fail him. For the second time, he appealed to the Duke to form a government.

The Duke, whose simple creed it was that 'The King's government must be carried on', agreed to try, but he held it to be essential that any Tory Cabinet should include Peel, and Peel would have none of it. He had shared in the change of front over Catholic Emancipation and he had no wish to be called 'Turncoat' again. The Duke bravely trailed his net again without bringing up anything more hopeful than his old friend, Sir Henry Hardinge, Mr. Baring the banker, and Manners Sutton, the late Speaker. Hardinge would follow the Duke in any capacity, and Baring would have made an excellent Chancellor of the Exchequer, but Sutton, who thought that he would make an excellent Prime Minister, was disgusted to find that he was only to be asked to lead the Commons. The Duke's last chance seemed to be fading.

All through these 'May Days', while Parliamentary parties manœuvred and bargained, the temper of the country was steadily rising. There was little rioting—the situation was too serious for sporadic outbreaks—but Francis Place spoke confidently of a rising of the whole country unless the Bill were to be passed at once. Birmingham, where Joseph Parkes and Attwood presided over the biggest political union in England, was ready to support it and with them were the unions of Manchester, Hull, and Sheffield. Place's plans for a run on the banks, under his slogan of 'To stop the Duke, go for gold' were already in operation, and there was a rapid fall in the Funds.

The whole financial weight of the Barings and Rothschilds and of the other anti-Reform bankers was thrown into an attempt to keep prices steady, but another and bigger fall followed Grey's announcement of the Government's resignation. At the same time, Provincial banks began to report heavy withdrawals of gold. At Birmingham, £20,000 was withdrawn in one day, and in two days the Bank of England paid out several hundreds of thousands of pounds. 'There is no doubt,' Butler writes, 'that the run on the banks was considerable and was believed to be greater.'

The Duke had grimly remarked that, 'The people of England will be quiet if they are left alone; and if they will not, there is a way to make them'. All over the country, officers' leave was stopped and troops were confined to barracks. Alexander Somerville tells, in his *Autobiography of a Working Man*, how, at Birmingham, where he was then serving with the Scots Greys, the troop horses stood for two days saddled and bridled in the stables; and how, one Sunday, the barrack gates were shut and the men were ordered to rough-sharpen their swords so that they might inflict jagged wounds. The old soldiers were able to tell the recruits that the last time that such an order had been given was on the night before Waterloo. Somerville writes that the troops were not to be relied upon. Some of his own troop had written to Lord Hill, the Commander-in-Chief, that, 'The Greys would do their duty if riots and outrages were committed, but they would not draw swords or triggers upon a deliberative public meeting, or kill the people of Birmingham for attempting to leave their town with a petition to London'. (Somerville himself was implicated and, after a perfunctory court-martial, received two hundred lashes.)

Politically the impasse was now complete. Late in the night of 14 May, the Tory leaders met at Apsley House, and next day the Duke told the King that he had failed. The King had no option but to summon Grey, but he was still obdurate about the creation of peers, and the Cabinet, not even Richmond dissenting this time, refused to take office on any other terms.

A week of wild rumours followed, while, all over the country, mass meetings demanded the creation, or stoppage of supplies and, Butler says, 'very nearly the abolition of the Monarchy itself'. The run on the banks went on, and on 17 May, the Manchester *Correspondent* reported that 620 depositors had given notice to withdraw £16,700.

In thousands of houses, window placards announced 'No taxes paid here', and Lord Milton, the heir of Earl Fitzwilliam, informed a cheering House of Commons that 'he had asked the taxgatherer to call again'. 'I never before,' Henry Cockburn noted in his journal, 'actually *felt* the immediate pressure of a great popular crisis. . . . There was nothing to distract the attention or to break the terrible silence—nothing but grave looks and orderly public meetings, unconquerable resolution and the absolute certainty that, if any accident had made resistance begin anywhere, it would have run like an electric shock in a moment.'

The popular newspapers were unrestrained in their language and some of them openly threatened the King. On 19 May, the *New Weekly Messenger* said: 'We are monarchists . . . but if monarchy can only subsist with Wellingtons, Cumberlands, Lyndhursts, ambitious bastards and German women for its ministers and its love, with rotten boroughs, enormous pensions and desolating taxes for its appendages . . . let monarchy go to the right-about and the lesser evil of Republicanism be dominant in England.'

Panic and anger swept in alternate waves through the King's court. The King was furious at the public abuse of his wife, disgusted with both Whigs and Tories and still determined not to create new peers. Cam Hobhouse told Place that secret arrangements had been made for getting the King and Queen away to Hanover. Lord Munster, the eldest of the King's 'ambitious bastards', added to the confusion with an unscrupulous and futile plan for spying on his father's interviews with Grey and reporting the result to Wellington. The Duke of Buckingham, too, was implicated in the scheme, which was foiled by the Duke's uncompromising honesty in writing to Sir Herbert Taylor that, since he could not form a government, it would only be proper that all communication between the Palace and Apsley House should cease at once.

On Thursday, 18 May, it seemed that there was no way out and that revolution was inevitable. Yet, as so often happens in England there was a way found, and, when found, it was so simple that no one could understand why it had not been tried before. Nor has anyone, then or later, been able to assign the credit for its discovery. It may first have seen the light in a chance suggestion made in a speech by Baring, that the Whigs should remain in office to pass the Bill, and should drop their demand for new peers on the understanding that the Tories would not oppose Schedule A in the Lords. The King himself later took credit for the suggestion, which others have ascribed to Taylor, largely on the strength of the daring action which he took to further it. It did not come from the Whigs—most certainly not from Lord Durham, who had taken his stand upon the creation and was immovable. He was still, in spite of his threat of resignation, a member of the Cabinet, since Russell had said that if Durham resigned, he must follow him. Durham was too loyal a Reformer to deprive the cause of two of its best fighters at the height of the battle.

The simple solution was that the anti-Reform peers should abstain from voting when the Bill came up again, and the King wrote to Wellington to beg him to agree to this. He also authorized Taylor to write to several other peers to the same effect and to let Grey know what he had done. He asked Grey to make a statement in the Lords that the Government would continue in office and to tell Althorp to make one in the Commons as soon as he learned that Grey had spoken. Grey believed that at last the battle was won. But there was to be one more in the long series of misunderstandings which punctuated the arrangements between King and Prime Minister. Either Grey misunderstood the King or Althorp misunderstood Grey. Whatever was the reason, Althorp made his statement in the Commons without waiting for the message from the Lords. The message never came, because Grey had never been in a position to make his own statement.

He should have spoken to a silent and half-empty House, bereft of the Duke and his adherents. Instead the House was full and both Wellington and Lyndhurst spoke strongly against the Bill, without the least suggestion of giving way. Grey was nonplussed and could only wonder dismally what was happening in the Commons.

Hobhouse tells the story in his Memoirs. He had come into the House of Commons and taken his seat beside Althorp, to whom he told the news of the debate which was raging in the Lords, and of which he himself had only heard just before he entered the Chamber. 'He said,' Hobhouse writes, ' "So much the better; but it is rather a bore to have spoken with so much confidence. Now I shall have my shooting." "You may," I said. "The Pitchforks will be here." "Not here," he replied, "the other house." ' And Althorp, having done his duty, went happily off to clean his guns.

The blame for the miscarriage of the arrangement lay neither with the King nor with Grey, but with the Duke of Wellington's outraged sense of propriety. On receipt of the King's letter he had replied stiffly that, 'as a private individual' he should abstain from voting at the King's request but that it was not a course which he thought proper to recommend as leader of his Party. He regarded it as an act of treachery, and though, from loyalty to his master, he was ready to do violence to his conscience, he would not further burden it by leading his friends into shame. He had therefore come into the Lords, resolved to retire as soon as the House divided, but up to that moment to do all that he could to defeat the detestable thing. He had not, of course, seen fit to mention the King's request to any of his colleagues.

Grey was furious at what he thought to be yet another piece of royal treachery, and next day went with Brougham to the Palace and presented the King with a choice between creation of peers or inevitable revolution of the whole country. The Whigs had done all that they could to save their King's face, but they had had enough of his equivocation. The King, since he could do nothing else, again gave his promise. The Lord Chancellor, with more prudence than tact, asked for it in writing. The King, bitterly ashamed and angry, asked Grey whether he did not trust his word. Grey did not, but he was too polite to say so, and confined himself to supporting the Chancellor's request without comment. Next day, they had the King's assurance in writing that he would create as many peers as they wanted.

There was one more person concerned, who knew the King too well to rely on his constancy, and that was his private secretary, Sir Herbert Taylor. All through the negotiations he had been invaluable as a link between the King and the Government. Now he took it upon himself, without authority, to ensure that there should be no further danger of a misunderstanding. He wrote to Wellington and to several more of the Tory peers and told them what the King had done. He took a fearful risk in so forcing the King's hand, and it might well have been the end of his career. When the Reform Bill came up for its third reading in the Lords, the Opposition benches were almost empty, and the Bill passed the House by a huge majority.

There was still to be one more attempt to make it appear that the King had agreed to Reform for the sake of his people, and Grey and Althorp were determined to make it. They believed that if he would come down to Westminster in person to signify the Royal Assent to the Bill, he might still regain some of his lost popularity. For his own sake, they begged him to do it. But the King had had enough of Reform and Reformers. He brusquely refused to have anything more to do with the damned Bill. On 7 June, it received the Royal Assent by a Commission, of which Lord Durham was a member, and became law.

CHAPTER IX

'It was not a good Bill,' John Bright wrote many years later, 'but it was a great Bill when it passed.' It was great in his sense, because it was the beginning of everything which led to Universal Suffrage, but it was not good because it took so small a step at the start. It is surprising to think that this Bill, which aroused so much enthusiasm and so much opposition, made in fact very little difference to the composition of the House of Commons. It is still more surprising to read of the wild enthusiasm for it which prevailed throughout the country and most of all among those who could not expect to benefit from it. It was to take many years still for the workmen in the towns and the labourers in the fields to be allowed to have a voice in the choosing of their representatives. All that the Bill did immediately was cautiously to admit to the suffrage a proportion of the middle classes and the more prosperous tradesmen. Yet it was the first step and it made future progress inevitable. The Whigs, who had introduced it were, in fact, as anxious as the Tories that there should be no extension, though in this, as in so many things, Lord Durham differed from his colleagues. No one fought more strongly for the Bill than Lord Grey, but even he looked on it as the utmost that ought ever to be conceded. He agreed to a stronger measure than he personally welcomed for that very reason and, in a letter in which he gave Durham instructions, he wrote that it should be 'large enough to satisfy public opinion and to afford some grounds of resistance to further innovation'.

Russell, the chief draughtsman of the Bill, was even more definite in his opinion and was so much opposed to any extension of the suffrage that he came to be known as Finality Jack.

It was never Lord Durham's idea that this was to be anything but a first step and, before more than a year or two had passed, he was to start agitating for further measures of Reform. He never forgave the Cabinet for abandoning the idea of the ballot, which was his first demand, but, beyond that, he seems to have kept steadily in view the idea of gradually extending the franchise, though probably not to the point of universal suffrage. It is curious that he should have been in so many things so impatient a man, so determined to force his own ideas on to the world, and yet have had this fund of patience in really important matters, as he was again to show in Canada. With all his faults of temper and his arrogance, there was sometimes in him a breadth of vision and a length of sight which enabled him to accept an inadequate temporary measure for the sake of a long-term gain. Grey and the rest had fufilled their pledge and were content. Durham was pleased with what they had got and almost at once began to scheme for the next advance. After all, the family motto was *Le Jour Viendra* and the day would surely come for a wider franchise—as for a Commonwealth of Nations—though it might not be in his time.

The enthusiasm throughout the country could hardly have been greater had the Bill been about to introduce the millennium. Not only did the middle class greet it with acclaim but steel-workers in Sheffield, cotton-hands in Manchester, and miners in Durham held mass meetings in support of the Bill, and in many of these meetings they spoke of further extensions and even of a vote for every man. It was after one of these, held at Sunderland, that Morton wrote to Lord Durham that 'Universal Suffrage was proposed by a man of the name of McLeod', who 'has been exchequered about a dozen times for defrauding the Excise but is better known as Radical Jack'.

It was fortunate for Lord Durham that at this time, when his political duties and his health and above all his family anxieties left him so little time for looking after his vast property that he should have had as agent a man of the calibre of Henry

Morton. Throughout the years 1830 and 1831 Lord Durham was almost continuously in London and it was left to Morton to watch over the Lambton properties in one of the most stormy times in the history of the County of Durham. His immense correspondence shows how efficiently and bravely he carried out his difficult task.

They were the days of the Durham pitmen's strike which began in 1830 and lasted intermittently through much of the following year. The Combination Laws had been repealed in 1825 and almost at once the men began to organize into Unions. The first in that district, the Colliers' United Association, only lasted for a few years and was succeeded in 1830 by the 'Pitmen's Union of the Tyne and Wear'. At the end of 1830, wages in the district had fallen so much that, in some collieries, men had to be content with eight or ten shillings a week. In addition to this there were other grievances, notably that of the owner's 'Tommy Shop' at which the men were more or less forced to spend their meagre wages on meat, drink, and candles. The feeling among the men was so near to desperation that, as 'binding day' drew near at the beginning of 1830 most of them agreed to refuse to be 'bound' any longer on such terms. The owners would not discuss any others and throughout January and February in 1831 almost every pit in the district stood idle. One of the few exceptions was the Lambton pit, where Morton continued to report that most, sometimes all the men were at work. It was inevitable that the next step should be an attempt by the other pitmen to persuade or force their colleagues at Lambton to stop work in sympathy with them, and Morton—who must have been a man of extraordinary courage—went about for some weeks in danger of his life, literally in danger, for the men were desperate and there was no limit to the means which they might use to enforce their will. There is, in the Lambton papers a scrawled letter, dated 3 April 1831, which even after so long has power to chill the blood of any reader:

'John Radison you give these lins to the workman Or els you will suffer byb the by we suppose you Are bound against your grements you think you have don right but when our turns is out if you dont come among the men the forst generall meeting you and your brother will ly in one Churchyeard and that will be such a church as a number of men like

you has not lane in this long time . . . if you don't think fit
to come after these Directions we must forse you to the grand-
stand and you must take the punishment put upon you. . . .
We suppose that B culbert Skipsey was the first that got
bound and if he does not come a monge the men he shall be
the first that will die.'

They were no empty threats. There had been occasions when
pitmen had defied their leaders and gone to work against their
orders and had later been clubbed or stabbed to death on some
desolate moor. Punishments less than death, too, had a savagery
which was only to be expected among men who lived always on
or near the starvation level and whose lives were harsh and
incessantly in danger. Morton, in one of his letters to Lord
Durham, wrote that a man who voted against the majority at a
meeting had been 'stript of his clothes and badly beaten', and
Lord Durham himself, two years later, spoke of men who had
done the same thing and had been stripped naked and flogged
down their village streets while men and women looked on and
applauded.

Yet the Lambton men were at work, and in the spring of
1831, Morton was able to report that they were all 'bound'. It
is no mean tribute to both owner and agent that the men continued at work almost throughout the strike in spite of efforts to
bring them out. Morton must have had some exciting times
though he seems not to have been at all afraid of the men in
the Lambton pits. He wrote in March 1831: 'I am pretty
certain that by reasoning the matter coolly but decidedly with
them that I shall undermine them on general points that the
leaders have imposed upon them. . . . I do not fear that they
will attempt any violence against me—they may perhaps hiss
me or even pelt me with mud.' It is surely a fair inference that
such confidence could not exist at a pit where the men had
reason to hate their employer.

The danger lay in the men from the neighbouring pits and
Morton writes of nights spent in the colliery buildings with a
few helpers armed with shot-guns and of watching, as he rode
across the moors, long columns of men winding towards the pit
heads, so that he had to ride for help to the nearest place where
there were troops. There were cavalry at Morpeth and, when
danger seemed to be very near, a troop of dragoons was

stationed in Houghton, only a mile or two from the pits. That was Lord Durham's doing. If his men wanted to work, then no one should interfere with them and he first asked the Home Office to supply policemen such as Sir Robert Peel had just instituted in London. They were not available, and Morton suggested the use of Militia or Volunteers. Lord Durham would have none of it. He had not forgotten the disastrous efforts of the Yeomanry at Manchester in 1819. He wanted no Peterloo Massacre in his own countryside. Regular troops could be trusted to carry out their duty without prejudice or local feeling, so troopers lounged and waited for something to happen at Houghton or Burnmoor and bored subalterns rode races on the Lambton course.

Up to this time, Lord Durham had not been closely concerned in foreign affairs. He had perhaps hoped that Lord Grey would offer him the Foreign Office, but there must be few politicians who have not, at one time or another, seen themselves as heaven-sent foreign secretaries. Durham was too busily engaged in the cares of Reform to take any more active part in foreign affairs than was involved in routine attendance at Cabinet meetings, but his connection with King Leopold gave him a special interest in Belgium and, unofficially, he acted as adviser to Leopold. They had been friends for many years while Leopold was living alone and rather miserably in England after Princess Charlotte's death. It was probably by Durham's advice that he refused the crown of Greece and to him he turned again in 1830 when the Belgian crown was offered to him. Now that he had a chance of an active career it is evident from his letters that he was reluctant to take any decisive step without Durham's approval. In April of that year, Durham sent him the draft of a constitution for Belgium and Leopold wrote in reply:

'My dear Durham,
  I return you the constitution you had the kindness to communicate to me. My prayer is that you, who have of late had much more to do about constitutions than any man, would also give this Belgian Constitution a moment's attention. It is made in opposition and hatred of Kingcraft, the object was to make the position as like a president as possible.'

In June he wrote to say that the Belgian question was coming to a head and that the delegation were on the point of arriving to offer him the crown. 'May I repeat my petition today,' he wrote, 'they will probably arrive tomorrow. Perhaps you will permit me to call on you tomorrow at some hour which may suit you.'

The offer was made and accepted. Leopold became a king and the letters continue in a spate from Brussels. They must have been sometimes a little embarrassing to their recipient, since Leopold felt far from secure on his new throne and regarded Lord Durham as the member of the British Cabinet whose duty it was to keep him there. Leopold's position was not enviable. Holland was always threatening, France was incalculable, Russia was a mystery. Great Britain, with some justice, he regarded as half-hearted, as long as the man whom he called the 'Thane of Aberdeen' was Foreign Minister. Things would, he hoped, be a little better under a Whig Government, though he seemed to have difficulty in grasping the idea that it was not within the competence of the Lord Privy Seal to order the British Fleet into the Scheldt whenever he pleased: 'You may be quickly sending a fleet to the Scheldt and the coast of Holland to put a stop to the warlike spirit of my neighbour—the moral effect of even a few frigates will be very great. If you consider the immense importance of the present crisis of trust you will press the Government to act quickly. If a British naval force appears immediately on the coast of Holland . . .' Then there are endless references to two fortresses, Marienburg and Philippsville, which should have been demolished under the terms of the Powers' agreement but which France subsequently wished to retain as a matter of sentiment and a *'point d'honneur'*. Leopold may perhaps be excused for his suspicions of the French sentiment, and the question of the fortresses seems to have got thoroughly on his nerves: 'I have been tormented with these fortresses since the month of August and they appear to be a constant stumbling block. I beseech you, my dear Durham, help me to this additional act in the way I wish it.'

'In the way I wish it' fairly describes Leopold's attitude towards all foreign policy as letter after letter bombarded Lord Durham—letters as full of underlining as any that Queen Victoria was ever to write, full of complaints about the writer's ill-health and ill-luck and finally reinforced by a formidable contribution from Baron Stockmar, that *soi-disant* expert in the art of ruling. There are urgent requests to Lord Durham to interfere in domestic matters at Kensington Palace where the young Victoria was living—'I still see symptoms of a determination of getting rid of Baroness Lehzen, that *must not be* on any account and I put in my positive veto'.

There must have been times when Lord Durham wearied of his unsought position as Leopold's agent in England, but he displayed a surprising patience and found time to take part in the management of the Claremont Trust which controlled the property and money which Leopold still owned in England. Leopold's tone is often querulous and sometimes absurd, but his letters express a genuine gratitude for all that Durham had done and was trying to do for him and when Charles Lambton died in 1831 he wrote sympathetically, though even then not without reference to his own 'misfortunes equally severe'.

'. . . I am going,' he wrote on 20 October, 'to propose to you a measure which I am extremely anxious to see you adopt and which I earnestly press upon you. Pray let me induce you to come to me as soon as you can. You will find the climate agreeable and the town pretty. Your visit would gain me the assistance of the truest friend I have and to you the change of air and scene could not be but favourable.'

Out of the depths of his despair, Lord Durham answered:

'I feel most grateful to your Majesty for your kind and gracious letter which I received last night—as you too truly observe none but those who have experienced similar calamities know how severe is the blow which at once lacerates our warmest affections and destroys our dearest hopes.

'Did not a sense of duty towards those who are spared urge me to reject the feelings of my heart, I should covet the hours which removed me from this world. . . . I will come to Brussels and if the result of my visit should prove of the slightest advantage to your Majesty I should feel what little consolation my present circumstances would admit of.'

Lord Durham went to Brussels and the change undoubtedly helped him to return in good enough health to play a decisive part in the last fights for the Reform Bill. The friendship with Leopold remained unbroken until Durham's death.

PART THREE

'Radical Jack'

1833–1837

Whenever we improve, it is right to leave room for a further improvement. It is right to consider, to look about us, to examine the effect of what we have done—Then we can proceed with confidence, because we can proceed with intelligence.

EDMUND BURKE. *A Plan for the better security of the Independence of Parliament.*

Certainly, great persons had need to borrow other men's opinions to think themselves happy; for if they judge by their own feeling they cannot find it. . . . For they are the first that find their own griefs, though they be the last that find their own faults. . . . Certainly men in great fortunes are strangers to themselves, and while they are in the puzzle of business they have no time to tend their health, either of body or mind.

FRANCIS BACON. *Of Great Place.*

CHAPTER I

'The Bill to give everybody everything' had passed into law and the Millennium had arrived. There would be no more unemployment, no more high prices, no more war. Bread would be cheap and meat within the reach of every man's pocket. So, at least, the people of England believed in that bright dawn of 1832.

They were encouraged in this delusion by the election which followed the passing of the Bill. It was fought with better temper than its predecessor, though with no less vigour and bribery. Lord Durham had long realized that there could never be an honest election without the ballot. As long as a man's vote was open and public, so long would it have a cash value. The only difference between this election and its predecessor was that more candidates were bribing more electors.

The people of England were delighted. To their future of high wages and cheap food there was added the prospect of frequent elections with votes at top prices. It was not until the first reformed Parliament met in 1833 that they suffered their first disillusionment. Its composition was strangely like that of the last unreformed Parliament. There were a few changes in it, even one or two oddities. By some elective chance, which neither he nor his friends could understand, John Gully, the pugilist, bookmaker, and racehorse owner, came in for Pontefract. Macaulay defeated Sadler at Leeds and Cobbett won Oldham. There was a first glimpse of a great Parliamentarian of the future, when Newark returned W. E. Gladstone.

But, on the whole, the new House was the comfortably familiar assembly of landed proprietors, country squires, and sons of peers, with Althorp leading them as before.

The Peers were unchanged. The King's treachery, as they considered it, had saved them from an infusion of new and dubious blood, and they remained as alert as ever to hinder the first sign of progress in any direction, but they were not quite what they had been in spirit. The danger had been averted shamefully and almost too late. They had had to face the hard fact that there was a limit to their powers of obstruction, and, though the threat had receded into the background—it was not to be heard again till the year 1910—it would not quite disappear.

Outwardly all was as it had been before. Earl Grey still sat on the front bench with his legs crossed and his back turned towards his colleagues, Philpott's dark face still scowled among the white-sleeved bishops. Melbourne laughed and joked in deceptive indolence and Brougham, the Lord Chancellor, alternately displayed the brilliance of his oratory and the limitations of his knowledge of law. Among the Opposition the Duke was as erect as ever and as spruce in his blue frock-coat and white trousers. Only Lord Durham was seldom in his usual place, and their Lordships' stately debates were less often enlivened by that most mellifluous of voices and least accommodating of tempers. He was still Lord Privy Seal, but for the next few months he was to have little time to spare for his public duties as bereavement and sorrow continued to accumulate in his family.

At the end of the previous year, he had lost his eldest son, and during the same year, his mother, Lady Anne Wyndham. They had never been close to one another, but he loved her and she was a part of that Lambton tradition which was his greatest pride. In 1832, too, the second daughter of his first marriage, Georgina Sarah, died of consumption. On 12 June, ten days after the enactment of the Reform Bill, he wrote to Grey:

'I am in despair. In eight months I have lost son, mother and daughter. When and where is it to end? I shudder to think who is to be the next victim. I have borne up as long as I could and, with exertions hardly to be described, have gone through all the turmoil and agitation of public life.'

It was his black period and, in little more than another year he was to lose his third daughter, Harriet, and within another twelve months, his sister, Frances Charlotte, Countess of Bessborough. It was the more bitter because it all came upon him at what should have been the time of his greatest triumph and at the height of his popularity in the country.

That was real enough. The name of Radical Jack was blessed in innumerable homes throughout England and there was much talk of Grey resigning and of his succeeding to the Premiership. In November 1833, the *Morning Post* protested:

'It has for some time been rumoured that Lord Durham will be Premier before the opening of the next session of Parliament. . . . But, setting aside the truth or falsehood of the report, we think the existence of that report itself a fearful sign. Lord Durham's appointment may or may not have been contemplated. That it has been thought certain by a few is pitiful; that it has been considered probable by many is yet more sad; that it seems to none of us impossible is as strong a proof as we can anticipate of the perilous position in which at this time, the nation is placed.'

It was a combination of Grey's affection—much tried but never failing—and Palmerston's desire to remove a possible competitor which roused Lord Durham from his despair and set him to a task which was suited to his ability and was exacting enough to call for all his energy and determination. In 1833, there was urgent need for a British statesman of rank and authority at the court of St. Petersburg, to persuade the Emperor Nicholas to take his part in the resettlement of Europe and the preservation of peace.

The Belgian crisis seemed to have passed, but Nicholas had given no sign of recognition of the new King of the Belgians, and, by reason of his family connections, he was very much more inclined to favour the Dutch. France was in one of her more chauvinistic moods and the restraint which Russia could have exercised on her would have been enough to dissuade her from any more attempts to dominate Belgium. The Powers of Europe needed Nicholas's help, or at least, if that were unobtainable, the assurance of his neutrality.

Then there was further need for talks with Russia because of her recent conquest of Poland and the brutality of her treatment of the vanquished Poles. In 1815, at the height of the usual post-war scramble to reconstruct Europe, Alexander of Russia had granted a constitution to Poland which he ruled thereafter as a national kingdom, not as a part of his Russian dominions. Fifteen years later, when the yeast of rebellion was working all over Europe, the Poles rose in revolt at Warsaw and assembled over 50,000 troops to fight for their independence. There was justification for the rebellion, for Alexander, having granted them a constitution, had first suspended it and then altered it to a form in which the Polish Diet lost all its power and was restricted to the discussion of purely formal measures. Nicholas had continued the process of repression, because, as Lord Byron observed in *Don Juan*, he

> *Had no objection to true liberty,*
> *Except that it would make the nations free.*

In September 1830 the Russians marched into Poland, captured Warsaw, and destroyed the last faint remnants of Polish liberty. Poland lapsed into the state of a Russian province, under the brutal rule of a Russian Archduke. The Powers had agreed to Poland's national status and Britain and France protested against this violation of it, while the systematic Russian cruelty shocked the conscience of every civilized nation.

It was to be not the least of Lord Durham's delicate and difficult tasks to prevail on the Emperor Nicholas to put an end to these cruelties. *The Times* of 27 June, in referring to his mission, went so far as to call for 'a direct and strenuous interference on the part of this country in favour of the glorious and deeply outraged Poles'. On the same day, the Princess Lieven wrote to Grey and called his attention to the article.

'I had only heard,' she wrote, 'Lord Durham's mission spoken of vaguely and as a possibility. They will wonder at it in Russia, and do more than wonder if the object of his mission were really that of which the *Times* of this morning speaks. But, for the first time, I think the *Times* has not told the truth. In any case I regret the article, for it may create a bad impression.'

They did indeed wonder in Russia, where Lord Durham had a reputation as an anarchist and a fire-brand. In so autocratic a country, his support of Reform was enough to damn him as an enemy to all kings and all governments and as an inciter of the rabble. The bad impression, of which the Princess was afraid, was much increased by the ill-mannered debate which arose in the House of Commons on 28 June, when O'Connell referred to the Emperor as a 'miscreant', and, on being mildly reproved by Palmerston, was supported by Hume, who offered to call the Emperor not only a 'miscreant' but also 'a monster in human form'. Nothing, it would seem, was being left undone to ensure a thoroughly unpleasant reception for Lord Durham on his arrival in Russia.

A further complication was that Britain had no ambassador at the Russian court. Sir George Heytesbury had resigned in 1832, and no successor had yet been appointed. When Heytesbury was on the point of retiring, Princess Lieven, who could never refrain from interfering, had warned Nesselrode, the Russian Foreign Minister, that Palmerston was going to send Sir Stratford Canning to replace him. Canning was an extremely able man, who had just distinguished himself greatly in a special mission to Spain, and had previously served on the embassy staff at St. Petersburg. He would have been an ideal choice as ambassador, were it not that he was unacceptable to the Emperor, whom he had offended on his previous visit, which had been before Nicholas had succeeded to the throne.

The whole thing had been a triviality. Owing to an oversight, Canning had omitted the Grand Duke Nicholas from the round of formal calls which protocol required him to pay when about to leave the country. So rigid was the Russian idea of etiquette that the petty slight had been magnified into a studied insult.

Nesselrode, in replying to the Princess's letter wrote: 'Don't let it be Canning. He is a most impracticable person, *soupconneux, pointilleux, défiant.*' He reinforced his request with a revival of the old story of the insult and with the threat that if Canning were to arrive, no one would receive him.

The position was at its most awkward when the time came for Durham to go to Russia. Palmerston had not yet made the appointment, but it was no secret that he still meant to send Canning.

The absence of a British Ambassador would throw an extra burden on Lord Durham and the strained relations caused by Palmerston's unhelpful action about Canning would call for an extraordinary discretion. The recent behaviour of the House of Commons would only make the situation more unpleasant for him. Princess Lieven, who was having the time of her life, warned Grey: 'How deeply I regret the discussion which took place yesterday in the House of Commons, and above all, the silence of Ministers. Hitherto, any such language personally insulting to a Sovereign in friendly alliance has always met with reproval in the Government papers.' With characteristic impudence, she advised Grey to tell Althorp or Russell to say 'a few words' to repair Palmerston's omission.

Palmerston, admittedly, had reproved O'Connell, but half-heartedly and more on the score of a breach of Parliamentary behaviour than of an insult to a friendly sovereign. Grey knew this and answered: 'I have just seen Palmerston and, if an opportunity is given him, he will state more strongly his disapprobation of the language used last night.'

The correspondence between Grey and Palmerston proves fairly conclusively that the idea of asking Durham to go to Russia originated with Grey. Palmerston agreed at first with reluctance. He did not trust Durham and he was still new enough at the Foreign Office to resent suggestions even from the Prime Minister. He consented to the appointment because Durham would fill in the awkward gap which his failure to appoint an ambassador had caused. Possibly, too, he was glad of the opportunity of removing from the country a man who would gladly have held the position of Foreign Secretary, but Palmerston was too conscientious to send any man abroad to represent his country unless he were satisfied of his ability.

Grey had suffered much from his son-in-law, but he did not forget, that, whatever their differences might have been, Durham had always supported him loyally in public, and, if he had had to put up with the more troublesome side of his character, he knew better than anyone his real ability as well as his charm. For personal reasons he was glad to recommend Durham for a position in which his finest qualities would find full scope, though he dreaded the separation from his daughter which her residence in Russia must mean. Those very qualities which hampered Durham in the rough and tumble of political life were to be assets to him in his new work. His inordinate pride of family was not out of place in the stiffest court in Europe. The Czar of all the Russias was an almost omnipotent autocrat, but Lambton of Lambton could show a pedigree quite as long and certainly much more respectable than could the haughtiest Romanov. His obstinate liking for his own way became tempered to a just firmness when he spoke not for himself but for his country. His outbursts of temper had almost always been the result of illness or mental suffering, or sometimes of the most petty of irritations. Change of scene and the prospect of high responsibility gave him restored health and a new poise, and the temper now showed only—and not without effect—as a smouldering glow which warned men not to take him lightly. The darkness began to fall from his spirit and in this new and exacting environment, his many good qualities shone out clearly. The Russians had expected to see a wild and turbulent revolutionary; they saw instead a fastidious aristocrat of extraordinary charm and great personal beauty, a patient and skilful negotiator, and above all, a man of absolute integrity. In the House of Lords, Lord Durham had been a firebrand, in the Cabinet room he was an irritation and a perpetual menace to his colleagues. But, on the heights where emperors walk, and in the rarefied air which autocrats breathe, Radical Jack was at home.

CHAPTER II

It is a pity that the Princess Lieven, who was so prolific a letter-writer and so well placed to observe all that went on in the diplomatic world, should be such an unreliable witness, since her letters are the most constant source of information about Lord Durham during the next few months. History has never been quite able to account for the extraordinary fascination which she exercised over a long series of Prime Ministers and Foreign Secretaries. Wellington, Grey, Aberdeen, Palmerston—all in their turns were taken into her confidence and fell under her spell. She was not, by contemporary accounts, very witty or entertaining, nor, by the standard of contemporary portraits, was she a beauty. On the other hand, she was officious, meddlesome, and endowed with an inflated idea of her importance. She was known to have been, at one time, the mistress of Guizot, the French Minister, but there was little evidence of sex in her attraction for the various British Ministers who became her friends. Charming she must have been and not only to men, since she was a member of the ladies' committee of Almacks which was a coveted distinction among British aristocrats and one which was rarely given to a foreigner.

Whatever her virtues and her charms may have been, sincerity was not one of them. Yet she has much value as a recorder of contemporary opinion about the great personalites of the political and diplomatic world. She was such a weather-cock, changing with every gust of favour or disfavour, that a reference to her diary can establish the popularity or unpopularity of almost any great figure at the time when she wrote, though her tone may have changed a month later, with a like change in public feeling.

It would be rash to attach much importance to the Princess's own opinion of Lord Durham, yet she faithfully indicates all the changes in his fortunes, by the warmth or frigidity of her comments. In 1831, when he was becoming an object of dislike to the fashionable world, she had written petulantly to her brother in Russia, General Beckendorf, complaining that Durham was always interfering between Earl Grey and herself. 'I am always,' she wrote in 1832, 'on the best terms with him [Lord Grey] and I shall see him today. He listens when I am speaking, but it only lasts half an hour, for then his accursed son-in-law—Lord Durham—comes along and carries him off and he becomes either a Jacobin or a child, as it suits the other.' A year later, when Durham seemed to be at the bottom of his fortunes, Princess Lieven abuses him to her brother with increased acerbity: 'The man's vanity is proverbial! He is the haughtiest aristocrat. . . . Here he is cordially and universally detested. The King, in speaking of him, never alludes to him otherwise than as "Robert Le Diable".' She adds that the King spoke with the liveliest anticipation of the joy of getting rid of Durham, to which she answered that it was a pity that it had to be at her country's expense. But times had changed and Lord Durham was on the upward grade. Princess Lieven's opinion rose with him, and she retailed for Grey's benefit every kind word which was spoken in Russia and every opinion favourable to the new arrival at the Russian court. Even before he had left England her tune was changing and she was full of concern about the possible damage which might have been caused by the wild speaking in the Commons.

Grey, though he was too polite to say so, did not need any advice from the Princess about the duties of a Prime Minister. He took a very early opportunity of disavowing in the Lords and on behalf of the Government, the language which had been used in the Commons about the Russian Emperor, though, as he wrote to the Princess: 'The effect of what I said would have been better if the Duke of Wellington had not thought proper to do all that he could to diminish it.' 'I trust,' he added, 'that Lord Durham's mission will prove useful, though I know (not from the communication alone which you made to me), the strength of the prejudice against him. I know too that this extends beyond his person; that your Government entertains something like horror of the principles and measures of the present Government.'

Whatever prejudice may have existed in Russia against Lord Durham and the Whig Government, the Emperor Nicholas was statesman enough to ignore it and to make a great effort to create a friendly feeling at the beginning of Durham's mission. Durham told the story of their first meeting in an official letter to the Foreign Office and also in a personal note to Grey, which Grey forwarded to Princess Lieven: 'I enclose a note,' he wrote, 'which Lambton wrote to me after his arrival at Petersburg, which will show you how much pleased he was with the Emperor's reception of him. For the particulars, I must wait until I see Palmerston's letter.'

The Princess declared herself 'enchanted that he should have been so pleased at the reception the Emperor gave him', adding unnecessarily: 'I am very curious to know what Lord Palmerston has heard.' In her letter of the following day, she repeated the request: 'If you have seen Lord Durham's letter to Lord Palmerston, pray give me an account of it.' Lord Grey, infatuated as he was, had not lost discretion so far as to show confidential Foreign Office documents to the Princess, and wrote, with a trace of coldness. 'I have not seen Lord Durham's *private* letter to Lord Palmerston yet', but, at the same time told her the gist of as much of the official despatch as was by that time common knowledge.

H.M.S. *Talavera*, with Lord and Lady Durham on board, had arrived at Cronstadt when a division of the Russian Fleet lay in the harbour, awaiting inspection by the Emperor. The Emperor arrived on 17 June and, Grey wrote, 'sent an officer on board the *Talavera* to express his wish to receive Lord Durham as a private individual, for the purpose of making his acquaintance before he presented his credentials as ambassador.' (It must be noted that, though the Emperor often referred to Lord Durham as 'Ambassador', it was not his official title, since he had come on a special mission and was not to stay in Russia after its completion. He is more correctly referred to in Foreign Office correspondence as 'Special Envoy'.)

The British papers had stated incorrectly that the Emperor himself had gone aboard the *Talavera*. In fact, Durham, in response to this invitation, boarded the Imperial yacht and, Grey continued, 'had a long conversation with His Majesty, which principally turned on the affairs of Belgium'. Grey forestalled the Princess's inevitable request by adding: 'for the details of which I have not time.' 'Nothing,' he continued, 'could be more cordial and gracious than the Emperor's reception of Lord Durham, accompanied by the expression of a wish that the interview between His Majesty and him should be of the most unreserved nature and deprived of all ceremony. . . . At the conclusion of the interview, which was of considerable duration, Lord Durham adds, "His Imperial Majesty's manner was most gracious, repeatedly shaking me by the hand, when declaring both his personal kindly disposition toward myself individually and my country generally."'

It is clear from the correspondence that Lord Durham arrived in St. Petersburg after having created a favourable impression, and that he himself was delighted with the cordiality which greeted him. On the domestic side, the family's arrival was less happy, since it turned out that no house had been got ready for them. Instructions had been sent to the British Consul to make preparations for them, but, by some mischance, the letter had miscarried and did not arrive until after they did. Lady Durham wrote to her parents that she was delighted with the novelty of everything, but already she found the cold trying. It was then the height of summer, and she must have looked forward with deep misgiving to the grim Russian winter and especially to the harm which it might to do her husband's precarious health.

The Emperor's marked courtesy to Lord Durham at Cronstadt was at once reflected in the attitude of the society of St. Petersburg, and, as soon as the Consul had found a suitable residence for him, Lord Durham set up his establishment with his usual magnificence. Both Lady Durham and he were impressed with the Russian court, which they found very different from the niggardly and ill-organized establishments at Windsor and St. James's. 'We have letters tonight,' Grey wrote, 'from my daughter, giving an account of their introduction to Peterhof, where they dined and were at a ball. She speaks in raptures of the Emperor and Empress and gives the preference to your court very much to ours.'

The Russian court of that date was the most ceremonious and rigid in Europe, and, in that charmed circle of privilege, Lord and Lady Durham moved as easily and naturally as dancers in a minuet. Once more, on 6 August, Grey wrote to Princess Lieven, telling her that 'they both speak with raptures of everything they have seen and met with'. A few days later, Sir George Heytesbury, the retiring ambassador, reached England with his own confirmatory report of the Durhams' successful début. He assured Grey that the Russians thought Durham 'extremely clever', an opinion which Princess Lieven reinforced from the news which friends in St. Petersburg sent to her. 'Shall I say, my dear Lord, that you are satisfied? They are so, certainly, in my country at the way Lord Durham deals with business and treats of all political questions. They think him remarkably clever and say that he has a manner of discussing affairs which is both straightforward and honest.'

Dining, dancing, and the endless ceremonies of the court did not absorb all Lord Durham's time. In conference with the Emperor and Nesselrode, he was steadily at work. It is difficult, even today, to estimate what he achieved during the few months of his mission. His own account of it is in the Foreign Office records and he does not conceal his conviction of his success. He had never been given to boasting of his own ability or achievements, fiendishly proud as he could be of his family and possessions, and his tendency in public affairs was rather to underrate himself. He probably did not exaggerate now, for Palmerston spoke with warm approval of his reports, and William IV, who hated him, sent him a message of congratulation. Princess Lieven's evidence, varying with the fashion of the day, is always suspect, but she wrote consistently to Grey in praise of him. Grey's answers, guarded as they are, show that he too was well satisfied with Lord Durham's progress. On 2 September, referring to a despatch of Nesselrode's, Grey wrote that 'he was much gratified by the proof which it afforded of the favourable impression which Lord Durham had made'; and again, on 3 October, a letter from Count Orloff is 'very gratifying as to the testimony it bears to the manner in which Lord Durham has conducted himself'.

Lord Durham's main task was to further good relations with Russia and to ensure that Russia should lend no support—should even show no approval—to Holland's truculent attitude towards the new Kingdom of Belgium. His secondary, and far more difficult task, was to obtain more merciful treatment for the unhappy Poles.

In this second task, it must be conceded that he accomplished nothing and deluded himself that he had accomplished a good deal. To attempt to interfere in what was, after all, a domestic matter of the Russians, was a delicate task, and one which could only be attempted by a man who enjoyed exceptional personal favour at the court. Even Durham did not feel it advisable to broach the question until he had been several weeks in Russia and was sure of his standing. It says much for his tact and persistence that he induced the Emperor to publish what in a letter to Palmerston he calls a 'merciful Ukase' ordering better treatment of the Poles. The Ukase was antedated to remove any suspicion that it had been promulgated after Durham's request, though it made little difference when it was dated, since the Poles were treated as brutally after it as before. It was obviously only a friendly gesture on the Emperor's part towards Durham and an attempt to pacify humanitarian sentiment in England. In the country of its origin, it was tacitly accepted as a piece of diplomatic politeness which was not meant to be translated into action.

Durham was mistaking a gesture for a reality in accepting the promise of a Russian autocrat as though it were the word of an English gentleman. He had done all that he could, and his personal friendship with the Emperor had enabled him to go further than most ambassadors would have dared. This was emphatically a case where achievement must be assessed in proportion to the difficulty or impossibility of the task. It is surely too much to expect any man in a matter of a few weeks to

eradicate the age-long tradition of cruelty in a nation. In pleading for the Poles, it was unlikely that Durham or anyone would
succeed, since the only argument was that of humanity, a plea
which seldom arouses response in the hearts of autocrats and
still less often in Russians

Things were going badly in the Low Countries. The settlement which the British Cabinet, with the support of France,
Prussia, and Austria, had engineered was threatened by the
intransigence of the Dutch. The King of Holland was in no
way reconciled to the idea of an independent kingdom of
Belgium and openly proclaimed his belief that the waters of the
Scheldt were his private possession and his intention of so keeping them. France, in one of her belligerent moods, was quite
prepared to fight Holland, but the other Powers felt no confidence that she would restore any territory which she might
acquire in the course of the war. Austria was loyal but ineffective, and Prussia was too much occupied by the danger of
revolutions in the lesser German states to pay much attention
to anything further away. So far Russia had not shown her
hand.

Russia's silence prompted the Dutch to further obstinacy.
They relied on the family connection between their royal
family and Russia's, which, so far, had restrained the Emperor
Nicholas from adding his country's weight to that of the other
Powers. Durham explained this difficulty in a letter to Lord
Grey:

'The great difficulty in getting them to act with us in the
Belgian business arises, as you may well imagine, from
the family ties and domestic influence which surround the
Emperor on all sides. I am certain that he thinks force ought
to be used if necessary, and will be glad when it has produced
its effect, but wishes to avoid the odium of himself outraging
the feelings of his relations and connections.'

Most of the Powers were in agreement that the time to use
force had come, but none of them was prepared to use it
except France, whom none of the others trusted. The situation
had become so tense that Grey, in one of those fits of despon-
dency which often attacked him at a moment of crisis, told
Princess Lieven that the only solution was to draw a ring round
Holland and Belgium and leave them to fight it out. The

Emperor Nicholas appeared to favour the use of force as long as his own country was not involved and as long as it did not result in any advantage to France, a country on which he looked with horror as the home of Jacobinism and of every sort of anarchy and evil. His simple suggestion was that Britain should act alone.

He had already proposed it to Lord Durham during the long talk in the harbour of Cronstadt, urging that Britain should occupy Antwerp by way of warning to Holland. 'He seemed much alarmed,' Durham had reported to Palmerston, 'at the notion of a French army again entering Belgium and pressed on me with the greatest earnestness the propriety of our occupying Antwerp and garrisoning it with British troops.'

That was the first that Lord Durham had heard of the idea and he lost no time in rejecting it, arguing that the best hope of preserving order lay in joint action by the Powers. 'As long as Russia holds back,' he told the Emperor, 'the King of Holland will still entertain hopes of assistance from that quarter.'

Nicholas had not abandoned his idea and, in August, Nesselrode brought it forward again, since, from Russia's point of view, it was an ideal solution. Holland would probably yield, Britain was to be trusted, and France would be kept in the background. Nesselrode and his master were still as frightened of France as they had once been of Britain and there was no Lord Durham at St. Petersburg to speak for France and assure them that a country might have reformed its own Parliamentary system and still have no desire to interfere with its neighbours'. Nesselrode overrated either his own astuteness or Lord Durham's simplicity when he presented his idea in the form of a not very skilfully concealed trap.

His ingenuous suggestion was that he should communicate the Emperor's wish for a British occupation of Antwerp to the King of Holland, and let it be understood—quite unofficially, of course—that it had been discussed with His Britannic Majesty's representative at St. Petersburg, who had raised no objection.

Lord Durham lacked experience, but he was not the simpleton that Nesselrode thought him, and his essentially straightforward nature made him treat the suggestion with something like open contempt. As he wrote to Palmerston on 2 August, he at once told Nesselrode that, while Britain was ready to use force if necessary, she would use it only in conjunction with France and the other Powers; meanwhile, as he had told the Emperor at Cronstadt, the best solution of the problem was for Russia to abandon her seclusion and announce her open support of the Powers. In fact, Lord Durham's answer, when stripped of the elegant verbiage of diplomacy, amounted to nothing more than a flat refusal to commit Britain to the role of Russia's cat's paw.

He was even more outspoken a few hours later on the same day to the Dutch Ambassador, who had called to apologize for the violent things which had been said in his country about Britain.

'I told him,' Durham wrote to Grey, 'England could have no object in the part which she had taken but the equitable settlement of the unfortunate affair, the consideration of which had been forced upon us. That the prosperity of Holland was as much an object of interest to us as that of Britain—but that we were bound in honour to carry into effect a treaty, the execution of which we had guaranteed; and that I must fairly tell him that the conduct of the Dutch Government had been such as to leave me no doubt that their object never had been a bona fide settlement of the question. We parted good friends.'

CHAPTER III

Lady Durham's diary of the Russian mission, which is preserved at Lambton, is full of information about their household in St. Petersburg and the details of their domestic life. She was a shrewd and amused observer of everything that she saw and kept her record with an agreeable informality so that a recipe for 'making 54 gallons of malt liquor' rubs shoulders with her description of the Easter Festival in the Russian Church. Two impressions which especially remain after reading it are the enormous amount of work which Lord Durham had to get through and the excessively high cost of living, especially of living in the style which Lord Durham thought proper for his position. The account books at Lambton show how much of this expense must have come out of his own pocket, for the sum which his mission cost the Government was modest in comparison with recent missions of the same sort. In 1826, Wellington's visit of a few weeks' duration, cost the country over £4,500, only £900 less than the cost of all the months which Lord Durham spent there, and it must be remembered that Wellington stayed as a guest of the Russian Marshals, so that he was not incurring the expense to which Lord Durham was put for a house and servants and all their food and maintenance. The Duke of Devonshire, in the same year, sent in to the country a bill for £10,000 for an even shorter visit. The total for Lord Durham's mission of £5,440 13s. 6d. seems extraordinarily reasonable and must have been supplemented by many thousands of pounds of his own money.

Russia was then a country in which what was called bribery in more scrupulous parts of the world was the accepted and indeed the only way of getting things done. Many officials, even high officials, were paid only nominal salaries and left to make the rest of their living as best they could. Even the simple procedure of Lord Durham's presentation of his credentials cost him 2,160 roubles, most of which went on gifts of gold snuff-boxes to court officials, while he was presented with a bill from the Imperial Stables for the carriage and the horses which took him to the Palace, as well as for the wages of the various grooms and strappers who prepared them. Hospitality too, was a heavy charge, since the Russian taste was for immensely long and elaborate dinners and the Russian thirst was unquenchable. In Lady Durham's diary there is a note of a dinner which they gave on 4 March 1834 to twenty-six guests, when the menu included '*Olla Podrida Complete à l'Espagnole avec Garbauzos, Chozzos, sauce au tomates*' while the sweet champagne which they had to provide was always an offence to Lord Durham's sensitive palate. A note in another hand which has been slipped into the pages of the diary seems to have been a list of dishes for another dinner—a list drawn up by an illiterate, or more probably a foreign chef, since the list of fishes includes 'Bake Hake, Boil Eela, Stew Salmon and Turkie Boil'.

This style of living was in sharp contrast to the straits to which they were put during their occasional carriage tours through the countryside, when they were often hard put to it to get the simplest of food. Lady Durham records her 'recipe for getting fresh eggs in a Russian village where you intend to pass the night.' 'On arriving in the evening, offer a reward for every egg that is brought you and buy them all up; in the morning, if there are any eggs to be had, you will get them fresh.'

Her list of the tasks which were thrust upon Lord Durham, as acting ambassador, is formidable in its length and variety and all these had to be undertaken in addition to his work as special envoy. Many of them, it would seem, might have been attended to by a junior official at the Embassy, or even by the British Consul, but the Russians could seldom be content in the smallest matters unless His Excellency had himself looked into them, and the British residents were insatiable in their demands on his time and energy, though it is impossible to blame them, when for a long time there had been nobody with real authority to speak for them.

The Debating Society of the British Residents attracted the attention of the Russian Police, who darkly suspected them of plotting revolution and massacre and were convinced that they were a secret society of the most dangerous sort. The Society appealed to Lord Durham, who was able to appease the police by showing them the list of subjects to be debated during the coming season. These included such innocent topics as 'Whether the introduction of machinery into a country would be beneficial or not'; 'Whether talent is natural or acquired'; 'Whether the establishment of Temperance Societies is desirable in any part of the world'; and 'Whether Matrimony be preferable to Celibacy'.

There was further trouble in the literary and intellectual circles of the residents when the Royal Society wrote from London to complain that the Imperial Academy of St. Petersburg had not acknowledged receipt of a volume of the last literary transactions of their body. Lord Durham passed the complaint on to the Academy who replied with chilly dignity that 'Les Sociétés Savantes n'échangent pas de simples lettres de remerciement'.

Support for the Scottish Missionary Society, who wanted to buy land from the Russian Government, was rather more like the normal duty of an ambassador, but Lord Durham's next request for help in a matter of religion was something of a puzzle. A British 'artizan' who had been arrested for theft informed the prison authorities that he had never been baptized and refused all offers of spiritual consolation from any of the priests or ministers who attended the gaol. The authorities asked Lord Durham to confirm the man's story, which he was unable to do from his own knowledge, never having heard of the man before. He sent for a Protestant minister and told him to deal with the question. There were constant applications made to him by the police, who regarded the British Ambassador as being there for their convenience in matters of the very slightest importance. Once he had to intervene for 'two or three youths about fifteen years of age', who had been throwing ice at windows.

There was an occasional matter which really aroused his pity and interest, as when he was appealed to by Polish refugees whom the Austrians had handed over to Russia, and many of commercial importance, one of which must have brought back memories of County Durham and Mr. Morton. The Ship-owners Association of Sunderland, whom Mr. Morton considered 'a very ignorant, selfish and unreasonable lot of people', were in constant collision with the Russian Customs authorities and Lord Durham took up their case and managed to get concessions for them. Then he was beset by inventors. An Ionian subject, Papadofoulo Vereto, had invented a 'certain warlike device' which the Board of Ordnance in London had refused to look at and apparently thought that the British Ambassador in Russia ought to make up for their neglect by pushing his case with the Russians. Lord Durham knew as well as anyone the habit of the Board of Ordnance of rejecting all 'warlike devices' at the first offering, but did not feel called upon to intercede for an Ionian subject in what was none of his business. He also extricated himself with some skill from an imbroglio in which the Church of Armenia sought to involve him over an extremely complicated dispute with the schismatic Armenians who had omitted from their public prayers the name of the Categhogos of Etchinasia, a place which was much venerated in their Church because it was near Mount Ararat.

It is little to be wondered at that, when he was continually pestered by anyone who had a grievance or a request, genuine or imaginary, Lord Durham should have found life at times very exhausting and should have succumbed to his neuralgic pains. Yet even in sickness he was not free from inventors and enthusiasts. Prince Kosloffsky, hearing of his indisposition, rushed to his aid with a 'recipe for headache from the King of Wurtemburg's Doctor, a very learned physician—to exclude all air from my chamber and fill it with strong perfume of burned feathers'.

Among the other papers relating to this visit is an interesting list of books which were sent out to him. He was always a lover of books and this list shows the range of his interests and the way in which, even in Russia, he managed to keep abreast of the literary world of London. There are more books of travel and history than of any other sort, but sport is represented by Nimrod's *Chase, Turf and Road*, fiction by Lady Blessington's *Victims of Society*, and politics by Cooke's *History of Party* and Fonblanque's *England under the Seven Years' Administration*. For biography, he had *The Life of Sir Walter Scott* in three volumes, *Attila* in three and three more of Jack Bray's *Illustrations of Human Life*. That his reading was often related to the work in hand is shown by the preponderance of books about the Near East, that perpetual source of anxiety to all who dealt in Russian foreign policy—Scott's *Egypt and Candia*, Pashley's *Travels* (three volumes), Bacon's *First Impressions of Hindustan*. Lighter reading presumably accounted for *Gentleman Jack* (three volumes by 'The Author of *Cavendish*'). Wherever Radical Jack might find himself, there was sure to flourish a vigorous social and intellectual life, which must have done much to sustain him when he plunged once more into the tortuous world of Russian diplomacy.

CHAPTER IV

The plan which the Powers of Europe had accepted for the settlement of the Dutch-Belgian problem was the production of the British Cabinet and the diplomacy which set it and maintained it in motion was Lord Palmerston's. Both have a right to their full share of credit for its eventual success, but it is unfair to diminish the share which undoubtedly belongs to Lord Durham. The plan required for its success that, if Russia would not actively support the other Powers, she should at least remain neutral and refrain from any action or words which might seem to suggest that she favoured Holland.

For a few months during that year of 1833, the peace of Europe hung not on the resolution of a Cabinet nor the skill of a Foreign Minister, but on the tact and resolution of Britain's Ambassador to the Court of Russia. Palmerston's diplomacy, admirable as it was, would have been robbed of its effect had not Lord Durham kept a cool head and an unswerving purpose; had he not, above all, been able to convince the Emperor Nicholas and his Foreign Minister of his country's determination and of his own integrity. It was his first diplomatic appointment and he had to hold his own in negotiation with such skilful veterans as Nesselrode and Pozza di Borgio, against the influence of Metternich and the almost legendary Talleyrand. He lacked their experience and something of their skill, but in discretion and firmness he was their equal as in honesty he was infinitely their superior. He was subjected to direct pressure from Nesselrode at St. Petersburg and to more remote pressure from the courts of Holland, France, and Austria. There was even a danger that his old friendship for Leopold of Belgium might have coloured his views and brought upon him the suspicion of prejudice, a suspicion which any one of those skilled diplomatists would have been swift to use for his own profit. Lord Durham kept his head and—to the surprise of many who knew him—his temper. He was determined that Holland should yield to pressure but equally determined that it should be to the concerted pressure of the Powers and not to Britain alone. He gave no encouragement to the Emperor's repeated suggestions that Britain should take it upon herself to bring Holland to heel.

With patience and courtesy, yet without a hint of compromise, he insisted that the peace of Europe was the affair of the Powers of Europe, and that Russia, if she would not help, must at any rate refrain from even the appearance of hindering.

The result of his mission was one of those diplomatic triumphs which nearly always escape the notice of history because they result in inaction, whereas a treaty or a battle has a date and a certain historical value in its own right. Russia could have done much to help and still more to hinder, and Lord Durham's achievement lay in the fact that she did nothing at all. Had she actively supported the others the result would have been the same as it was, though the settlement would have come sooner. Had she given any show of support to her old friend, Holland, the only consequence could have been war. She held her hand, and though the negotiations dragged on for some months after Lord Durham's return to England their success was never any longer in doubt. It was, as it happened, hastened by King Leopold's betrothal to a French Princess, which brought France into line with Britain and restrained her from any attempt at a purely selfish policy. It is not making any extravagant claim for Lord Durham's diplomacy to say that he played an important part in securing Russia's neutrality and that his personal influence over the Emperor was a valuable asset to his country. Foreign Office correspondence shows that he also used this influence in a less conspicuous way by explaining to the Emperor the working methods of the French and British constitutions. Nicholas was most deeply suspicious of the French, especially since their latest revolution. It had ended in a limited monarchy, but in Russian eyes, it appeared as nothing but a continuance of the Jacobinism of 1792, nor was Russian opinion any better pleased with the Reform Bill which seemed to add Britain to those countries which were ready to throw off the rule of monarchy and submit to the mob.

Lord Durham, much as he hated all Bourbons, had always been a lover of France and an admirer of the French people. His influence, as his letters to Palmerston show, was used to convince the Emperor that, though the French monarchy was in no danger, it would be all the stronger for Russia's support, and that it was sound policy for Russia to lean towards France rather than Austria. Nicholas's preference had been for Austria as an old established monarchy and he had not considered that it would be to his interest to strengthen the cause of monarchy where it was weak rather than where it was already strong. Lord Durham appealed to both reason and sentiment when he pleaded that the greatest autocrat in Europe should lend his countenance where it was most needed and where it would do most good. By ignoring France, Nicholas might drive her into new folly and produce just the effect which he feared. 'I begged him to consider,' Lord Durham wrote, 'whether that very result might not be produced which he so much deprecated.'

With one of those flashes of foresight which sometimes distinguished him, he added a warning that, if France and Russia were to go to war, and Russian soldiers to be taken prisoner, they might return to their country imbued with those very ideas which Nicholas so much detested. (The world had not yet learned to talk of 'indoctrination'.) He also warned the Emperor that, while 'Russia might be and was very useful to Austria, Austria never could be to her—showed him how impossible it was from their geographical position that their interests could ever be the same'.

Few men were better qualified than Durham to instruct the Emperor about the state of Britain after her experience of Parliamentary Reform. In the Lambton MSS. there is a letter of his to Palmerston in which he describes the effect produced on the Emperor by his account of the men who formed the new Parliament—men, who, as their own countrymen were beginning to realize, were not very different from those who had represented them before. Nicholas was deeply impressed by the number of landed proprietors, aristocrats and sons of peers who filled the Commons, and by the control which was still exercised by the quite unreformed House of Lords.

Unhappily the end of Lord Durham's stay in Russia was marred by continued unpleasantness about Canning's appointment. The Emperor still refused to receive him as ambassador and Palmerston was by this time quite determined that, if the Emperor would not have Canning, he should have no one else. Palmerston was just beginning to display the first signs of that arrogance which was to spoil so much of his later work at the Foreign Office. Princess Lieven, as was her habit, meddled unceasingly and Durham's position grew more and more embarrassing. He had won the Emperor's friendship and, in his heart, he agreed with him about Canning, but he was at St. Petersburg as his country's servant and he had to follow Palmerston's instructions.

While officially he maintained his country's attitude on the matter, he continued to bombard Palmerston with arguments and protests, which unfortunately only had the effect of stiffening Palmerston's obstinacy. Palmerston did not like Durham and still felt that Earl Grey had forced him upon the Foreign Office. He had formed the ridiculous opinion that Durham was infatuated with Princess Lieven and was pressing her interests rather than those of his country. Palmerston, to do him credit, was one of the Princess's rare failures. He succumbed to her charm for a time, but soon began to see through her, and at last contrived to get her husband recalled to Russia as the only way of getting rid of her.

The question of an ambassador remained insoluble. Palmerston, against all advice, appointed Canning. The Emperor refused to receive him. Lord Durham wrote, in his diary:

'When it became a question of who was to be Ambassador after my leaving St. Petersburg, Lord Palmerston was told that there was only one man in England to whom the Emperor objected, namely Canning. In despite of this, Palmerston gazetted Canning without even conveying any notice of his intention to do so to Lord Grey. When remonstrated with by Lieven he said, "Canning is of my party and I must provide for him." '

The result of Palmerston's devotion to his party was that for two years there was no British Ambassador at St. Petersburg where British interests were left to a chargé d'affaires, and that, as Durham wrote, 'The result was the suspension of all confidential intercourse between the governments at a time when, in the interests of the peace of Europe, harmony between them was most necessary.' Intercourse was not, as a matter of fact, restored until 1835, and the next ambassador was the Earl of Durham.

CHAPTER V

Lord Durham returned to the world of intrigue and jealousy from which he had briefly escaped and found it as he had left it, but he viewed it now with even less tolerance and with an even less purely party interest. Before the summer of that year of 1833 had changed into autumn, he was once again the querulous semi-invalid who had left England in May of the previous year.

He had talked with kings and met on equal terms Europe's most celebrated diplomatists. Now he sat again in the Cabinet room in London and listened to Grey's vacillations, watched Palmerston's growing self-importance, Althorp's laborious efforts to expound a policy of which he had not grasped the first principle, Brougham's uneasy assertiveness, Holland's old-fashioned prosiness and timidity. Even his old friend and ally, Russell, became more and more the embodiment of a priggish manner and a mincing voice. There was a new source of irritation in Stanley's attempts to combine liberality of speech with the most unliberal of measures in Ireland. Ireland was to be the beginning of the Cabinet's undoing, though in the last election, eighty-two of the 105 Irish members returned had been Whigs, and though it would have seemed that the Whigs had a great opportunity of mending the relations between the two countries.

Such a chance for healing old wounds might not occur again for many years and a generous and humane policy might have done untold and permanent good, but the Whigs, under the direction of a Prime Minister who did not like Ireland, not only failed to take their chance but made things worse by adopting a repressive policy which was strongly reminiscent of that of Pitt in England in 1812.

In the Cabinet, Durham opposed it hotly. He had seen too much tyranny in his own country and abroad to acquiesce in it from his own party. He fought it with all his strength, backed by his memory of Bourbon cruelty in France and Spain and of the sabres of the Yeomanry at Peterloo, reinforced by his recent knowledge of Russian brutality in Poland. He had believed that he could count on Grey's support, but Grey was wavering towards Stanley's policy and once more there were hard words between father and son-in-law. It was at this time that Lord Durham earned his new nickname of 'The Dissenting Minister' by being perpetually at loggerheads with one or all of his colleagues on some point or other of Cabinet policy.

He had only been at home for a few weeks and already he was thinking of resigning. Lord Broughton, in his memoirs, writes that Lord Durham told him at this time that he was going to resign, but that he would choose his own time for announcing it—'He would not let the fellows know his determination sooner than he could help. He would keep them in hot water as long as he could'—a sentiment which Broughton, who was always censorious of his colleagues' motives, attributed to 'the natural consequences of disappointed vanity'. Durham then had a bitter argument with Grey over the retention of Stanley at the Irish Office, refusing to continue as Privy Seal unless he were removed. A new coolness grew up between him and Palmerston, though they had got on tolerably well together during his mission to Russia, and though a colleague, who achieved the difficult task of being a friend of both, said that 'they would have been very good friends if they had ever understood one another'. Unhappily they were to drift farther apart during the next few years. They were too sharply divided on home affairs for any permanent alliance; Palmerston thought Durham a dangerous revolutionary and Durham thought Palmerston a hopeless reactionary. So the breach widened, with Palmerston and Melbourne on one side, and Durham alone on the other.

The second Irish measure which was engaging the government's attention was the Bill to regulate the Establishment of the Irish Church. Since most of the Irish were Roman Catholics, the Established Protestant Church was rich in everything except parsons and congregations. From a purely economic point of view, it was plainly absurd that so large a revenue should belong to a Church where in many parishes the parson preached his Sunday sermon to a dozen or less of the faithful, while many churches remained empty and locked from year's end to year's end. The Whigs were agreed that something must be done to reform the Establishment, though they differed strongly as to what should be the solution.

There were two schools of thought. One, which Durham

favoured, wanted a complete reorganization of the Irish Church and a redistribution of its funds in such a way as to secure some sort of equity in the value of benefices. They proposed to use surplus funds for the general good of the Church and especially for lightening the burden of tithes which bore hardly on so many of the Catholic farmers. They held that the funds of the Church were her inalienable property and could not be diverted to any other use, however deserving the cause might sound, and they could claim good scriptural warrant for their view.

The opposing school, to whom the word 'Corban' meant nothing, were not in the least concerned with the spiritual needs of the Irish, but very much with the surplus income which might be diverted to other causes, not by any means necessarily in Ireland. Lord John Russell was the leader of this school of thought and was strongly supported by the English nonconformists. Russell's strong speech in the House did much to embarrass the Cabinet, who had not agreed on a common policy, and gave rise to Graham's celebrated comment that 'Johnny has upset the coach'. It seemed doubtful whether the coach could go on much further and Lord Durham's resignation in 1834, though it lightened the load and pleased the passengers, did nothing to restore the vehicle's equilibrium. As individuals, nearly all the members of the Whig Party were delighted to be rid of a domineering and quarrelsome colleague. Collectively they were uneasy. Radical Jack was still a power in the country, especially in the North. *The Times* had already mentioned him as a possible successor to Grey as Prime Minister, and the political unions in the newly enfranchised cities were solidly on his side. If he really chose to exert himself, he could command as much or more support in the country as any living politician.

Grey, who knew him better than any of them, could have told them how remote was the danger, for only Grey of his colleagues knew how sick a man his son-in-law was, how weary and pain-racked in body and disillusioned in spirit. At the moment, as Grey knew, Lord Durham was both mentally and physically incapable of the effort required for the transaction of ordinary day-to-day business—much less of heading a movement or entering on a political venture. He did not question the truth of Durham's statement when he wrote that his health made his resignation from the Cabinet an absolute necessity.

Other members of the party were more sceptical. Broughton wrote that 'Durham called on me at the War Office and used language calculated to alarm anyone that gave him much credit for foresight'. 'Bear' Ellice, Durham's brother-in-law with whom he was alternately friendly and not on speaking terms, asserted that Durham's reason for resigning was the old grudge which he bore Grey for refusing him the earldom which he had so openly coveted. In 1834, Grey persuaded the King to bestow on his son-in-law this coveted honour of the Earldom of Durham, and William, counting it a small price to pay for being rid of him, consented. Creevey, spiteful as ever, noted in his diary: 'So Lambton goes out with an Earldom to soothe his aching head. A pretty physic!'

The Cabinet received Lord Durham's resignation with barely concealed relief, but, when he left their counsels, their last claim to liberality of thought or action or name went with him.

His own share of the correspondence about Ireland is typical of his frame of mind at that time and, it must be added, of his innate tendency to see abstract questions in the light of his own personal dignity. He was perfectly sincere about his objections to Stanley's Irish policy, but he resented the way in which, as he thought, he had been ignored in the discussions. In October 1832, Stanley, having, as he had reason to believe, agreed on a general policy with the Cabinet, went to Ireland to discuss it with Lord Anglesey, the Viceroy. Before leaving he had embodied his plan in a memorandum which had been circulated to the Cabinet. Durham took exception to some of the suggestions and, not having been well enough to attend recent meetings, still thought that the Cabinet should have waited for his consent before committing themselves to a policy. In November he sent to Stanley in Ireland a set of comments on his plan and, perhaps thoughtlessly, asked him to pass them on to Lord Anglesey. To this Stanley demurred, writing: 'I must beg to decline being the channel through which your paper is to be laid before Lord Anglesey, if upon further consideration you think that it should be so laid. But is it expedient that he should be put in possession of a document—not being the decision of the Cabinet, but submitted to their consideration by one of their members?'

No doubt, from the strict viewpoint of propriety, Stanley was right, but Lord Durham was not in a temper to stand on such niceties. . . . He wrote in a memorandum to the Cabinet:

'I cannot but feel much surprise at the objection which Mr. Stanley has raised to the propriety of submitting observations to the Cabinet on a plan decided on, as he says, previous to his departure for Ireland. Whatever may have been the discussions on the subject in the Cabinet, the printed plan itself was not circulated until after Mr. Stanley's departure. Until the appearance of that document therefore any remarks were impossible. For what purposes was it circulated if not for those of information and discussion? Of what use is the deliberative character of a Cabinet if every member of it is not at liberty to offer whatever remarks reflexion may suggest to him. . . .?'

Stanley had written that one of the proposals, that of reducing the stipend of three bishoprics, was 'proposed and agreed, tho' after the plan was printed for the Cabinet', a rather careless statement which roused Durham to the acid inquiry: 'Proposed by whom—agreed to by whom? Neither the fact of the proposal or the agreement was communicated to me. This circumstance, however, shows the advantage of further discussion.' There is perhaps something to be said on Lord Durham's side, but his unfortunate tendency towards personal grievances is shown by the fact that in all his next letters to Grey the Irish question is referred to as 'the difference between Stanley and me' or 'the point at issue between Stanley and me'. In January 1833, for instance, he wrote to Grey,

'Dear Lord Grey,
I regret to be obliged to trouble you but I can not remain any longer in ignorance of what has been done in the Cabinet on the question pending between Mr. Stanley and myself.
Since his threat to bring the matter under discussion I have never recd. the slightest communication respecting it— and the time is now come when it must be settled. I must therefore beg you to name an hour at which I may have an interview with you.'

On the following day, 30 January, Grey, pacific as ever, answered:

'My dear Lambton,

The melancholy circumstances which have prevented you from attending the Cabinet will sufficiently account for nothing having been done upon the question which you state to be pending between Stanley and you.'

He pointed out most reasonably that the proposals had not yet been completed as a Bill and that 'when the Bill is completed as I believe it is, or nearly so, any member of the Cabinet who may wish to do so will, of course, have an opportunity of objecting to it'. He added, with his usual courtesy, though with what inward weariness can be imagined, 'I shall of course be happy to see you at any time that you may wish. I must be at the House of Lords for the Commission at two, and after that I shall be at your orders at any time before dinner.'

Yet, if there was pique in Lord Durham's attitude, there was reason too and the objections which he put forward in his memorandum show that he had lost nothing of his ability to argue and to state his argument in lucid prose, or even of his occasional gift of humour. One proposal of Stanley's, optimistically headed 'Proselytism', had been to establish a Protestant Church and a beneficed clergyman in every parish in Ireland where there lived one Protestant. Of this monstrous piece of extravagance, Durham wrote:

'The Plan proposes in other words . . . that a fixed salary should be given to a man for doing nothing in hopes that he may find something to do. . . . Will the enjoyment of a good income unburthened with any duties render its possessor anxious to change his condition and augment his labour?—whilst by so doing he does not augment his reward? Will giving a man salary without work make him desirous of work without salary? If,' he added, 'Proselytism is to take place, it will be carried on by the Religious Enthusiast or the needy preacher whose gains depend on his success. The first the Church is not likely to get—the other it is impossible it should have since the Plan prevents it.'

Not for the first time Lord Durham had stirred his colleagues and for two days Russell and Duncannon were pleading with him. They were both colleagues of the Reform Bill days and were closer to him than any of the Cabinet except Grey. For this was always the difficulty which faced any colleagues of

Radical Jack. They might disagree with him, even dislike him, but they could never ignore him. It was not only that, out of favour as he was and out of sorts with the world, he could be obstructive and dangerous. He could be and frequently was both, but the real danger was that he was seldom obstructive without some good reason. His opposition might be stiffened by personal pique, but it was always based on solid reason and integrity. The real difference between him and most of them was his obstinate refusal to make any concessions to the tactics of the moment, so that he insisted on things that were in themselves right and necessary but were premature or temporarily impossible—as he had fought for his ballot proposal, ignoring the danger that it would wreck the whole Reform Bill; as he was soon to fight for his own ideas in Canada in defiance of the whole Cabinet. But, though he was capable of being as unreasonable as any man living about getting his own way or preserving his own dignity, he could be made to see reason. And they could not deny that there was much reason in his objections to a good deal of Stanley's plan. There have been few better instances of that divided nature of his than this, when, having roundly asserted his own will, he gave in to the pleas and arguments of his colleagues. On 30 January, before he was to have seen Grey, he wrote to him:

'Duncannon has given me an account of the conversation which he has had with you this morning which has gratified me very much for it has convinced me that I had formed an erroneous impression yesterday with respect to your sentiments towards me—both as regards my public and private position. I can have no hesitation in saying that the certainty of the existence of those feelings in your mind renders it a matter of duty as well as pleasure for me to exert myself to the utmost of my power in your service.

'I may take this opportunity of saying that after the explanation I had with Ld. J. Russell yesterday I shall be enabled on the same grounds as he does to support the Irish Church Reform Bill—and, this cause of difference being removed, to which or any other I hope never to recur, I know of nothing which should prevent my earnest co-operation in all the measures of your Government.'

Yet, at the end, he makes it clear that he cannot expect

indefinitely to remain in the Cabinet and asks for continued leave of absence: 'My feelings have been so much harassed and my health suffered so much of late that I require quiet and repose if it can be granted to me.'

Lord Durham's letter of resignation mentioned only his health as the reason and in this spirit Grey answered it in a letter of sympathy and kindness, but it is obvious in the correspondence which had recently passed between them and Stanley about Ireland that ill-health was not the only and probably not the chief reason for Durham's feeling that he could no longer remain a member of the Cabinet.

CHAPTER VI

The Earl of Durham had time now to look after his private property and affairs and he spent much of the next few months at Lambton, where he was chiefly concerned with the business of his collieries. During this time he formed the Lambton Collieries Association, an enterprise of astonishing vision and modernity, which provided compensation in cases of accident and sickness and even a rudimentary form of retirement pension, and he insisted that the men must have a share in the administration of the Association's funds and in its management. The management committee was composed of fifty miners, all of whom were elected by their fellows and, to inaugurate the scheme, he entertained them to a magnificent banquet at Lambton Castle and himself took the chair. After dinner he spoke to them and proposed the toast of the Association in words which were not only graceful but also unmistakably sincere. Ever afterwards, when his public duties allowed him the time, he took a personal interest in all the affairs of the Association, to which he contributed annually a generous sum out of his own pocket.

Lady Durham was at home again and there were guests at Lambton. Harriet Martineau stayed there during one of her tours which she was making in the industrial districts of England while she was studying the wages and working conditions of the people. She left in her autobiography an account of a conversation which she had with Lord Durham, which shows how much he trusted Brougham almost up to the time when their serious quarrel began. The talk at Lambton Castle had turned on the Society for the Diffusion of Useful Knowledge. Miss Martineau said hotly that 'the surest way *not* to reach the people' was to use the Society, as they had a widespread and very reasonable distrust of Lord Brougham 'and his teaching and preaching clique'.

Lord Durham had not been taking part in the conversation, but later, when he was alone with her, asked her why she had been so fierce about the Society. Miss Martineau burst into one of her passionate tirades against Brougham, but Lord Durham stopped her when she accused Brougham of dishonesty and self-seeking. 'Brougham,' he said, 'has done and will do foolish things enough, but it would cut me to the heart to think that Brougham was false.' A few minutes later, he said again, 'It would cut me to the heart.'

If Miss Martineau wanted to study labour troubles, she could hardly have come to Lambton at a better moment. The men in Lord Durham's pits were at work and were earning good wages, but the rest of their Union was ill-disposed to them, probably because they had worked steadily during the unrest of the previous two years. Lord Durham and Mr. Morton were much troubled about the situation and especially about the brutal methods which the Union leaders used to enforce their will on reluctant members. Morton, who seems to have been a man of great discretion as well as of cool courage, took these incidents as part of the ordinary troubles of commercial life, though he never failed to do all that he could to uphold his own men and to prevent interference. Unhappily, Lord Durham was still in that frame of mind in which any annoyance was aggravated out of all proportion and had recently made some public and scarifying references to the union leaders. It was inevitable that these should have been misrepresented and a version of them spread abroad which suggested that his attack had been made not on the leaders but on all Unions. There was an alternative version which alleged that what he had actually said about the leaders of the Durham and Northumberland Unions was meant for the whole of the country. In January 1834, he had written to Morton in angry protest:

'My observations applied only to the Delegates of this district—elsewhere they may be honest but mistaken men— here I know them by their acts to be most unprincipled rascals.'

He was more deeply wounded by a story which was put about in his own countryside that the men in the Lambton pits were ill-treated and dissatisfied. After all that he had tried to do for them and was still trying to do, such a suggestion was intolerable and he protested hotly: 'I know that there is no Proprietor of Mines in England with whom his workmen are better off or whose comforts and happiness are more studiously consulted.' He spoke nothing but the literal truth, but he would have done better to have said nothing at all, for it brought his critics and enemies out against him. The most extravagant rumours were printed in the less scrupulous papers and were taken up by the Tory Press and, almost at once, repeated by the Whigs. One rumour told of a tricolour flag on his yacht and of his revolutionary tendencies which were fast driving him into violent action. Another paper revived an old fiction about the painting of the French Revolutionary emblems on his carriage doors, when last he had been in Paris. It could not have surprised him that the Tory papers should have taken advantage of this crop of scandal—'What *Villains* these Tories are!' was his comment —but the alacrity with which the Whig Press joined in was a shock to him. He did not yet understand that to the official Whig party he was now a liability.

If he had been in better health and less generally depressed and nervous, he might have ignored the unpleasantness and it would then have died down, but he was far from well and the darkness still hung over his spirit. He acted wildly, threatening libel actions against the papers which had attacked him and so gave them some welcome encouragement. Lady Durham and his friends tried to persuade him that it was not a battle worth fighting and he yielded so far as not to press the actions which he had begun. But it was a bad time for him and the gulf between him and the official Whigs grew wider, while he would not bestir himself to draw nearer to the Radicals who would have welcomed him. He grew restless at Lambton—and that in itself was a sign of some deep inward turmoil—and began to spend more time in London. He made frequent appearances in society and less frequent visits to the Court at Windsor or St. James's.

Holland House and Devonshire House were still the great centres of political hospitality, but he preferred the livelier entertainment which was to be found at Lady Blessington's. Wellington was a visitor, Count D'Orsay, exquisitely cravated and bewhiskered, Long Wellesley, solemnly asserting that 'a man could not live like a gentleman in London on less than £10,000 a year'. There was Paganini, the violinist, of whom the suffering Althorp said that 'he made every noise that could be made with a fiddle and several that couldn't': Lord Brougham and Vaux, over-assertive and a little awkward, and young Mr. Disraeli, fantastically overdressed, and always to be observed threading his way through the crowd in the direction of anyone whom he thought might be of use to him; Edward Bulwer, talking of his latest historical novel and smarting under the vicious criticism of J. G. Lockhart. And once there was an American journalist, who watched the arrival of 'a man of middle stature and of naturally cold address' and noticed that 'Bulwer spoke to him but he was introduced to no one'. The journalist asked his name and was told that it was Lord Durham, but by this time Disraeli had spotted his objective for that night. A rising young politician, especially if he were a Jew whom nobody liked, needed a patron, and either Whig or Tory would serve for a springboard.

'I dined yesterday with Lady Blessington,' Disraeli confided to his diary, 'and Durham among the guests and he talked to me nearly the whole evening.'

Probably Disraeli did more than his share of the talking, but he did not find a patron. Lord Durham was polite and went so far as to murmur a few conventional words about 'Happy to be of use if he should find an occasion'. It may be that he did not find Disraeli's overwhelming charm much to his fastidious taste, for soon Disraeli began to write in his diary in a very different strain: 'Interviews with O'Connell, Bedfors and Lord Durham. The first is the man of the greatest genius, the second of the greatest taste, and the third of the greatest ambition.'

The same American journalist, alert as journalists must be for the latest gossip, made a note of the meeting and commented, 'With D'Israeli in Parliament and Lord Durham on the last round but one of the ladder of greatness, the Viceroy will be Premier, no doubt.'

Among all those who gathered at Lady Blessington's, only Bulwer was on intimate terms with Lord Durham. He had entered Parliament three years earlier as a supporter of Reform and, at the time of the Bill's first rejection, he had given great help by publishing a pamphlet called 'A letter to a late Cabinet Minister on the present Crisis'. Bulwer did not stay long in politics which interfered too much with the production of the long series of his historical novels, but, when he was raised to the Peerage as Lord Lytton, he remained a supporter of the Whigs in the House of Lords. At the time of the Reform Bill he had first met Durham in Lady Blessington's house. Durham, who had greatly admired the 'Letter to a Cabinet Minister', had asked her to arrange the meeting. It seems strange to read in her letter to Bulwer that she hesitated to arrange it because she was nervous about his possible response to Lord Durham's approach. Bulwer was never at his ease when meeting strangers and she begged him: 'You are going to meet Durham and he is prepared to admire and like you. Pray don't be supercilious to him as you are to most people.' The meeting was a success and for the next few years the two men were good friends. Bulwer was by ten years the younger and looked up to Durham with open admiration. He strongly supported the Radicals in their desire that Durham should put himself forward as their leader and as a candidate for the Premiership. In a letter to Lady Blessington he wrote:

'Durham has written his horoscope on the people's hearts and they only want the occasion to tell him of his destiny.'

There were in the Commons a number of young members who were either Radicals or in sympathy with Radical views— men such as Bulwer, Sir William Molesworth, and Raikes—all of whom would have supported Radical Jack if he had beckoned to them. Behind them were the political associations of the great towns, particularly Birmingham where their leaders Attwood and Parkes were urging their huge membership to call for Durham's leadership. Joseph Parkes, the Birmingham solicitor, had got to know him personally and for many years they wrote constantly to each other about politics and municipal reform.

All the time that Durham was in Russia and again when he was in Canada, Parkes kept him up to date with the latest moves in political opinion. Attwood and he were pressing for the Reform of municipal government which was only the logical continuance of Parliamentary reform and they shared Lord Durham's anxiety for the vote by ballot. It was certain that neither Whig nor Tory governments would ever consider the idea and its only hope lay in the formation of an entirely new party.

It seemed in that year that Lord Durham was the only possible head of such a party and indeed the only man who could bring it into being. None of the professed Radicals had enough standing in Parliament or enough following in the country. Radical Jack had the middle classes and the workmen's associations behind him. He might be unpopular at Westminster, but he was still a great figure there. The North Country was solidly behind him and he enjoyed everywhere the enormous prestige which the Reform Bill had won for him. Above all, he had, with all his faults, the qualities which a leader needs—ability, honesty, courage, and pugnacity, as well as the undoubted charm which he could exercise among men whom he trusted.

It seems possible that, if he had cared to put himself forward that year, he would have had half England with him and might have become her first Radical Premier. How long he would have lasted as that, must always remain a matter of speculation, but, however long or short the time, there would have been nothing of the political stagnation which was to persist through the next ten years when alternating Whig and Tory governments had no thought except to hold on to their uncertain positions.

Neither in 1834, nor again in 1839, could Lord Durham bring himself to desert the party of which he was still a member. Even if he had been tempted—and there is nothing to show that he was—he would do nothing against the Whig Government as long as Grey was its leader. When the Government's Irish Bill came up for debate, Lord Durham had been ill again and was at Cowes, from where he wrote to Grey:

'I tell you fairly that the fact of your being at the head of the Government alone had prevented me from coming up to London to oppose the Bill altogether. As long as you are in this situation, I will never do any public act that may be construed as one of opposition.'

On 9 July, the Government were defeated and Grey resigned. Althorp, loyal as ever, went with him and this was a worse blow to the Government, since Althorp was the only member of the Cabinet in whom the King felt any confidence. He had less than none in Brougham, and yet it was Brougham who now saved the Whigs by persuading the King that the Commons would not endure either Wellington or Peel as Prime Minister and that the only solution was for the Whigs to remain in office and for Melbourne to take Grey's place.

The King hated Brougham, but he was no match for him in argument, and at last gave his consent, reluctantly and only on condition that Althorp should retract his resignation and continue to lead the Commons. Althorp, who had seen a chance of a full season's shooting, was even more reluctant, but obedient as ever to his sense of duty, and the Administration was reformed with Melbourne as Prime Minister.

The crisis had provoked an outburst of invective from the popular Press exceeding anything that had been heard even at the time of the Reform Bill. Every paper had its candidate for the Premiership and its scapegoat. The *Morning Chronicle* had always been a Tory paper, but had recently changed hands and now came out strongly in favour of Lord Durham. The *Globe* clamoured for Palmerston. *The Times*, which had lately been regarded as Brougham's mouthpiece, suddenly turned against him and attacked him with astonishing bitterness; while, at the same time, it began to speak favourably of Lord Durham.

This *volte-face* of *The Times* has never been satisfactorily explained. A story which was current at the time, but which seems to have had little truth in it, attributed it to a contemptible intrigue by which Barnes, the Editor, bought, through an intermediary, the contents of Brougham's wastepaper basket, in which he found scraps of a correspondence between Brougham and Althorp about 'declaring war on *The Times*'. The scrap on which this phrase was written is preserved and in its margin there is a pencil note saying: 'Picked up by a Friend and sent thinking it may be of service as a private principle of action.'

The most probable explanation is that the letter referred to *The Times*' criticism of the Government's new Poor Law, though Brougham accounted for Barnes's change of front as being a response to his own recent attack upon the paper in the Libel Committee and to his perpetual fight to put an end to the heavy tax on newspapers which had crippled the less wealthy papers and seemed likely to lead to something dangerously like a monopoly in favour of *The Times*. Brougham had lost much of his influence with *The Times* a few months earlier when his brother, who had been on its staff, had died. Whatever may have been the true explanation, *The Times* was henceforward merciless towards Brougham.

Grey never believed that Brougham had tried to get rid of him, though it was and remained an article of faith with the rest of the Grey family and connection. In fact he wrote on 4 November a magnanimous letter to Brougham in which he acquitted him of the charge:

'I have at all times disdained all suspicion and belief, though these things had made my retirement immediately unavoidable, that they were intended to produce that result. Of that intention, whatever share you might have had in the previous transaction, I entirely acquitted you, having in my possession what I consider as the strongest proof of your wish for my continuance in office.'

The letter was characteristic of the quiet dignity with which at last Grey withdrew from politics. His career had been long and distinguished and, whatever may have been his failings in temperament, his integrity and goodness of heart had never been in doubt. When he left there left with him the last trace of that aristocratic Whig tradition which had dominated the politics of the country since the revolution of 1688.

CHAPTER VII

It was already probable that neither Lord Durham nor Lord Brougham would find a place in Melbourne's Cabinet. In the farcical interlude which diverted the country during the last months of 1834, they made sure of their exclusion. During those months both of them disported themselves in a way which has ever since been the despair of their biographers. Their quarrel was as undignified as it was public and as trivial as it was unnecessary. The most serious result of it was that, while in Lord Durham's memory it burnt itself out and was forgotten, in Brougham's it was nourished and kept warm, until it was time for it to burst into new flame four years later.

In a speech at Gateshead, Lord Durham had recently given a most injudicious account of the preparation of the Reform Bill during which he implied that it was almost exclusively his own achievement. Not content with that, he had explained in great detail the points where the Bill fell short of what he had intended and had more than hinted that it would have been a much better Bill if he had had all his own way.

In the summer of 1834, Melbourne had written to Grey: 'I will have nothing to do with Brougham. I need not state to you the reasons of my determination. They reduce themselves readily under two heads—viz. his whole character and his whole conduct. I will have nothing to do with Durham. For obvious reasons I forbear to state to you my reasons for this decision.'

There was no need for Melbourne to state them. Grey knew them only too well. In November he wrote sadly to Russell of 'the new impetus given to Radical agitation by Durham' and, in the following year, he seemed to have given up all hope of him, when he wrote to Melbourne: 'O'Connell and Lambton are both to be considered as Radicals, with whom I must regard our difference as no less decided and ought to be as strongly marked as with the Tories.'

Earl Grey had been a Reformer, but he had finished reforming. He had fulfilled his pledge in the passing of the Bill and there was no more to be done—then or in the future.

Lord Durham, on the other hand, had only just started. He had never ceased to clamour for more Reform and for all those parts of his original Bill which the Cabinet had struck out. In June 1834, the month of Grey's resignation, Disraeli, still little known, but a shrewd observer, wrote:

'The Whigs can not exist as a party without taking in Lord Durham and the King will not consent to it. Durham is not in a hurry and becomes every day more violent in his demands. Triennial Parliaments to be a Cabinet measure, an extension of the Constituency, the ballot to stand on its merits—in short, a Revolution.'

The outbreak which those who knew Durham and Brougham had long expected, came at Edinburgh in September, at a dinner which had been arranged to honour Earl Grey. Brougham was in the north of England, speaking at a series of meetings. He was not wanted at the Grey dinner in Edinburgh, since all Grey's supporters still blamed him for causing Grey's resignation, but Lord Brougham was not a man to be deterred by fanciful notions of delicacy. He not only invited himself to the dinner, but spoke there at great length, paying a most eloquent tribute to Grey, while not overlooking his own merits. During his speech, he used certain expressions which Lord Durham—why it is difficult to see—took as a personal attack on himself and resented with all his usual violence. Brougham referred to:

'A great number of honest and conscientious men, I have no doubt, men, generally speaking, of sound opinions, but somewhat unreflecting, who think action and execution everything and all the time that is spent on deliberation thrown away . . . they are in such a hurry to get to the goal that they will not wait to see whether the lynch-pins are in the wheel. . . . I wholly respect the good intentions of these men . . . but, when they ask me to get into their carriage, I must decline to accompany them.'

Brougham did not mention Lord Durham by name and always afterwards maintained that he was not talking about him. The speech presented the cartoonists, especially Doyle, with an unending source of fun in the Whig Coach, which was generally shown thundering down the precipice with Lord Grey vainly tugging at the reins, and with as many of his colleagues on the box or inside the coach as could be conveniently crowded in. Lord Durham was a favourite passenger in Doyle's cartoons, in which the King often appears, as an unwilling and frightened passenger.

Durham was indignant that Brougham should have intruded upon a company where he was neither wanted nor expected and his accumulated anger led him to take as a personal affront words which, in a calmer mood, he might not have felt called

upon to resent. After his tribute to Grey he ended his speech
with a reply to the Chancellor:

'My learned friend the Chancellor has been pleased to give
some sound advice to certain classes of persons of whom, I
confess I know nothing, except that they are persons whom
he considers as evincing too much impatience. I will freely
own to you that I am one of those who see with regret every
hour which passes over the existence of acknowledged but
unreformed abuses. . . . I object to the compromise of
principles. I do not object to the deliberation with which
reforms are conducted; but I do object to the compromise of
principles. I object to the clipping and paring and the
mutilating which must inevitably follow any attempt to
conciliate enemies, who are not to be gained and who will
requite your advances by pointing out your inconsistency,
your abandonment of your friends and principles and then
ascribe the discontent created in your own ranks by these
proceedings to the decay of liberal feeling in the country. . . .'

There does not, at first sight, seem to be in this speech, any
more than in Brougham's, anything personal or violent enough
to start such a resounding quarrel as was to follow. Durham
himself did not think that he had done any more than express
his dissent from the cautious policy about Reform which
Brougham was advocating. As he wrote soon afterwards to
Parkes: 'I was not personal.' Even the Press, as a whole, though
they reported both speeches at some length, did not indulge in
much comment on either, nor seem to regard them as of
especial importance and certainly saw nothing personal in
them. The *Spectator*, which was favourable to Lord Durham,
remarked that 'Lord Brougham delivered at Edinburgh what
was felt to be an insidious speech against the great body of the
Reformers. . . . Lord Durham was not personally attacked, but
the Reformers of England were ill-used by the Chancellor.'
It is a pity that so great a scandal should have had so trivial
a beginning, but both men were strained to the point of
desperation and, during the next few weeks, they bandied
defiance and denunciation at each other across the breadth of
Great Britain. Their language grew wilder and more personal
as their anger mounted, and Brougham especially, forgetting
the dignity of a Lord Chancellor, but carrying the Great Seal

with him, delivered a series of speeches in the Midlands and West which earned him one of *The Times's* most imperial rebukes:

'When a whale has been wounded in the Northern seas, it often is found afterwards in more southern latitudes, rolling and tumbling and writhing in agony, unable to shake from its filthy carcase the barbed and inextricable harpoon. So the extraordinary fish harpooned at Edinburgh some weeks ago has already spouted forth brine and bitterness on the Avon.'

The most bitter attack of the campaign was delivered not in a speech but in an article in the *Edinburgh Review*, which, though unsigned, was generally accepted as Brougham's work. Its text was that passage in Durham's Edinburgh speech which referred to the 'clipping and paring' by which the supporters of Bills tried to make them acceptable to their enemies. It was an obvious reference to the omission of the ballot from the Reform Bill and to the alteration of the franchise qualification, both of which had been carried against Durham's unsupported opposition. The *Edinburgh Review* pointed out that Lord Durham had supported the Bill, imperfect though he now considered it, and went on to denounce his Edinburgh speech. It compared his words with some which he had spoken on the subject of Reform more than fifteen years before—an insidious form of attack which can on occasion trip up any politician who has ever lived—and concluded:

'But Lord Durham, in his vehement love of whole and entire measures and his "impatience of every month that passes" without something being done, chose to read a lecture against "clipping" and, above all, against making use of the time taken for digesting any measure, in order to make it acceptable to such a number of persons as may suffice to carry it through Parliament. [He and his friends] look down from this elevation of pure, rigorous, unbending principle on which they are pleased to plant themselves, with an amazing self-complacency upon the rational, practical and consistent men, who have disdained to commit no such vagaries; thanking God that they are not as others are—clippers, compromisers, men of expediency!'

This was open war and Lord Durham unhesitatingly

accepted it as such. He wrote to Parkes: 'The Government have declared war on me through their mouthpiece, the Chancellor, and I must buckle on my armour. I will accept his challenge at Westminster—but he shall hear of me first a little further north.'

The Whigs of Glasgow had arranged a great festival in Lord Durham's honour for 29 October, at which he was expected to make four or possibly six speeches, the most important of them at the banquet which was to end the day. It was this banquet which he chose for the final answer to the Chancellor.

The Whig leaders watched with growing concern. No one was more anxious than Earl Grey, who felt that his son-in-law was endangering his party's success, his family's repute, and his own prospects. He poured out his grief and resentment in a series of letters to the Princess Lieven, to whom the whole business was a godsent feast of scandal. On 20 October, he wrote:

'The thing that at this moment interests us all and at the same time annoys me most is the war that is going on between the Chancellor and Durham. You will see in the papers the manner, little creditable to either, in which they are attacking and answering each other at public meetings. Both, as generally happens in such cases, are in the wrong, but the Chancellor most so if it be true—and it is hardly possible to doubt it—that he is the author of an article in the *Edinboro' Review*, in which, for the purpose of attacking Lambton, he states very incorrectly what passed in the Cabinet in the preparation of the Reform Bill. Lambton will be here on his way to Glasgow for the dinner for which he goes and which will probably cause more mischief.'

Grey's foreboding was justified. On 4 November he wrote in grave disapproval:

'I could have anticipated nothing so bad as what has happened. No respectable person attended him at the meeting. It was completely Radical and he has entirely joined himself to that class.'

The Durham Dinner at Glasgow was a formidable affair. At six o'clock in the evening 1,700 diners sat down at twenty-two tables and the programme included thirty-nine toasts, which included, beside the usual loyal sentiments, 'The People—the Only True Source of Political Power' and, perhaps a little menacingly, 'Lord Melbourne and His Majesty's Ministers, and we trust that their practice in power may be in accordance with their principle in opposition.' The last toast, proposed from the Chair, was 'The Earl of Durham' and, before Lord Durham rose to reply a glee-party contributed a song which had been specially composed for the occasion.

Welcome, Durham to our land,
First of Freedom's sacred band!

Lord Durham began with a reasoned answer to the attack which the *Edinburgh Review* had launched and stated with his usual directness his own views on Reform. Having stated his conviction, he turned to the congenial task of refuting Brougham's accusation of impatience:

'Now as to the charge of impatience. It has lately been brought against me by one most eminent person in no very complimentary terms. But I will not follow the example which he has set us, and nothing shall fall from my lips inconsistent with his high station and his former services in the cause of his country. He has been pleased . . . to challenge me to meet him in the House of Lords. I know well the meaning of the taunt. He is aware of his infinite superiority over me in one respect and so am I. He is a practised orator and a powerful debater. I am not. I speak but seldom in the House of Lords and always with reluctance in an assembly where I meet with no sympathy from an unwilling majority. . . . He knows full well the advantage that he has over me. He knows that in any attack which he may make on me in the House of Lords, he will be warmly and cordially supported by them. With all these manifold advantages, almost overwhelming, I fear him not; and I will meet him there.'

One of the chief causes of the quarrel was that both men were disposed to claim rather more than their fair share of the credit of having introduced Reform, even to the point of ignoring the claim of Russell, who, as Princess Lieven remarked, 'found himself sitting between Lord Durham and Lord Brougham, who fought like two vultures for the honour of Reform, leaving John and his glory and his reform entirely neglected'. Lord Durham, in his anxiety to dispose of his rival's claim to be the chief Reformer had written to Russell to enlist his support. Russell was magnanimous enough to say nothing about his own share and ill-advised enough to suggest a course which would decide the question beyond further dispute. He suggested that a simultaneous statement should be made by Durham in the Lords and himself in the Commons telling the detailed story of the Cabinet's deliberations over the Bill and finally allocating the credit for its passing. But such a procedure would involve the disclosure of Cabinet secrets and memoranda, permission for which would have to be obtained from the King.

Russell, who was entirely on Durham's side, undertook to do this, but, by an oversight, did not first get the Prime Minister's approval, an entirely unintentional discourtesy for which he apologized as soon as he realized what he had done.

The King disliked Russell, Durham, and Brougham equally, but grudgingly gave permission, only to withdraw it on receiving an energetic protest from Melbourne, who justly observed:

'If the arguments in Cabinet are no longer to be protected by an impenetrable veil of secrecy, there will be no place left on the public councils for the free investigation of truth and the unshackled exercise of the understanding.'

CHAPTER VIII

For some weeks of that winter of 1834 Durham was confined to his house in London, where he spent most of the day in bed in a darkened room and could take no food except tea and a little bread. Above all was the desolation caused by the loss of his eldest son. At the turn of the year he felt a little stronger and moved to Cowes where he had a house and where his yacht, the *Louisa*, was laid up for the winter. There his spirits began to revive. A man of less courage might have been crushed by such a load of trouble and have withdrawn altogether from public affairs, but there was always a toughness and resilience in his nature which would not let him give in as long as he could find useful work to do.

That might have seemed an impossibility, but it had not struck him in that light, for Cam Hobhouse, who called upon him before he left London for Cowes, noted that 'he expressed his earnest wish to be employed under our Government and as a means of regaining his old friends'. Hobhouse adds, in that tone of patronage which makes his diary so irritating to read, 'His tone was quite different from what it was formerly and I could not help believing him sincere.'

'To regain his old friends' was always uppermost in Lord Durham's mind. Few men who quarrelled as often and as violently as he would have been so anxious to make amends and to patch up broken friendships. Passionate and belligerent as his nature was, resentment and malice had no part in it.

There was already in Parliament the nucleus of a new party, who were known as the Philosophic Radicals. Their leaders were the men who had supported Reform and had seen with disillusioned eyes, the removal from Melbourne's Cabinet of the great figures of the fight for Reform. Their spokesmen in the Commons were Charles Buller, Edward Bulwer, and several more of the younger men whom Reform had brought into the House. In the country they had the support of the growing Political Unions in such towns as Manchester and Birmingham and of men like Attwood, Francis Place, and Joseph Parkes.

They were strong in numbers and determined in policy but they lacked a leader. Their principal supporters in Parliament were more or less unknown and they had no great figure behind whom they could rally. A section of the more advanced Press was clamouring for new leadership and the most out-spoken and most influential was John Stuart Mill, who wrote in the *Westminster Gazette*. Even the *Spectator*, which was always uncertain and had lately been speaking harshly of Lord Durham, began to mention him as the best hope for the country. It seemed that just at the moment when he had apparently lost all his hope of political power, he might be reinstated by the overwhelming desire of thousands who were weary of the old contest between Whig and Tory and longed for someone who could see further than the immediate tactical needs of party warfare.

The Philosophical Radicals were naturally anxious to sound him as to his willingness to take the lead and they assigned the

task to Edward Bulwer, who had met Durham during the
Reform struggle, had often been in his company at Lady
Blessington's, and was almost a personal friend. Early in 1835
Bulwer wrote to Lord Durham a letter, which purported to be a
request for advice, and asked whether Lord Durham thought
that he would be well advised to join them. Durham's answer
spoke without enthusiasm of the new Radicals and advised
Bulwer to have nothing to do with them, at any rate until he
had made much more careful inquiry about their membership
and the type of support which they could command. He left
Bulwer in no doubt at all that he would have to look elsewhere for a leader.

It was a set-back for the Radicals and yet no more than they
might have expected, had they known Lord Durham a little
better. Even his enemies admitted that he was entirely free
from self-seeking and he was too honest and too farsighted to
put himself at the head of any movement until he was quite
sure of whom it consisted and in what direction it was going.
He had been a great party fighter, but he was moving beyond
the realm of party politics. It is not too much to say that the
years which saw his eclipse as a politician saw his emergence as
a statesman.

His experience of foreign policy in the affair of Belgium and
still more his diplomatic experience in Russia had introduced
him to a wider world than that of domestic policy and had
given him an opportunity of showing the direction in which his
greatest talents lay.

His mind, lively as ever, and now ranging farther abroad
soon began to turn to the problems of Britain's overseas
Colonies, a subject which occupied very little of Parliament's
time or interest. He became the President of the recently
formed Colonization Society which Edward Gibbon Wakefield
had founded while serving a term of imprisonment for the
abduction of an heiress. Another member of the society was
William Turton, who had been at Eton with Durham, and who,
like Wakefield, had been at one time involved in a serious
scandal over women. Two more associates were Charles Buller
and his brother William, both of whom were to give him such
valuable help in Canada two years later.

Melbourne was not interested in the Colonies, which he had

entrusted to the care of Lord Glenelg, but he was still very much interested in Lord Durham, as he was in anyone who might trouble his own security or interfere with his own pleasant existence. To him, and to all the official Whig party, Durham was an impossibility in office and, out of it, a perpetual threat.

Lord Durham had rebuffed the new Radicals, but there was no knowing when his mind might change. Politically he seemed to be a spent force, but his popularity in the country was still immense and was growing as men realized that he, alone of the Reformers of 1832, was determined to press on to the next step in his programme. Melbourne would not employ him and dared not let him be idle. He decided that it was absolutely necessary to find for him some position which would keep him occupied and at the same time keep him from interfering in home politics.

As it happened, the ideal position lay vacant and ready to hand. Owing to Palmerston's intransigence about the appointment of Sir Strafford Canning, Britain was still without an ambassador at the Court of St. Petersburg. Fear of Russia was seldom absent from British minds and lately there had been unusually disquieting rumours of troop movements behind the western frontier of Russia and of naval activity in the Black Sea. Russia's covetous glances in the direction of Constantinople had been a cause of British anxiety any time these past ten years, and there remained the permanent threat to Persia and, through Persia, to India.

Melbourne and Palmerston agreed and sounded Grey about Durham's probable reaction to the offer of the post. Grey hesitated, though mainly for personal reasons. He had washed his hands of Durham as a politician, but he still kept a certain affection for him and still more for his own daughter. He did not think it likely that Durham would refuse the appointment, nor did he doubt his ability to carry out its duties, whatever might be his shortcomings in home affairs. But he doubted very seriously whether his health would be equal to the task and to the terrible Russian winters. He agreed that the offer should be made, but he did so with reluctance.

Palmerston and Melbourne were in such a hurry to get rid of Durham that they took the extraordinary step of sounding the Emperor's opinion of the appointment before consulting their own master. Palmerston knew how much the King hated Durham and probably felt that it would save trouble to make all the arrangements before presenting the King with the suggestion. The King was naturally furious and there were scenes of recrimination which nearly wrecked the scheme and which called on all Melbourne's reserves of tact and persuasion before at last the King gave a grudging consent.

The reaction in Russia was prompt and cordial. The Emperor Nicholas gave prompt assent to the appointment and, in July, Grey wrote to the Princess Lieven, who was now back in St. Petersburg: 'Durham is delighted with his appointment and more especially with the gracious manner in which it was received by your Emperor.' He added severely that, 'I should also be very glad of the arrangement which removes Durham from a scene in which he has very imprudently brought himself into a false position.'

Lord Durham was delighted but he was under no illusion as to the reason for his selection. He told Hobhouse that he knew that he was only being sent out of the country for the sake of getting rid of him. At the same time he welcomed a chance of returning to the world of public affairs and to an active career. He knew that he had no prospect of employment at home and all summer he had chafed at his enforced idleness. On 7 June, while he was at Cowes, he had written to a friend: 'Now that I am getting better, which I am every day, I am overcome with horror at my hopeless idleness and inactivity. I cannot be employed at home and don't like being idle. The only language I have heard from those who profess to be my friends is "We don't wish to see you in office—your time has not yet come." This feeling has been acted upon by the Government also and I am thus put out of the pale of home politics.' And—perhaps because experience had taught him a self-criticism which had been lacking in his impetuous youth—he added, 'Perhaps it was necessary. I owe them no grudge and am ready at a moment's notice to do whatever is deemed right.'

CHAPTER IX

In that summer of the year 1835 the British Government were more than usually apprehensive about Russian intentions and especially about her relations with Turkey. The Sultan of Turkey had recently been hard put to it to subdue the revolt of Mehemet Ali and had received valuable support from Russia, while Britain and France had looked on with neutrality tinged with secret sympathy for Mehemet. Now the statesmen of Europe had visions of a strong alliance between Russia and Turkey with its probable consequence of a hostile bloc extending from the Baltic to the Dardanelles and perhaps southward to Persia and the borders of Afghanistan.

Palmerston loaded Lord Durham with instructions and special warnings. He was above all things to inquire into Russia's state of preparedness for making war and to report all movements and concentrations of troops, all new accumulations of stores and workshops, and all assemblages of ships or of land transport. For this purpose he asked Durham to make his entry to Russia by the port of Odessa and to undertake the long and weary journey to St. Petersburg by road, for the better observance of the offensive preparations which were certainly going forward. He further desired Durham to call at Athens and Constantinople on the way in the hope that he might pick up some useful information at one or the other place.

It was extremely inconvenient for Lord Durham and would involve his leaving his wife and children to travel alone by the Baltic route, since he refused to subject them to the miseries of land travel in Russia further than was unavoidable. It was imprudent even for him to undergo so much extra fatigue, especially when Britain had ambassadors at Athens and Constantinople, who had far deeper knowledge of their respective courts and were regularly reporting on them. But Lord Durham had spoken no more than the truth when he professed himself ready to go wherever he might best be of use nor did he allow the uncertainty of his health to weigh with him.

Lord Durham's suite included an unusually large number of naval and military officers, who were to act as his expert advisers when he had to report troop movements and his brother-in-law, Edward Ellice, who had big interests in the Russian fur trade had volunteered to accompany the party as far as Constantinople.

Lord Durham suffered badly from neuralgia during the voyage and was prostrated for several days on his arrival at Athens, but he recovered in time for formal conversations with the young King Otto and his foreign minister, D'Armansperg, and conferences with Sir Edmund Lyons, the British Minister in Greece.

King Otto, a Bavarian whom the Great Powers for some reason which has never been fully explained had planted on the throne in Athens, was a man of many troubles, nearly all of them financial. His financial minister, another Bavarian, applied to all of them the same simple remedy of raising one loan after another as long as he could find any one to borrow from. The Greek people, burdened with an ever increasing load of interest and seeing no compensating benefit to themselves, were convinced that the revenues of their country were being devoted more to Bavarian interests than to their own. Lord Durham reported severely to Palmerston on this financial trickery, and gave Otto some much-needed instruction about democracy and the advantages of a balanced budget, finding him, as he said, 'anxious to learn but not over bright'. He then went on to Constantinople, where the Sultan, though bright enough, was so little anxious to learn that he had lately refused to see the British Minister with whom he would only communicate through the medium of his court jester. It was not, he found, so easy to deny himself to the Earl of Durham, who insisted on and obtained an interview, though he accomplished nothing by it. Durham finally arrived at Odessa, where he submitted to the required quarantine of fourteen days, and from where he sent his respectful greetings to the Emperor, who was then at Kieff. His naval and military staff dispersed in various directions to hunt for the suspected invasion forces and he himself started on the long and weary journey across Russia. Day after day the carriage jolted across the mud-tracks which wound over the interminable flatness of the Steppes, blinded by dust in fine weather and bogged down to the axles after rain. It was a nightmare journey for the man who had been used to driving through Durham in his own carriage with outriders and who had breakfasted, even in the heart of the Yorkshire Dales, off butter, eggs, and bread from his own farms at Lambton, as Creevey had recalled. At last, more dead than alive, he crawled into St. Petersburg. He had faithfully followed his instructions to go by the longest route and to observe the country and especially to look out for military moves or preparations, and he had seen a few thousand square miles of dun coloured flat earth and perhaps less than a brigade of troops. It must have been with unspeakable relief that he arrived to find that Lady Durham and his family were already installed in a house in the capital.

The popularity which Lord Durham had won on his previous mission to Russia had not diminished during his absence, and the court of St. Petersburg were openly delighted to receive an ambassador whom they knew and trusted—the more so for the unhappy difference of opinion with Palmerston about Canning's appointment. Nesselrode, the Foreign Secretary, was cordial and the Emperor himself showed to Lord Durham marks of favour which soon became almost embarrassing. Lord Durham found that he could be admitted to the Emperor's presence at almost any time without the strict etiquette and protocol which bound the other ambassadors. Indeed he soon found it tactful to drop a discreet hint that the special favour accorded to him was becoming a matter of comment and to suggest that for the sake of good relations with the rest of the Diplomatic Corps, he ought to conform more strictly to the usual custom. At the same time he occasionally found that this easy access to the Emperor was of great use to him and of service to British interests, and he did not fail to make use of it when he saw a chance of helping a British subject or preventing an injustice. During his first few months there were two instances when he used his interest with the Emperor to arrange the settlement of long outstanding claims. In one case, a British merchant, Alexander Grant, had for years been pressing a perfectly just claim for payment against the Russian Government. It was a very serious matter for Mr. Grant, since it involved many thousands of roubles and in despair he laid his case before Lord Durham and begged for his help. Durham, though he was a great aristocrat, never forgot that he was also a great capitalist. He knew the ways of business and honoured his responsibility to other men of business who needed his support. He interviewed Grant and got from him all the papers concerning the case, which he studied until he was perfectly familiar with them. The Russian authorities were at first delighted that Lord Durham had taken up the case. Since it was their simple policy to yield on any point in proportion to the bribes which they were offered, they saw a rich chance of gain from the English Milor, who was reputed to be one of the richest men in his own country.

They were soon to find that Lord Durham had no intention of bribing anybody and also that he was prepared to press Mr. Grant's claim until he was satisfied with the justice of the settlement. They tried to obstruct him with the plea that an Imperial edict had been given and that only the Emperor could rescind it, only to find that the Ambassador was ready and willing to take the case up himself with the Emperor and that his influence would make it an easy thing to do.

The Russian finance minister was strongly opposed to any revision and advised the Emperor against it, but Durham's influence was too strong for him and the Emperor rescinded his edict. The finance minister even went so far as to argue that there was no precedent for the rescinding of such an edict, but the Emperor was fully convinced by Durham's advocacy and dismissed this objection for the trivial quibble which it was. 'I care not,' he said, 'for the want of a precedent. If I have unintentionally sanctioned an act of injustice, the sooner I repair the evil the better. I am sure Durham would not call my attention to this matter if he were not fully persuaded of the justice of Mr. Grant's claim. Let the whole affair be again referred to the Council of State for examination.' The Council of State, who had enough sense to know their duty, reversed their own decision and Mr. Grant got full settlement of his claim.

The Emperor's remark about Lord Durham was not mere politeness nor kindly yielding to a friend. It was based on the assurance that in fact Durham did not press any claim until he had personally and most thoroughly examined it and satisfied himself of its justice. He gave clear proof of this in the affair of the British ship *Vixen* which was already causing friction between the two countries and might, but for his firm handling of the case, have resulted in serious international trouble.

The *Vixen*, carrying a cargo of contraband goods, had put in at Sardjouk-Kalch, a Black Sea port, where the Russian Customs men, acting within their rights, had detained her crew and seized both ship and cargo. Palmerston was at first disposed to accept the version put forward by the captain of the *Vixen* and to take a strong line in his instructions to Durham. But Durham had shown his usual care in investigating the incident and had come to the conclusion that the *Vixen* was in the wrong. The English newspapers had begun to clamour for strong action and were indulging in their only too familiar clichés about 'the honour of the Neutral Flag'.

Durham ignored the ill-informed agitation and told Palmerston clearly that he would not support a claim which he knew to be unjustifiable. He wrote that the *Vixen's* action was 'indisputably and knowingly in contravention of the Russian tariff and there is no ground for regarding the seizure of the ship in the light in which the English newspapers put it'. Palmerston accepted his advice and the incident ended there.

Throughout this time, Palmerston and Durham worked together more amicably than might have been expected from two men so different and so irreconcilable in home affairs. Palmerston did not like Durham, but he knew his value as an ambassador. He later remarked to a friend: 'Russia is coquetting with Durham and, in order to cajole him, she is obliged to be civil to us—so the appointment has answered.'

Durham did not share Palmerston's apprehensions about Russia's warlike intentions and plainly told him so, but he painstakingly observed and reported on the state of the Russian forces and his papers are full of lists of stores and depots and of the disposition of divisions and batteries. He submitted to Palmerston a full report on the subject, which even Palmerston called 'the best report which has ever been sent to the Foreign Office'. Durham wrote with respect of the Russian Army and especially of the quality of the infantry whom he found to be well drilled, clothed and equipped, but he could see no sign of their being on anything like a war footing nor any provision for transport and forage more than was required for their ordinary duties. Of the Russian Navy he wrote with less respect. He had seen it at Cronstadt on his previous visit and, since then, he had taken care to get information about the fleets in the Baltic and Black Seas.

'These are,' he wrote, 'fairly embedded in ice seven months out of the twelve; when at sea for a summer cruise, the men exhibit all the symptoms of rawness and inefficiency which must naturally be expected . . . not one of them from Prince Menschikoff downwards, anticipates the possibility of its ever being made use of as a means of attack or defence.'

Palmerston accepted this opinion and tried to impart it to his master, who at last went so far as to tell him that he might inform Lord Durham that 'His Majesty had been much pleased with his report'. Yet even now the King could not free himself from his terror of Russia and his dislike of Durham. Ellice reported in a letter to Durham that 'I understand that the King made the remark on some of your papers that they are rather like the composition of a Russian than an Englishman'.

Even Melbourne could not refrain from approving Durham's work in Russia and wrote to him:

'I consider you as rendering the greatest service to your country and the world by taking a sober and rational view . . . and by trying to check the extreme violence of feeling and the unnecessary prejudice and suspicion which prevail in this country.'

Durham had no patience with English Russophobia and said so with his usual freedom. He wrote to Melbourne:

'Every disturbance which takes place in any remote province in the East is attributed to "Russian intrigue". . . . If the Sultan complies with our request on the Monday, it is attributed to "Russian influence"; if he changes his mind on the Tuesday, "Russian influence", if the wind blows from the West or East or North or South, no matter, the compass is under "Russian influence". All this would be very absurd if it were not so dangerous and would have ended, if I had not interfered, in a war with that country in which all Europe would have been involved.'

It was of supreme importance to the peace of Europe that there should be at the court of St. Petersburg a man who commanded the respect and truth of its Emperor, who could hold himself above prejudice and racial hatred and who was not afraid to tell his countrymen in vigorous words when and how they were going wrong. Nor was he any more tender of the Emperor's feelings when the occasion called for strong words and did not scruple to tell him on one occasion that the British would never tolerate a Russian move against Constantinople 'as long as we have a drop of blood in our veins or a guinea in our Treasury'. His popularity at the court was certainly not due to any attempt to ingratiate himself or to court the Emperor's favour; indeed, when the need was there he could speak as one autocrat to another.

CHAPTER X

Lord Durham's immense mass of correspondence shows how much his mind was still occupied with home politics while he was in Russia. He had already come to the conclusion that he had no hope of employment at home under the existing Whig Government, but he seems never to have given up hope of a change in its composition or of a complete change of administration. The Tories were out of the question as far as he was concerned and he watched with interest the tentative struggles of the new Philosophic Radicals. He was corresponding freely with Edward Bulwer and Joseph Parkes, particularly about the Reform of municipal government which was to be the natural result of Parliamentary Reform. The new Radicals were strong enough to make their influence felt in Parliament though their numbers were far too small to give them any immediate hope of power. Above all, they lacked a leader and Bulwer was still hopeful of persuading Lord Durham to take the position. Durham, it is clear from his letters, watched their progress with sympathy as well as interest and wished them well, but it is equally clear that he had no intention of committing himself to them in any way until he knew a good deal more about them and was satisfied that their aims were constitutional and that they were not just an irresponsible body of cranks.

Parkes sent him much useful information about the state of party feeling at home and more than once gave him warning that he had still one implacable enemy there in Lord Brougham, whom he described as 'like a tiger in the jungle, dealing out death wherever he fixed his prodigious claws'. Durham was never inclined to think much about his own safety. He was a long way from England and it was not likely that Brougham could do him much harm. He himself was a man of quick and terrible rages but not of long resentments and he completely underestimated Brougham's tenacity and his almost illimitable power of bearing malice. Bitterly as he could resent a slight he could never keep for long the memory of it and he was always anxious to patch up a quarrel and to renew a friendship. At the moment, as he reflected, Brougham was not a danger, but he would have done well later to heed Parkes's warnings and to watch Brougham carefully, for it was that long enduring malice which was to bring him down in all but ruin only a few years later.

There is much family correspondence, especially during the first few months of Durham's residence in Russia, with his brother Hedworth, who had succeeded to his elder brother's seat in the Commons as member for County Durham. Hedworth was never an enthusiastic politician, spoke rarely in the House, and only retained his seat because it was right that a Lambton should hold it. He was one of those invaluable members of a family who are always at hand in time of trouble, who are perhaps little regarded at other times but have an astonishing fund of competence and kindness always at the disposal of their friends and relatives. He was sorely needed all that late summer and winter of the year 1835, when the threat of another tragedy overhung Lord Durham's family. His eldest daughter by his first wife had married the Hon. J. G. Ponsonby and was now very ill, another victim of the family curse of consumption. She was then with her husband in Ireland and Hedworth went to stay with them to give what help he could and to keep Durham informed about her condition.

As the year drew to a close Lady Frances grew rapidly worse and on 17 December she died. Such griefs were always an agony to Durham's loving heart and intense family feeling. In despair he wrote to Hedworth on 30 December a letter which recalls his terrible outburst to Grey after his son's death in 1831.

As ever, grief affected his health and Lady Durham's letters to her father spoke of her anxiety about him. The Russian winter had brought on a return of his neuralgia and now he felt the first symptoms of that rheumatic fever which was almost to cripple him and was at last to enforce his retirement before his work in Russia was over. All through the winter of 1835 he was intermittently an invalid, confined to his house and unable to fulfil his more arduous duties, though he worked steadily at home and took every opportunity that his health afforded him of appearing at court and of meeting Nesselrode and the other diplomatists.

In the spring of 1836 he was stronger and able to resume his full duties, though he still suffered at times from his excruciating headaches. When June came he was much cheered by the first real sign that his incessant care for the oppressed Poles was likely to achieve some measure of relief. On his previous visit he had worked hard for them without success and Palmerston had instructed him to renew his efforts. The people and the Press in England had taken the cause of Poland to heart and were clamouring for more merciful treatment with a violence which proved their goodwill but, at the same time, did not help their Ambassador in making a tactful approach.

It was a matter which had to be handled with the utmost care, since Russia considered it as a purely domestic affair which was no concern of any country but her own. Durham wrote to Palmerston and warned him that Britain must not press too far or ask too much, adding the pertinent question, 'May they not retort upon us about Ireland?'

In June of that year his tact and persistence began to make progress and he was delighted to hear from the Emperor himself of certain new appointments which were about to be announced for the government of Poland. The new governor was to be Marshal Paskievich, and Prince Koziloffsky, a noted friend and lover of the Poles, was given a seat on his council. The Emperor told Lord Durham that the appointments had been made by his personal order and that the object of them was to ensure a more humane policy.

It was a tribute to Lord Durham's diplomacy, and Palmerston acknowledged it as such. The pity was that he could not stay longer to keep an eye on the Polish situation and see how far the Emperor's humane intentions were translated into action.

In the early autumn he had to consider how much longer he could stand the climate and the life of Russia. He was stronger but he had never fully recovered his health after the breakdown of the winter and, as the short summer waned and the first flurries of snow swept down the streets of St. Petersburg, he became seriously ill again with rheumatic fever. For weeks he lay abed and both Lady Durham and he feared that he would never survive the darkness and cold of another Russian winter. Lady Durham begged him to ask for his recall, but he would not do that, feeling that he had still much work to do before he could rest. But he was so ill and so constantly in pain that eventually he was forced to write to Palmerston to ask for a provisional leave of absence, 'to be used only in case I find myself utterly unable to support the severity of the climate as the winter advances'.

In his letter, which was a private one, he referred to the King's notorious dislike of him, but Palmerston in his reply of 24 September was able to reassure him. He admitted that the King had felt 'irritation'—it was, he said, a better description than 'dislike'—but that had passed off; 'whenever your name is mentioned it is with perfect good humour'. The King, Palmerston wrote, had begun to realize what good work Durham was doing—'Your despatches are praised as being ably written, though,' he added, 'there is an impression that you take too favourable and indulgent a view of Russian policy.' But this was mild criticism from the King compared with his opinion of the rest of the Whig Government, for Palmerston wrote: 'The King and the Court hate us and wish us all at the Devil.' Palmerston further added the good advice that, should Durham find that he had to come home on leave, he should first of all send a despatch renewing his belief in Russia's pacific aims but adding a warning to the Foreign Office that this belief 'ought not to induce us to relax in any degree the vigilance with which the proceedings of Russia in all parts of her extreme frontier ought to be watched'.

Durham gladly accepted these 'friendly hints', as Palmerston called them. They coincided with his own opinion, for he had never thought that Russia's friendly attitude was necessarily permanent nor had he suggested any relaxation of vigilance. All he had wanted was to ensure that the vigilance should be as unobtrusive as possible and that the British Press should be more restrained in their comments. He wrote the suggested despatch and Palmerston wrote in cordial approval.

In October and November Lord Durham was feeling much stronger than he had dared to hope and felt fairly confident of being able to stay through the winter. He knew that much of the present good relations between the two countries depended on his personal interest at the Russian court and he was determined not to cut short his mission if it were possible to avoid it. Not even the Foreign Office realized the importance of the Ambassador's personal relations with the Emperor; an ambassador whom he did not like might pack his bags and go home at once for all the good that he could do. Also Lord Durham was resolute not to give up his post until he had satisfied himself that his successor would be equally acceptable. He wanted no repetition of Palmerston's obstinacy about Sir Stratford Canning.

There was still one aspect of Russian policy which gave him some anxiety and that political farsightedness of his showed it to him years before it became a worry and finally an obsession to Britain for nearly a century. He dismissed as ridiculous the vague alarms of Russian fleets in the Channel or Russian divisions crossing the Eastern border to march across Europe. He paid not much more attention to the danger of Constantinople, which was then the greatest fear among his colleagues. His eyes were fixed on a spot far beyond that, on the road to Persia and Afghanistan and so to India. In what was to prove his last important despatch from Russia he called Palmerston's attention to this possible threat. That was in May 1837 and he had given the matter such concentrated thought that he was able to send to Palmerston a list of Russia's probable routes and movements should she turn her thoughts that way. Palmerston agreed: 'It seems pretty clear that sooner or later the Cossack and the Sepoy, the man from the Baltic and the man from the British Islands will meet in the centre of Asia.'

CHAPTER XI

Lord Durham had overestimated the improvement in his health and, as soon as the year 1837 began, he knew that he could not stay in Russia for much longer. On 26 January, he wrote:

'My mission is nearly over. I have done all the good that in present circumstances can be affected and my health has been so seriously injured by this atrocious climate that my physician will not allow me any longer to delay seeking a change.'

In fact his doctors had told him plainly that they would not be responsible for his life unless he would leave Russia as soon as he could. When the late spring made it easier for him to get about, he began to wind up his affairs and prepared to leave in June. Palmerston wrote sympathetically, approving of his return, and told him that the King, in recognition of his work, had been pleased to bestow on him the Grand Cross of the Order of the Bath. On 10 June, the Emperor of Russia honoured him with the cross of the Order of St. Andrew. William IV was very near to his death and, in his last hours, seems to have realized how harshly he had judged Lord Durham and to want to make amends to him. Lord Erroll wrote to tell him 'how kindly His Majesty spoke of you a very short time before his death'.

That Grand Cross was the last order that William was to bestow. When, after a pathetic request to his doctors to 'patch him up for a few days longer' so that he might see another Waterloo anniversary, he died, Lord Durham was already on his way home. Next month he received his Cross from the hands of the new Queen, at her first investiture.

In those early days Lord Durham had every reason to expect that the Queen would look kindly on him. He had been one of the few who had persistently shown kindness to her when she was an obscure Princess; one of the still fewer who had treated her mother with courtesy and kindness, when the King insulted her on every possible public occasion and grudged her the meanest necessities of life in the Palace of Kensington which he had given her. The Princess Victoria had grown up with pleasant memories of Lord Durham's visits to Kensington and of the interest which he took in her reading and her study of history. She remembered too with gratitude the occasional visits of Lady Durham and one of her first acts as a Queen was to appoint her a Lady-in-waiting.

The story of Lord Durham's last years is one of the enmity between him and those two old colleagues, Melbourne and Brougham. It was none of his seeking, for, though in his time he had quarrelled with both of them, he bore no malice and would not have attacked either. Melbourne, to do him justice, was no aggressor. He hated Durham but would not have gone out of his way to destroy him had it not seemed to him to be necessary for the preservation of his own position. The rancour and the aggression lay all with Brougham. They had smouldered in that implacable heart, fed with memories of old differences, until the time could come for them to burst into flame and exact revenge. He was still furiously angry with Durham but still more with Melbourne and he waited with savage patience for an opportunity to wound them. It was his undeserved good fortune that the opportunity, when it came, involved them both and enabled him to strike with one blow. And, at the end of the story Melbourne, whose instinct of self-preservation was abnormally developed, would succeed in extricating himself and in leaving Lord Durham to suffer the whole weight.

None of this would have been possible without Melbourne's almost total ascendancy over the Queen in the opening years of her reign. Melbourne had already decided that Lord Durham must be found a high-sounding post somewhere as far away from Britain as possible. For a time he seems to have hoped that he would be able to go back to Russia, but the doctors emphatically forbade it. The answer to the other problem came unexpectedly and from a quarter where he could never have believed that it would come, if only for the reason that it was a quarter to which he gave as little attention as possible. As Prime Minister, he was naturally aware that Her Majesty owned certain provinces in North America, usually known as Lower and Upper Canada. The inhabitants of these provinces were (apparently) becoming dissatisfied and impudent and were already talking of throwing off their allegiance.

For himself, Melbourne would not mind that at all. As he

THE COUNTESS OF DURHAM
From a portrait by Sir Thomas Lawrence

was later to write to Lord Durham, 'The separation might not be detrimental'. In December 1837 there was a serious threat of rebellion in Canada and the Government were forced to make some display of interest in the situation. How lightly the responsibility had rested on Melbourne's shoulders is shown by a letter which Lord Howick, Earl Grey's son and a member of the Government, wrote to him, 'You will excuse my saying that in my opinion you ought much sooner to have given your serious attention to the affairs of this Colony in connection with which you must be aware that you have given no real assistance to Glenelg.'

Melbourne's whole conduct and attitude to Colonial affairs both before, during and after the Canadian crisis justify this startling rebuke from a subordinate. He was not interested in any of the Colonies and made no pretence that he was. But he was interested in his own survival and now he realized that a failure to hold Canada, though it 'might not be detrimental', would probably involve the fall of the Whig Government. Reluctantly he bestirred himself. Canada was a long way away, but the Canadian crisis was suddenly very near and it threatened his own position. The Whigs were in an awkward position between the Tories and the Radicals, who had not yet combined against them, but would probably do so over Canada, since the Radicals were in favour of Emancipation and would vote with the Tories. The Tories cared as little about the Colonies as did Melbourne, but they were too well practised tacticians to miss such a chance of arranging a coalition for the pleasure of turning out the Government. Melbourne felt himself strong enough to cope with his enemies at home as long as he was constantly near to the Queen and could use his inordinate influence with her, but someone must go out to cope with her enemies abroad.

By the end of the year the two Canadas were in all but open revolt. Sir John Colborne, who commanded the British troops out there, had enough force and was a good enough soldier to suppress anything but full-scale rebellion, but what Melbourne needed was a statesman to prevent a rebellion. He must be one of real ability since his task would be in a few weeks to straighten out the tangle left by the indolence and callous neglect of a good many years.

'What then was Melbourne to do?' Sir Reginald Coupland writes, in his *The Durham Report*. 'The situation in Canada was slowly worsening; nobody in any party had any policy for dealing with it which held out any hope of success, but he and his colleagues would have to bear the brunt of failure. At his wits end, he conceived a brilliant idea.'

The brilliant idea was to send out Lord Durham. 'Lord Durham,' Coupland continues, 'had returned from his successful Embassy at St. Petersburg and, though Melbourne cordially disliked him, he recognized his capacity and his popularity with the left wing in the Commons and the electorate. Durham, if anyone, might throw light on the Canadian darkness and to call Durham to the Government's aid, irritating as it would be to the Tories, might go far to propitiate the Radicals.' It is important to remember that, in the opinion both of contemporaries and of later historians, Melbourne sent Durham to Canada for purely selfish reasons. Even Lord David Cecil, an indiscriminating admirer, admits it when he writes, 'Melbourne must indeed be blamed for sending out Durham in the first place. It is not right to appoint a man you distrust to an important public job just because it will ease the political situation at home.' Lord Durham knew it himself and it was freely stated in both Houses of Parliament during the ensuing debates. Lord John Russell showed his awareness of it in his famous panegyric on Lord Durham's work in Canada. Melbourne himself did not trouble to deny it.

Melbourne sent Durham to Canada for his own convenience and protection. He induced him to go by giving him a virtually free hand there and promising him, in his own words, 'the fullest and most unflinching support'. Lastly, to save his party and his own position, he betrayed and abandoned him. That is the end of the long antipathy between the two men who were so unlike in everything but in nothing more than their ideas of loyalty and honesty.

PART FOUR

'Lord High Seditioner'

1837–1838

Let the colonies always keep their idea of their civil rights associated with your government—they will cling and grapple to you; and no force under heaven would be of power to tear them from their allegiance. . . . Deny them this participation of freedom, and you break that sole bond, which originally made, and must still preserve the unity of the empire.

EDMUND BURKE. *On Conciliation with the Colonies.* 1775.

Mean men must adhere, but great men, that have strength in themselves, were better to maintain themselves indifferent and neutral.

FRANCIS BACON. . . . *Of Faction.*

CHAPTER I

Canada had become a British possession in 1763 and its constitution in the year 1837 was the result of the Quebec Act of 1774 and the Canada Act of 1791. The Imperial Parliament—the name which the British Parliament used for transacting colonial business—had passed both of them with the genuine intention of keeping a just balance between British and French inhabitants and particularly of removing the resentment of the French who regarded themselves, with some justice, as the original settlers.

The Quebec Act, in a spirit of real generosity, went far towards meeting French sentiment by recognizing the Roman Catholic Church as the official religion and by preserving most of the old French-Canadian civil law. Its generosity made no appeal to the growing numbers of British settlers, most of whom were Protestant and many of whom had come into the country after the American Revolution of 1783. These were British loyalists who had lived in the Thirteen Colonies and had, often at great personal sacrifice, crossed the border so that they might remain British subjects. Clearly the Imperial Government were bound to consider the interests of people who had given up so much for the sake of what they called 'the blessings of the British Constitution'.

The population of Canada soon began to show a preponderance of British subjects and it would have been unfair to insist indefinitely on the retention of French church and law. Inevitably there was friction between the two nationalities. The French were mostly farmers and fur-traders, while the British were engaging in all forms of commerce and especially in the export to Britain of wheat, timber, and furs. The position of the French would get worse as time went on since no new immigrants were coming from France to add to their numbers, while the British numbers grew steadily. Yet the French had still, on the whole, the better of the deal with their own Church and with commerce regulated by their own civil law. It was in an attempt to strike a fairer balance that Parliament passed the Canada Act of 1791, which adopted the important principle of partition between the nationalities. The principle had been tried and was working well in what had been the old province of Nova Scotia and was now divided into Nova Scotia and New Brunswick. Most of the British had settled in the western half, the renamed New Brunswick, while the French predominated in Nova Scotia.

The experiment was less happy in the great province of Quebec, in which, though most of the British had settled in the western half, there were many thousands of them in the eastern. The province was divided into Upper and Lower Canada, and partition, while it worked well in the western or Upper Canada, promised less well for the eastern or Lower Canada, where a minority of British found themselves surrounded by French. In Upper Canada British law was to prevail, but French law was retained in Lower Canada. Parliament, showing a wise tolerance, made no attempt to regulate religion in either province, and the Roman Church, though neither established nor endowed, remained the principal religion over the whole of both Canadas.

It was not an ideal solution. Probably there could be no ideal solution, but it was workable, which was as much as could be expected for the moment. It was at least an improvement on the old system. The less satisfactory part of Parliament's plan was the regulation of the internal government of each province and the relation of each with the Mother Country. It is perhaps enough to say that its chief defect was that it made no provision for representative government in either province and that all proceedings and all decisions taken by the provincial assemblies were liable to revision or cancellation by either the Lieutenant-Governor in Canada or by the Colonial Office and Imperial Parliament in London. One apparent concession, was an undertaking not to inflict direct taxation on the colonies, 'except for the purpose of regulating Trade'. This concession aroused more indignation than gratitude, for the Canadians were all traders and it seemed to grant them freedom from everything except the one kind of taxation that really mattered. It left Britain in fact in the position of being the sole power able to fix the taxes and duties on all her transactions with the Canadas. Canada could become a dumping ground for any unwanted British products while her own could be kept out of the British markets.

There was no feeling that this power would be abused, nor was it, but it was there and the colonists resented it. The British had sometimes very short memories. They might have recalled that the threat of taxation without representation had been the chief cause of their loss of the Thirteen Colonies, not many years before. There were still men living who had heard Burke's famous statement of the true principles of colonial government:

'My hold on the colonies is in the close affection which grows from common names, from kindred blood and equal protection. They are ties which, though light as air, are strong as links of iron. Let the colonies always keep their idea of their civil rights associated with your government—they will cling and grapple to you; and no force under Heaven would be of power to tear them from your allegiance.'

Burke's words had gone unheeded when they were spoken and were by now forgotten, or that obnoxious taxation rule would not have spoiled what was an honest attempt to deal fairly with both sides in Canada. Yet, by a mischance which was no fault of the Imperial Government, the Canada Act became obsolete almost as soon as it became law. In the following year the French Revolution began and its effect was drastic on both sides of the Atlantic. In Europe the struggle between France and the rest of the nations was beginning and England was soon too much engrossed in it to devote much attention to a problem in Canada which they believed that they had solved. In Canada the traditional hatred of the French for the English was sharpened by the long and bitter European wars and especially by the final defeat of France. The French-Canadians became more and more resentful of British rule and less disposed to see any good in the British Constitution.

The British settlers were changing as the old loyalists died out and men of a different type began to take their place. The new immigrants from England had seen the beginning of a new order. They had seen royalty destroyed in France and had heard the first stirrings of the threat to Privilege in their own country. They had known the bitterness of Tory oppression with its suppression of Habeas Corpus and its threat to their liberty. The new immigrants arrived with talk of the new men who were beginning to make themselves heard in England, Francis Place, William Cobbett, Burdett, and Hunt. They were not likely to take kindly to a system which, with all its benevolence, was rather less enlightened than that which had prevailed in their own country before the Revolution of 1688.

Another class of immigrant was trickling in from the United States. The Americans were, as young nations are apt to be, noisily self-confident, triumphant in their recent emancipation and—most ominous of all—in their right to unrestricted trade with Britain, while Canada was still bound by the British tariffs. Nor was the threat from America confined to noise and boasting. Their ships entered the Canadian rivers and bands of mounted men crossed the border to loot or possibly to reconnoitre for a later crossing in strength. America was already dreaming of a United States which should include the whole of the North Continent. In 1812 Britain, not content with having the Emperor Napoleon on her hands, went to war with the States and an American army marched into Canada. In face of the common danger French and British united and hustled the Americans back across the border. Peace was restored in 1814 and the bond of common feeling did not long outlive the common danger. Each nationality went back to its own grievances. The long fight between the Assemblies and the Executive Councils began in both provinces.

The Canada Act had granted constitutions to each province after the British model of Parliament, Cabinet, and King, represented by Assembly, Executive Council, and Lieutenant-Governor, but the Executive were appointed by the Governor and were not responsible to the Assembly, while the Governor could be overruled by several authorities at home. In Upper Canada, the British majority, with their traditional respect for old forms, were not dissatisfied except that they demanded that the Executive should be made responsible to the Assembly as the British Cabinet were to Parliament. The French, fired by the example of their Revolution, saw no virtue at all in the British Constitution and clamoured for a republican form of government. In both provinces, for all their differences, the demand was much the same. They wanted a sweeping reform which would make their government both representative and responsible to themselves, with the ultimate power, under the Throne, resting in the Assemblies.

Canadian hopes rose when in 1830 the Whigs came into power and at once began to reform their own electoral system. Such a party, the Canadians felt, could not refuse to a colony what they were giving to the Mother Country. They were the more disillusioned when they found that the Whigs were, if possible, less interested in their colonies than had been any Tory administration. Glenelg, at the Colonial Office, was a pleasant nonentity and the only other member of the Government who seemed to be aware of Canada's existence was Lord John Russell, whose liberal ideas at home contrasted strangely with the rigidity of his attitude to the Colonies.

The trouble, when at last it came to a head, was inevitably about taxation. In the past the Canadas had arranged their own taxes and duties and had contributed irregular but not ungenerous amounts to the Imperial Parliament. But the Napoleonic wars had so drained the exchequer that Britain turned her thoughts to other ways of getting money out of the Colonies. Lord Auckland was sent out as Lieutenant-Governor of Upper Canada with instructions to ask the Assembly to vote an annual Civil List as was done by the Imperial Parliament. He had no authority to compel it, but the Canadians were always aware of the threat which lurked in that phrase about taxation 'for the regulation of trade'. If they did not vote an adequate Civil List there was nothing to prevent the Imperial Parliament from imposing punitive import and export duties, until they complied.

The Canadas were disillusioned when they found that new Liberal was old Tory writ large. Their complaints had been ignored, their prayers refused, and now their pockets were threatened. Their one possible answer was to refuse to vote supplies to the Mother Country. In 1833 the Assembly of Lower Canada took this course. The loyalty of Upper Canada held out a little longer but in 1836 they too refused. Both Upper and Lower Assemblies then joined in warning the Imperial Government that no more supplies would be forthcoming until the constitutions of both provinces had been so altered as to make them representative of and responsible to the people of Canada.

The Whig Government could hardly ignore this threat, however contemptuously Russell might speak of it in the Commons. They appointed a Commission to inquire into the reason for grievances of which Burke had warned them more than fifty years before and which every Canadian despatch for the last ten years had been reiterating. They chose Lord Gosford to preside over it. The Commission went to Canada and began their inquiries. They were still patiently pursuing them when, two years later, Canada broke out in open rebellion.

CHAPTER II

In July 1837, Melbourne wrote to Lord Durham and asked him to go to Canada to report on the position there.

'The final separation of those colonies,' he wrote, 'might possibly not be of material detriment to the interests of the mother-country but it is clear that it would be a serious blow to the honour of Great Britain and certainly would be fatal to the character and existence of the Administration under which it took place.'

Lord Durham knew Melbourne and could not fail to see that he was more concerned with the future of his own party and his own position than with that of Canada. He declined the invitation. He does not seem to have given any reason for his refusal but probably the state of his health decided him. He had barely recovered from the rigours of the Russian climate and could not lightly contemplate a voyage across the Atlantic and an indefinite stay in a country whose winters were as cold as those of St. Petersburg. Nor was there any reason why he should endanger his life to oblige a Prime Minister and a Cabinet whose sole ambition was to get rid of him at any cost. Earl Grey was anxious that he should stay at home until his health was fully restored and he refers often in his letters to 'Lambton's frequent attacks of indisposition'. In one letter, referring to the Canadian project, he wrote that, 'What I fear most is the effect of the climate'.

So Melbourne's brilliant idea came to nothing and he had

nothing to replace it. All that summer and autumn he did nothing, while Canada drifted steadily towards rebellion and Sir John Colborne deployed his troops to cope with the threatened danger. Lord Gosford, having apparently finished his inquiries without coming to any conclusion, clamoured for his recall and returned, having accomplished nothing. Colborne had been on the point of returning after completing his tour of duty as Lieutenant-Governor of Upper Canada, but, at the request of the Government, he remained in Canada and took command of all the forces there. The first outbreaks were spasmodic and were all in Lower Canada. He suppressed them without any difficulty but there were signs that Upper Canada would soon join in the revolt. The whole of both provinces was seething with sedition in speeches, pamphlets, and various small acts of disobedience and defiance. The Executive Councils tried the effect of a few prosecutions as a deterrent, only to find that Canadian juries, however strong might be the evidence, would not convict in a single case. Any day might see the whole colony in rebellion, but the Imperial Parliament had no time to attend to such trivialities. In Britain a general election was in progress and honourable members were too busy in trying to keep or win seats to be distracted by the possible loss of an Empire. It was not until January 1838 that Parliament had leisure to consider the colonial problem.

When they did so, it was without energy or intelligence. The Radicals raised a new clamour for 'Emancipation' and Russell responded with a heroic but not very helpful piece of rhetoric in which he announced that Britain would never yield to force. But Melbourne had already seen the danger to his position. In December he had renewed his appeal to Lord Durham and, when Durham still hesitated, used all his influence with his infatuated Queen to get her to reinforce his own with her personal appeal.

Lord Durham hesitated for a fortnight before he answered, but the Queen's request was too much for him. On 15 January 1838, he wrote to Melbourne and agreed to go. He did not want the appointment. He feared for his strength to carry out the arduous duties and, strange as it may seem, he doubted whether he had the ability for so delicate a task. He was to make this clear later in one of his rare speeches in the House of

Lords, when he would speak of his reluctance to undertake the task and of his need for help and support from both political friends and enemies if he were to succeed in it. The sacrifice which he was making was immeasurable. It might well have cost him his life or at any rate turned him into a hopeless invalid. He might be facing a colossal failure and he had little reason to trust any promises of help from Melbourne. But one danger he overlooked. He forgot that the tiger was still crouching in the jungle, where Lord Brougham watched his every move and waited for him to make a false one. Nothing in Radical Jack's honourable career is more honourable to him than his willingness to attack so formidable a problem at so great a personal risk and sacrifice.

One thing he made clear to Melbourne. He would go on his own terms or not at all. He knew the magnitude of the task and questioned his own competence. He would attempt it only if he were allowed to use his own methods and were left unhampered in his choice of colleagues. On the same day as his letter of acceptance he wrote to Grey:

'I have stipulated with Melbourne that it is to be a temporary mission. I am not to be stinted in powers or money and am to have unstinted appointment of all civil officers whom I may think necessary for the efficient exercise of my duties. The undertaking is a fearfully arduous one and nothing but the extreme urgency of the case could induce me to make such a sacrifice, both public and private.'

Melbourne, in the thankful mood of the moment, was ready to promise anything. He replied at once to Durham's demands: 'I can assure you that I consider you as making a great sacrifice for the chance of doing an essential service to the country.' He added—in words which must be remembered in view of what was to follow—'As far as I am concerned, and I think I can answer for all my colleagues, you will receive the firmest and most unflinching support.'

On 17 January, Russell, for the Government, introduced into the Commons a measure which proposed to suspend the constitution of Lower Canada until November 1840 and to provide for its government by Lord Durham and a special council— five members of which were to form a quorum—which would have power to pass all necessary legislation as long as the constitution should remain suspended. The preamble of the Bill, as it was originally drafted, contained a clause, on which Lord Durham had insisted, giving him power to convene an assembly of either Province and all of its inhabitants, from which he could get information and through which he could test the feeling of the people. It was a reminder that the new Dictator was still the old Radical Jack; that the will of the people was still, as it had been in the days of the Reform Bill, of paramount importance to him; and that he still believed that only by personal contact with the people could he gain that understanding which was to him the essential of good government. The Tories, naturally enough, took fright at this alarming incitement to democracy and Peel led so strong a movement against it that it was struck out of the preamble.

Otherwise the Tories did not, at this stage, oppose the Bill, except for moving a few amendments when it reached the Committee stage. They were willing to embarrass the Government and more than willing to harass Lord Durham, but they were sorely handicapped by the eccentric attitude of their leader, the Duke of Wellington, who refused to make a party matter out of something which affected the welfare and honour of the country and willingly gave advice to the Whigs on the military necessities of the situation. The Duke had never been a wholly satisfactory party man and was liable to these disconcerting gestures. His followers shrugged their shoulders and waited for their chance.

The debate lasted for several days in both Houses and was only remarkable for two speeches. One was a characteristic outburst of spleen from Lord Brougham, in the course of which, however, he took occasion to speak in warm approval of Lord Durham's willingness to tackle a difficult situation which was none of his making. The other was Lord Durham's. He spoke only once during the debate and then only for a few minutes and in a tone of diffidence which astonished those who had only known him in his hot-headed and arrogant youth. In a passage which is moving because of its obvious sincerity, he appealed to men of all parties to give him their support in his most difficult task.

'I feel,' he said, 'that I can only accomplish it by the most

227

cordial and energetic support, a support which I am sure I shall obtain, of my noble friends, the members of Her Majesty's Cabinet; by the co-operation of the Imperial Parliament; and, permit me to say, by the generous forbearance of the noble Lords opposite, to whom I have always been politically opposed.' It was one of those moments of sincerity when the business of government seems to be lifted above the sordid routine of party strife, but not only noble Lords opposite but even Her Majesty's Cabinet were only too soon to show how incapable they were of rising to such impartiality.

Within a few days of the debate, Lord Durham received his Commission, the document which gave him his instructions and conferred on him his powers. Sir Reginald Coupland calls it 'elaborate and unprecedented' and Sir Charles Lucas writes that it was 'as futile a set of instructions as could be given to a strong man setting out on a difficult mission'. It gave him supreme executive authority in all British North American provinces and legislative authority in Lower Canada, while the constitution was suspended. In Lower Canada he was to have the assistance of a council, which he was to choose, and the additional power to grant or withhold pardon after sentence of death had been passed, without waiting 'until the Queen's pleasure should be known'. He was named as 'Captain-General and Governor in Chief in and over each of our provinces of Lower Canada, Upper Canada, Nova Scotia and New Brunswick, and over our Island of Prince Edward in North America'. Also he was to be 'High Commissioner for the adjustment of certain questions depending in the said provinces'. All 'Our Officers, Civil and Military, and all other inhabitants' were to be 'obedient, aiding and assisting unto' him. The only restriction was that he was to conform 'to such instructions as may from time to time be addressed to you for your guidance by us under our Sign manual or Signet' or through the usual channels of Privy Council or Secretary of State.

Coupland writes that the intention was that Lord Durham should himself rule in Lower Canada as absolute dictator and should rule the other provinces through their existing Lieutenant-Governors, leaving the details of administration to them but directing their general policy. Lord Durham had demanded full powers and he had got them in full measure. Their completeness caused a storm in Parliament and in both Houses speeches were made which deplored the concentration of so much power in one man. Brougham was especially eloquent in opposition, partly no doubt on personal grounds, but, to do him justice, almost as much because his whole life had been spent in opposition to tyranny and absolute power in any man. It is noticeable that, even in Brougham's speech, the objection was to the bestowal of such power on one man, and not at all to Lord Durham's fitness to exercise it. Francis Place, a lifelong opponent of tyranny, said that Lord Durham was the only man to whom he could bear to see such powers entrusted.

The general tone of the debate was unenthusiastic but resigned. Both parties deprecated such a dictatorship but realized that things in Canada had reached a pitch where, unless something exceptional were to be done, there was no hope of a successful solution. They agreed reluctantly, but they agreed and it seemed that Lord Durham's mission would start in an atmosphere of temperate good wishes and unity. But early in 1838 despatches from Sir John Colborne reported the total suppression of the revolt in Canada. The Tories breathed a sigh of relief and at once descended into the lowest depths of personal and party warfare.

CHAPTER III

Few things in the Tories' recent record, scandalous as it was, are more disgraceful than their sudden descent from fair criticism of colonial policy to the vicious attack which they were now to launch against Lord Durham. Colborne's despatches had convinced them that the trouble was over and they felt themselves free to turn their attention from matters of high policy to the more congenial details of harassing the Government. The Duke, indeed, remained as obstinate as ever not to prejudice the mission to Canada, but the less disinterested members of his party fell gleefully on the preparations which Lord Durham was making for his departure. It must be admitted that he gave them every opportunity. He had insisted on a free hand in matters of expense and, since he was an enormously rich man, he was prepared to bear a good share of the expense of the mission out of his own pocket. For this reason, he saw no need to stint himself and soon there were stories of the size of the suite and the luxury of the equipment which he was taking with him. The stories were not much exaggerated. During the weeks which elapsed before he sailed, the cases of silver and wine, of clothes and uniforms, the carriages, horses, and harness began to accumulate at Lambton, in London, and at the port of embarkation. His own wardrobe was such as would have sufficed for half a dozen ordinary Governors and his suspicion of Canadian taste in wine required the shipment of dozens of cases of dry champagne.

It was perhaps unnecessary, even a little ostentatious, but, since he was paying for most of it, it might be supposed to be his own affair. Yet it seemed to the Tories to justify an attack which might, so vicious was it, have had the disastrous effect of making him throw up the appointment and leaving them with the trouble unsolved on their hands. They opened their attack in April in the House of Commons, when Lord Chandos proposed a motion that the expenses of Lord Durham's mission should be on the scale of those lately approved for Lord Gosford's recent and abortive commission of inquiry. Gosford's expedition had undoubtedly been cheap, since he had lived in one room in Montreal throughout his visit and had rarely left the city, but cheapness had been its only merit. He had attempted little and achieved nothing and his only positive action when revolution threatened had been to proclaim martial law and to clamour for his recall. Chandos was ill-advised to set it up as a standard to which future missions should conform, but it served him and his friends for their immediate purpose which was to discredit the Government and to insult Lord Durham.

Once more, the personal relations between Melbourne and Durham must be noted at this early stage and borne in mind. Nearly all later historians have written as though their final rupture was the result of Durham's actions in Canada and of Melbourne's repudiation of them. They have not quoted those damning entries in the Queen's diary which reveal Melbourne's subtle depreciation of Durham at every opportunity. But the true cause of the rupture lay further back, in the history of their association and in the difference in their temperaments; it dated back to that painful scene at a Cabinet dinner when Lord Durham had insulted Lord Grey and Melbourne had later expressed a wish to knock him down. They must have been intensified by what can only have been Melbourne's jealousy of Lord and Lady Durham's standing with the Queen. Melbourne must always be first with her and could see in Lord Durham, a man of such charm and distinction, a possible rival in her favour. Perhaps he had never forgotten his wish to 'knock him down', and now his chance was coming.

Within the next few weeks Lord Durham began to appoint the staff who were to accompany him to Canada. He had demanded a free hand in this and had received a promise of 'the most unflinching support'. Yet, as soon as he named his first selections, he met with opposition which was unreasonable and, coming from Melbourne, surprising. The two appointments which aroused so much controversy were those of Edward Wakefield Gibbon and Thomas Turton. The reason for their selection was obvious. In the general apathy which existed among public men about everything to do with the Colonies, the only group who made a serious attempt to understand their needs was the little band of Radical Imperialists, from among whom Lord Durham also chose Charles Buller to be his secretary. Wakefield probably knew more at that time about the Colonies than any man in England. Turton was a barrister who had proved his ability at the time of the Reform Bill and had since done well at the Indian Bar. The objection to both men was that they both had disreputable sexual histories. Wakefield had been mixed up in a squalid affair about the abduction of an heiress, which had landed him in prison and Turton had been involved in a particularly unsavoury divorce case. In both cases the offence was one of many years before and both men had atoned for their wrongdoing and had been useful and honest members of society.

Lord Durham might have spared himself trouble had he consulted Melbourne before making the appointments, but he did not and apparently never meant to consult him. Melbourne's objection on moral grounds was the more irritating since there was no reason to think that he had any particular scruples. 'After all,' Coupland writes, 'this was Melbourne's day, not Gladstone's, it was the post-regency not the Victorian era.' No shadow of the Prince Consort's gloomy morality yet hung over the country. There were then, as Lord Durham was later with a certain waspishness to inform the Prime Minister, men holding high places in the country who 'were not free from the suspicion of adultery'. Melbourne himself, in spite of two rather surprising vindications in the Divorce Courts, had not previously shown any undue regard for morals private or public. But Melbourne was full of two thoughts. He honestly admired his young and virtuous Queen and wanted to protect her from any breath of scandal. Still more did he want to cling to his position at the head of a Whig Government, which might be endangered by these appointments. The Tories had displayed a commendable and quite unusual regard for economy in criticizing Lord Durham's personal expenditure. They could be expected to develop an even stronger sense of prudery when the names of Durham's assistants were announced. And the Whig Government was not in a position to stand any serious attacks. They had a bare majority and that only by the forbearance of the new Radical Group. The change of a few votes could easily defeat them. As a matter of fact the Tories very soon awoke to the opportunity which the appointments gave and the first attack was launched in Parliament as soon as Lord Durham had left the country. The trouble was to smoulder intermittently during all his time in Canada and to burst out again on his return, when any fuel was good enough to stoke the fires of Tory hatred.

Melbourne disliked the appointments and told Durham so and there was an acrimonious correspondence between them which ended with a meeting. In all this difference of opinion Lord Durham was not blameless. He did not show Melbourne any courtesy in consulting him about appointments and both then and later he showed a lamentable failure of the same sort in not troubling to keep him informed of his actions or to give him explanations of his policy. Characteristically, having demanded a free hand, he felt himself absolved from any obligation other than to tell the Prime Minister what he had done after he had done it.

Melbourne had at first refused to sanction Turton's name, and, finding that his sanction had not been asked, tried to get Lord Durham to withdraw. On 9 April, finding that his appeal was ignored, he wrote: 'If you have gone to this extent with him, I do not see what can be done.' Soon afterwards he had reversed that opinion and was pleading for the appointment to be cancelled, writing: 'The sooner and more quietly it is done the better.' But it was not going to be done, soon or late, quietly or with publicity. Lord Durham had made up his mind and refused to discuss it any longer. He did agree that the appointments were not to be announced before his mission had left England and that, when they were announced, they were to be appointments by the Governor-General of Canada and not to bear the approval of the British Government.

CHAPTER IV

Lord Durham had completed his preparations by early April in 1838. The *Hastings*, loaded with his plate and equipment lay waiting at Portsmouth while he went north for a last visit to Lambton and to the bedside of his uncle Ralph Lambton, who had been his guardian and was now dying. Charles Buller, in his diary of the mission left a moving description of the scene late at night when Lord and Lady Durham went on board with their children. Durham had been ill again that winter and spring and Buller noticed that he was white-faced and muffled to the ears in a huge cloak. There was, by Durham's order, a band of music on board to entertain the party during the long crossing. The *Hastings* sailed on 24 April. Four days later the first attack on the appointments to Durham's staff was launched in the House of Lords, when Lord Winchilsea called attention to the presence among the staff of Mr. Thomas Turton and demanded an assurance that he had been and would be given no office under the Crown. Melbourne's usual Parliamentary skill was quite equal to repelling this assault and gave the assurance that the Government had no intention of employing him—if indeed, he added, Mr. Turton were one of the party at all. His actual words are worth quoting in view of the agreement which he had made with Lord Durham.

'I say, first of all, that no situation whatever was offered by Her Majesty's Government to the gentleman to whom the noble earl had alluded; and next that he has gone out to Canada, if he has gone out at all, which I do not mean to deny, without any appointment, without any prospect of an appointment, and without any intention on the part of the Government, or on the part of my noble friend the Earl of Durham to appoint him to any public situation whatever.'

This strange piece of equivocation satisfied the Tory critics for the moment, but Melbourne had taken alarm and wrote hastily to Durham with the intention of covering himself still further.

'My dear Durham,
I write this in great anxiety and in hopes that it may reach you soon and in time entirely to prevent any hasty and indiscreet step. If I had not been able to say that Mr. Turton had gone out without any appointment and any prospect of an appointment, I am confident that we should have had motions made and carried in both Houses of Parliament to cancel the appointment and to remove Mr. Turton from it—as it is [the next words are illegible] by me that there is no intention either on the part of the Government or on yours to appoint Mr. Turton to any public situation in the colony, you must bear me out in this. . . .'
He then goes on to give Lord Durham some advice about the company which he should keep. 'Beware of scallywags and rogues . . . whatever their ability may be. . . .
'If you touch G. W. [Gibbon Wakefield] with a pair of tongs it is utter destruction, depend upon it. T. D. [Tommy Duncombe] is not so bad, but he is one of the same genus and can do nothing but harm.'

Not even Lord Durham's partiality for Tommy Duncombe had gone so far as to put his name forward for an appointment, the truth being that Duncombe was finding his creditors at home more than usually importunate and was minded to try the effect of a few months' absence. Melbourne's state of mind was not far removed from panic, and within a few days of writing this letter, both he and Lord Glenelg, the Colonial Secretary, were renewing their plea that neither Turton nor Wakefield should be employed on arrival. Lord Durham was urged to send both of them straight home again.

While this pitiful stream of entreaty was going out from England, Lord Durham was already at sea and there was little prospect of his getting the warning before he had had a chance of doing what he had always intended to do. But the appeals were on record and served later to show that the Government had done all that they could to restrain their headstrong Governor-General. Lord Durham did not reach Canada before the end of May, and by the time that he had read the first of Melbourne's sermons, he had already appointed Turton as his legal adviser. Turton, on learning of them, immediately offered to resign, but Durham refused to allow it or to be in any degree influenced by the warning tone of the correspondence. On 15 June, he wrote to Glenelg:

'If you, the Government at home, only support me and show a good front to the Tory marplots in England, I will answer for handing over to you in a few months all the North American provinces in a state of loyalty and content. If you cannot do this, but show the slightest want of confidence in me, you will do well immediately to replace me. . . .'

To Melbourne he wrote in even less accommodating manner:

'Really, if it were not very inconvenient all this would be very ludicrous. I am called upon to perform an almost super-human task. You provide me with no—or at least inadequate —means from yourselves, and you then interfere with the arrangements I make to supply myself with the best talent that I can find. . . . [Here] they believe in my good intentions toward all, and in my having support from home. See you to that; I will provide for the remainder. The Colonies are saved for England, as far as I am concerned, but you must be firm. Don't interfere with me when I am at work. After it is done, impeach me if you will. . . .'

It must be held to Lord Durham's great credit that he did, even then, try as far as he could to meet the Government's objections. As far as Turton was concerned, he had pledged himself to the appointment and he would not go back on his word. But there had been a little delay in appointing Wake-field and he found it possible to employ him without giving him any official title. With a final gesture of defiance he told Glenelg that he would require no salary from the Government for either of them, nor would he take any for himself. He proposed to pay both Turton and Wakefield out of his own pocket, though both of them declined to accept his salary and indeed showed throughout a devotion to their duty and to his person which does them great honour. The subject was dropped for the moment, but there must have been on both sides of the Atlantic a feeling that the last had not been heard of it, and the antipathy between Melbourne and Durham grew stronger. It was a sad end to Melbourne's promise of 'the most unflinching support'.

Though the *Hastings* took over a month to make the crossing, to judge by Lady Durham's letters and Buller's diary, they were anything but dull on board. The band played on deck when the weather permitted it and below deck for the Governor-General's dinner guests. Lord Durham had one very bad bout of his neuralgic pain but on the whole his health improved as the voyage went on and he took part in all the gaiety. There were private charades and theatricals organized by Wakefield and Buller. Durham was, Buller reported, 'In his most genial mood'. And every day there were long conferences in the Governor-General's day-cabin at which he and his staff began to lay their plans for the pacification and the good government of Canada.

The task which faced the mission was immense, since it was charged not only with those two essentials but with the reformation of all the economy and administration of the provinces and with the whole business of day-to-day government in Lower Canada. Legal problems were Turton's especial care, while Wakefield, the most experienced of them in colonial administration in general, dealt with such matters as immigration, land titles, and education. Lord Durham naturally held himself mainly responsible for high policy and constitutional matters. He proved, as he was over and again to prove, that he possessed supreme ability to delegate less important matters and to trust his staff to work without interference.

The main point which had to be discussed was naturally the

future relations between Upper and Lower Canada and between the British and French parties. So much is said about this in the final Durham Report that the only mention of it now need be the evidence which comes from the accounts of these discussions as to Lord Durham's feeling about it. During his last months in England he had taken every opportunity of discussing Canadian affairs with men who had lived there or had visited or who had other sources of knowledge. He had tried to draw knowledge from men of every party and shade of thought, but it was only to be expected that he should have heard more of the British side than of the French. Critics of his famous Report have written of the pro-British prejudice which he sometimes showed and have remarked that he gave to the division between the two nationalities in the provinces an importance which was more historical than contemporary. His own words in the early part of the Report show that he regarded it as the most important problem of all, when he wrote:

'I expected to find a contest between a government and a people; I found two nations warring in the bosom of a single state. I found a contest not of principle but of races.'

It is clear that before arriving in Canada he had made up his mind about the main principles which must guide him. He believed that the difference between the two nationalities lay at the root of every trouble, and he hoped to remove it by reverting to a single and united Canada. It was not his own idea, nor did he ever claim the credit for it. It was, in fact, a reversion to an earlier condition which had been discussed intermittently ever since the partition of the colony.

He realized that, in order to carry it out, he had to decide between two courses, which came to be called Federation and Union. Union would involve the complete fusion of the provinces under one central government. Federation was the principle of the United States of America, where separate states have their own government under a central authority.

It seems clear that during the discussions before landing Lord Durham was in favour of Federation as a first step, believing, as he did, that the enmity between the two races was so bitter and so complete that their fusion must be a matter of time and goodwill. In the Report, this final decision was for complete Union.

It is no criticism of him to say that this was a reversal of his original policy, since it was based on fuller knowledge and consultation with the peoples concerned. It is fair to say that, at this stage and before he had personal knowledge of the needs of Canada, he had decided on a provisional policy, which later he had the honesty and strength to discard where he thought it to be wrong. Of his whole attitude at this early stage there could be no fairer summary than his own words spoken in debate in the House of Lords a few weeks before sailing.

'I will know nothing of a French, British or Canadian party, but will look on them all as Her Majesty's subjects.'

That was at the back of all his planning and he was determined to make it clear to Canada from the beginning. During the discussions on board the *Hastings*, he conceived the idea of announcing his arrival with a proclamation which should explain freely and openly to the Canadians the methods which he meant to follow. Buller's evidence shows that Lord Durham personally drafted the proclamation, which is a characteristically plain and straightforward statement of policy. He promised mercy for the innocent, justice for the guilty, and above all he promised that he would learn from the people what their needs were and how they could best be met.

Since he had been charged with the whole government of Lower Canada, where discontent was strongest, he felt bound to make a provisional order for carrying it out until his own investigations could show him some more permanent scheme. From his talks in London with Canadian visitors he had gathered a true impression that the Council of Lower Canada were managing the affairs of the province in their own interests and that the official classes of Quebec were profiting by it in shameless fashion. The constitution of Lower Canada was suspended and his Commission left him free to administer it with a Council of whom five should form a quorum.

Characteristically, Lord Durham interpreted this to mean that a Council of five was quite enough, and, since he was free to choose them, he chose no Canadians at all, but men of his own staff, which had one advantage in that he would never fail to have a quorum. The only addition to these was Mr. Daly, the Secretary of the suspended Council and a man of such integrity that neither party had ever found a word to say against him. It is perhaps not surprising that Buller should have called Durham 'The Dictator' nor did he ever hide from the world that he meant to have his own way. He decided to dismiss the whole of the last Council except for Mr. Daly.

It was a bold decision, yet the way in which he carried it out proved that the words in his proclamation had not been empty and that behind the new dictator lay the old Radical Jack, who always knew that a nation or a party consisted of human beings with feelings and personal pride. His council of five of his own people could only be temporary, both on grounds of expediency and justice, and he was the last man to want to withhold from any people the right to govern themselves. He personally drafted a letter which he ordered Buller to send to every member of the old council explaining that his action was only temporary and that he would as soon as possible discuss with them the formation of a permanent and representative council. He thanked them gracefully for all their services and made it clear that he had no complaint against them nor any wish to get rid of them. His courtesy met with a full reward, for all of the members accepted their dismissal without demur and many of them later spoke of their gratitude for the open way in which he had dealt with them.

The *Hastings* arrived in the mouth of the St. Lawrence River on 27 May but Lord Durham remained on board for two more days while the immense store of baggage was put ashore and all preparations were made for the ceremonial entry, which both his policy and his personal tastes demanded. He was his Queen's personal representative and he meant that all Canada should know it. No doubt there was some personal vanity in it, but there was much practical statesmanship. He knew the world and knew what an important part on occasion the appearance of power can play. It was fitting that Canada should see the arrival of her Governor-General and Captain-General surrounded with as much of the form of grandeur as was due to his commission. So until the 29th the *Hastings* lay at anchor, 'amid', as Lady Durham noted in her journal, 'a whole fleet of men-of-war and under the guns of a magnificent fortress'. When the day came, the men-of-war were dressed over-all as the barge carrying the Governor-General passed through them and the batteries of the Fort of St. Louis roared in salute as he stepped ashore.

The Canadians had seen no such pageantry before. On the quay the guard of honour stood at the present and their band played the National Anthem. Then horses' hooves clattered on the cobble-stones as the mounted escort wheeled into position and the horses for the Governor-General and his suite were led forward. Lord Durham's horse was white, his staff wore the full dress uniforms of their regiments, the scarlet of the Guards and the Line, the blue of Hussars and Horse Artillery. He himself wore a magnificent uniform, heavily embroidered in silver, and the collar of the Order of the Bath. The crowd stared in amazement, but they raised a cheer as the procession moved off. The cheering grew as they rode through the streets and through the gate of the Fort of St. Louis.

CHAPTER V

The people of Quebec had enjoyed the ceremony and within a few days all Canada knew that a great man had come among them. But they were a hard-headed and suspicious people; they had had much to make them suspicious of anything to do with Britain. They waited to see what lay beneath the colour and the glitter and whether it were really a great man or just another figurehead.

In Quebec itself they had not long to wait. As soon as Lord Durham had taken the Oath, he published his proclamation to the people of Canada. They were stirred and interested and the favourable impression grew, but they were still suspicious— years of neglect and contempt are not wiped out by a few fair words, even though they come from a man with a reputation for fair dealing as well as words. They wanted more than assurance and, within a few hours they got it, when the news of the dismissal of the Council of Lower Canada became public.

Their hope became enthusiasm. It was not that they hated this council more than any other, but that at last someone had done something. Up to date they had had nothing but promises and those few and seldom kept. The new Governor had not been ashore for a day before he had shown them that he meant to act and act decisively.

Their satisfaction was shown in the newspapers during the next few days, and not only in the British papers but also in the French, which might have resented so drastic a dismissal of a predominantly French council. *Le Canadien* reminded its readers that the new Governor had been the leader of the Reform movement at home and that he had brought with him, as his staff, men who had worked in that movement with him. 'It seems', their leading article said, 'that the atmosphere has changed since the arrival of Lord Durham and that a refreshing breeze has reached even the most unfortunate.' The *Montreal Transcript*, a British paper, openly hailed with delight the dismissal of the Council: 'The days of Reform have indeed dawned upon this Colony, and we rejoice in our brightened prospects. . . . We duly appreciate the motives as well as the policy which has actuated the Earl of Durham.'

Le Canadien had spoken of a refreshing breeze, but to those at Quebec who had to carry out Lord Durham's orders it felt more like a hurricane. It had always been Radical Jack's way to go swiftly to the heart of a problem. He disposed in a few hours of the inevitable formalities and turned his attention at once to the most difficult and urgent of his problems, the disposal of the prisoners captured in the late rebellion and held for his decision. They had been arrested when military law was in force and Colborne, who ruled as long as it lasted, had wisely refused to embitter the situation further by a long series of courts-martial. The ordinary process of Canadian civil law would have been futile since he knew well enough that no Lower Canadian jury would convict even those prisoners who had been guilty of murder. The decision was a matter not only of justice but of statesmanship and ought to be left to the statesman who was coming to handle the situation.

The Imperial Parliament had concurred and it had been evident during their debates that they favoured as merciful a solution as possible. But the situation was a difficult one, since the laws must be upheld and rebellion punished. Lord Durham would never have considered courts-martial and was not minded to invite the defiance of Canadian juries. He had to find a solution of his own which should be merciful without being weak and should condemn the crime without destroying the criminals.

Lord Durham already had in mind the idea of a general amnesty which must exclude a few of those prisoners who had been most deeply implicated in the rebellion and, from motives of policy, was anxious to proclaim it on Queen Victoria's Coronation Day, 28 June. He had therefore no more than a month in which to act. Within a few days of his arrival he had consulted the Attorney-General of the province and learned from him of the numbers of prisoners held and released after examination. There were 161 then in gaol awaiting trial and Lord Durham sent for the depositions and the records of them all. He had no mind to dispense justice in bulk and went carefully through the details of every one of the 161 cases.

He called Buller and Turton in to advise him, but he knew that the decision was his alone and he rejected their advice, which was that he should introduce retrospective legislation, to enable him to punish them. Lord Durham refused to consider such an act of injustice. His Commission gave him wide powers to act during the suspension of Lower Canada's constitution and to do all things which had been within the power of the old Administration. He decided to settle this business in his own way and as speedily as possible. After an exhaustive review of all the cases he selected eight men who had been most deeply implicated in the rebellion, on all of whom lay the guilt of loss of life or destruction of property. He resolved to make an example of these eight, but even so, to be merciful. He demanded from them an admission of their guilt, and, on receipt of it, he would inflict no heavier punishment than banishment from the country. All the other prisoners were to be covered by his general amnesty.

It was a novel solution and not perhaps one which would have been approved by a strictly legal mind, since deep suspicion must always lie in cases where prisoners are persuaded to plead guilty. In this case it proved a satisfactory way out of an awkward situation. The British Canadians had been lustily calling for severe punishment for all the prisoners and Lord Durham tactfully sent Buller to explain his intention to them, with the result that they saw the wisdom of it and gave him their support. Buller's next errand was to the eight selected prisoners, who were so much delighted with the idea that they promptly drafted confessions of guilt in terms so impudent that Buller refused to accept them. (One phrase to which he particularly objected was 'if there be guilt in high aspirations, then we confess our guilt'.) Buller pointed out to them that, while Lord Durham was a merciful man, he was not one to tolerate impertinence, and the confessions were redrafted in terms rather less reminiscent of a political manifesto. Buller accepted these and submitted them to Lord Durham, who sentenced the men to life banishment on pain of death should they return to Canada. With some inconsequence—since he had no authority there—he appointed Bermuda as the place for their detention.

It never seems to have occurred to Lord Durham that he had no right to send his exiles there, but equally it never seems to have occurred to the Governor of Bermuda that there was anything odd in the proceeding. Durham was anxious that the whole business of the rebellion should be done away with and forgotten and he did not want to brand the eight scapegoats as felons by consigning them to a convict settlement. Indeed, he wrote to the Governor of Bermuda and asked him to treat them as well as possible short of letting them escape. No one in Canada commented on the selection of the place of exile and indeed the general feeling was one of astonishment and approval for such lenience.

There was one man in England who noted it, though he did not as yet make any public comment. Brougham had never ceased to watch either Melbourne or Durham and the illegality of the use of Bermuda was at once obvious to his legal mind. One of his friends has recorded that when Brougham read the news he rubbed his hands in delight and muttered to himself, 'Now, I've got them.' He had waited so long that he could afford to wait a little longer. Lord Durham's Ordinance was to be published on 28 June. Brougham meant to make no move until it had been made public and there would be no chance of any last-minute alteration.

It is strange that Lord Durham did not trouble himself to send home any details of his decision or to inform the Law Officers of the Crown of any of the depositions or the evidence against the accused. He had settled the business after his own manner and to his own satisfaction and saw no reason to report anything beyond the bare statement of what he had done. He had, it is true, a thousand other things to do and think of, but Buller, his secretary, or Turton, his legal adviser, ought surely to have had the sense to keep him straight on a legal matter and to remind him of the necessity of keeping the Home Government well informed about his actions. Yet the Home Government themselves did not apparently notice the omission until some weeks later when Brougham's sudden attack in the Lords set them searching frantically for any information which would help them to answer it.

Lord Durham was so deeply occupied with other important matters that it is quite possible that, having once settled this business, he forgot all about it. He had barely come to his decision when he was called upon to deal with an incident which might well have broken the already strained relations with the United States. Since the war of 1812 there had been an uneasy peace between the States and Canada and the border line between the two was a constant cause of friction, since there bandits and outlaws from both countries maintained a precarious existence by impartially raiding and plundering on one side or the other of it. Only a few hours after his arrival in Canada there had been an especially flagrant case of piracy, when a Canadian steamer, the *Sir Robert Peel*, which had tied up at a landing on the United States shore of the St. Lawrence, had been sacked and burned by a gang of ruffians who then fled into the States. Lord Durham saw at once that such an incident might easily be magnified out of all proportion in the atmosphere of suspicion which prevailed between the two countries and he acted with promptness and vigour. He offered a reward of £1,000 to anyone who could help to bring the criminals to justice and sent his brother-in-law, Charles Grey, who was a member of his staff, to Washington, to confer with the President about steps which could be jointly taken to prevent repetitions of such outrages and to discuss combined arrangements for patrolling the border regions by land and water. Grey handled his side of the negotiations with tact and ability and the American President was pleased with Lord Durham's approach and suggestion of co-operation. Lord Durham had been an ambassador and knew how much depends on the creation of a friendly atmosphere by personal contact. The Americans, on their side, were astonished by a Governor-General of Canada who seemed to realize the common bonds and interests of them both. The result was not only that free-booting on the border practically ceased from that moment but that the relations between Canada and the States began to improve. The improvement went steadily forward as long as Lord Durham was in Canada.

In spite of these distractions at the beginning of his mission, Durham had at once set in hand the work of reorganizing Canada's economy and administration and had set up a number of sub-commissions dealing with Crown Lands, immigration, law, and education, in which Buller and Turton found themselves fully engaged. Durham himself took in hand the formation of a police force, since he had found on his arrival that in the big cities there was nothing better than an antiquated system of Town Watch, as up to date and as efficient as Dogberry and Verges. He took as his model Peel's Metropolitan Police and, by the end of June, barely a month after his arrival, the system was becoming general throughout Lower Canada, from which it soon spread into the other provinces.

The Twenty-eighth of June was the day of Queen Victoria's coronation and on this day Lord Durham published his ordinance announcing a general amnesty for all who had taken part in the rebellion and promulgating sentence of banishment on the eight men of whom he had made an exception. There were also mentioned by name eight others who had been implicated but had managed to escape from Canada without being arrested. These sixteen were to be 'subjected to such restraint as may be needful to prevent their return to this province. . . .'; should they return without permission of the Governor, they 'shall, on conviction of being so found at large or coming within the said province', be declared guilty of high treason and 'suffer death accordingly'.

Lord Durham referred to his Ordinance in a private letter which he wrote to the Queen, congratulating her on her coronation, in which he said:

'I have been able to do this in your Majesty's name, without danger, because I have in my own done all that sound policy required in the way of punishment and security. Not one drop of blood has been shed. The guilty have received justice, the misguided mercy.'

It seemed, at this moment, that a difficult situation had been adroitly and humanely handled. The people of Canada recognized the generosity of the solution and the Press were almost unanimous in Lord Durham's praise. 'From that hour,' Buller wrote, 'the feelings of national jealousy and political sympathy gave way to that of admiration of Lord Durham.'

At home there was silence. The Government saw no wrong in the solution or in the Ordinance which ended it. Only Brougham rubbed his hands and turned again to the reading of precedents and the examination of relations with Bermuda and of Lord Durham's commission. Joseph Parkes had not been wrong in his simile of the tiger growling in the jungle. Now it was ready to spring.

In Canada all looked favourable. People realized that the new Governor was indeed a man of action and of mercy, and more of them were coming to know him personally, as night after night the windows of Fort St. Louis were ablaze with candle-light and the band played in the musicians' gallery while the Governor-General received his guests. Odd guests they were, some of them, as Lady Durham noted in her diary, for her husband had broken through the custom of entertaining only the official clique of Quebec, and Canadians of various backgrounds and wide social circles moved through the great rooms and gazed admiringly at 'the buffet spread with a maroon cloth' on which Lord Durham's racing trophies were displayed. The company were French and British, merchants and attorneys, soldiers and clergy, racing men and editors. 'The ladies,' Lady Durham remarked, 'had all done their best in dressing and were smarter than I expected, but seemed in a great fright.' And once, 'the highest person present', whom Lord Durham took in to dinner, 'attacked a plateful of jelly with a knife'.

Lady Durham was a charming hostess and hers was no light task, for the entertainment was incessant. In one of her letters to her mother, written many weeks after landing, she remarked that she had 'never seen Lambton dine out of uniform since they had arrived'. At present his health was good. He had had no neuralgia since that bout on board the *Hastings*, though once, a few weeks later, he ran a high temperature for days and the doctors could find no reason for it. Certainly the physical strain on him must have been immense, for his life was one round of meetings, conferences, and audiences, with those endless receptions where he must stand for hours in dress coat and high stock and at which he must eat interminable dinners and drink innumerable toasts. Yet when, at the end of June, they left Quebec for a tour of the provinces, Lady Durham was able to write to her mother: 'During all this time, he was generally well in health and in good spirits, pleased with the prospect of success.'

That letter is dated 2 July. On the same date, in his room at the Colonial Office in London, Lord Glenelg was writing another letter, to tell the Governor-General that the news of Mr. Turton's appointment had been given to Parliament and that the Tories were snarling again. (Brougham who had been very quiet and mysterious lately, had spoken to someone of a motion which he hoped to introduce in the Lords before the end of the month.)

CHAPTER VI

By the end of June Lord Durham's tremendous energy had accomplished so much of the preliminary work in Quebec, that he felt himself free to visit other parts of the colony, and early in July he set out on a tour which was to include Montreal, Western Canada, Kingstown, Niagara, and Queenstown. He was anxious to make a personal investigation of the transport systems of the provinces and, when he stopped at Buffalo, was particularly struck by the possibilities of the Welland Canal system. He instantly conceived the idea of a network of canals to link up the provinces and to provide cheap transport for goods both to and from the ports. This would undoubtedly be a slow method, but hardly slower than the hopeless tangle of unmetalled roads and the infrequent coaches for travellers and waggons for goods. He wrote at once to Glenelg asking him to propose to Parliament an immediate subsidy for opening the canals. It would cost a fabulous sum, but Lord Durham always looked on expenditure with the complaisant eye of a man who had never gone short of anything because he could not afford it. Glenelg had had a less expansive background and, in any case, was always in favour of doing nothing when possible. He promised to give the idea his attention and, in the meantime, gave Durham quite unnecessary permission to go on with his inquiries. Lord Durham, who knew both Glenelg and Parliament, was not to be put off with assurances, and so persisted that eventually Parliament agreed to send out a Colonel Philpott to make a report and submit estimates, which led to the grant of a sum substantial enough to begin the work and carry it some way towards completion. Few things during the whole of this time more impressed the merchants and manufacturers of Canada than the spectacle of a Governor who made such rapid decisions and insisted on the funds to carry them out being provided. They had seen enough of timid requests and contemptuous refusals. A Governor-General who sent a request to Parliament for hundreds of thousands of pounds as calmly as though he were sending an order to his hatter was an agreeable novelty.

One thing which was always in Lord Durham's mind was the furtherance of good relations with the United States, and, while he was on this tour, he took the opportunity of being at Niagara to make a demonstration of his goodwill, and accomplished in one day more than any previous Governor had attempted in a year.

15 July should be a memorable day in the history of North American relationships, for on that day for the first time a British Governor-General crossed the border and stood on American soil.

Those few days at Niagara, days which passed in a whirl of hospitality and a lavish display of military and civil ceremony, marked the highest point of Lord Durham's success and popularity in the New World. The scene on the Canadian bank of the river was like that of some high military occasion in Hyde Park or on Brighton Racecourse in the spacious days of the Prince Regent, when Lieutenant Lambton had been a subaltern in the 10th Hussars. The rising ground to the northward was white with the canvas of the camps of the King's Dragoon Guards and the 43rd foot. Day came in to the reveille of the cavalry trumpets and went out on the skirling of the highland pipes. Sir John Colborne and Sir George Arthur, the Lieutenant-Governor of Upper Canada, were in attendance on the Governor-General as he reviewed the troops on the flat ground below the encampments, where the roar of the falls sounded a *basso ostinato* below the shrilling of trumpet and fife.

Hundreds of men and women had crossed the river from the American side to see the display and for all of them Lord Durham had provided hospitality in his most princely style. Later Buchanan, the British Consul at New York, wrote to Colonel Cooper, Lord Durham's military secretary: 'The most violent democrats here are loudest in praise of Lord Durham's courteous manner and of his "Lordly Court", as they term the banquet they partook of at the Falls.'

The 'Lordly Court' was held on 17 July, two days after Lord and Lady Durham had crossed into American territory as the guests of the officer commanding Fort Niagara. There were anxious watchers on the Canadian bank when the Governor-General and his Lady, accompanied by the staff in full dress uniform, but without any escorting troops went over to the other side of the river. Sir John Colborne and Sir George Arthur were frankly apprehensive for their safety since the border district, though there had been little trouble there lately, was notoriously the home and refuge of fugitives and bad characters from both countries. Lady Durham, describing the scene to her mother, wrote: 'If Lambton had regularly consulted Sir John Colborne and the others he would have advised against it. . . . We heard afterwards that as soon as it was known we were gone across our return would have been watched for with some anxiety in Niagara.' It was not Lord Durham's habit to ask for advice about his own movements and, even had Colborne attempted to dissuade him, it would certainly have made no difference. As for Lady Durham, her place was always by her husband's side. However anxious she might be for him, she was fearless for herself.

But the anxiety was needless. The reception which greeted them was enthusiastic. Lady Durham remarked that some of the American men even removed their hats when she passed—

a common courtesy which, in their rather ostentatious reverence for democracy, they were reluctant to pay to anyone. 'There is no question indeed,' Coupland writes, 'that Durham's policy and personality went far to neutralize American sympathy with the Canadian rebellions and once again, on another continent, to prevent a war which to many observers, including the British Minister at Washington, had seemed imminent.'

Lord Durham's bold gesture had gained immediate and lasting success, and the British Consul at New York and Minister at Washington were left wondering at the effect which could be made on a truculent democracy by a combination of public display and personal charm. It was no surprise to Radical Jack, who knew more about democracy than any of them.

But there was one thing on which Lord Durham could never safely rely and that was his reserve of strength. After the visit to Niagara, he began to show the first signs, since his arrival, that his responsibility and the vigour which he brought to all his work were beginning to make too great a drain on its slender margin of safety. Neuralgic pains attacked him again and at Toronto, where next he stopped, he was in continual agony, though he went steadily through an exhausting programme of formalities. On his last full day there, he had to make three long public speeches and on the following morning he was receiving deputations and individuals until it was time for him to leave in the afternoon. In addition to all these, he was often writing despatches until the early hours of the morning, and, though he completed his programme at Toronto and went on to Montreal, he had to abandon the rest of his tour and return to Quebec. By this time he was utterly exhausted and Lady Durham was in continual anxiety about him.

There is little wonder that he should have suffered under the strain, for, in addition to the heavy load of his official duties, he was never free from the nagging knowledge that in England his enemies were once more baying after him. News had reached him of the Parliamentary debates about Turton and Wakefield, and from both Melbourne and Glenelg had come letters, ostensibly of warning and help, which showed something near to panic. If he had been in good health, he might have ignored these petty annoyances, but, as it was, they were an intolerable addition to the rest of his anxieties. Though he did not yet

know it, there was much worse to come. On 30 July, while he
lay in a darkened room in Fort St. Louis, prostrated by pain
and weariness, Brougham rose in the House of Lords to call
attention to the Ordinance of 27 June, of which he remarked,
that 'if the Noble Earl had given effect to it, he would have
been guilty of murder'.

If the activities of the Tory Party in the Imperial Parliament,
during the first weeks of Lord Durham's mission, make sorry
reading, those of the Whigs are no more creditable. Both
parties had at least one idea in common, their determination to
subordinate Crown, Empire, and Country to the immediate
chance of snatching or dodging a party victory or defeat. The
only difference between them was that the Tories saw in Lord
Durham's actions a chance of pulling down the Government,
while the Whigs were prepared to support him up to the point
when to do so might involve their own downfall. It seems in-
credible that men of the standing and traditions of Winchilsea,
Chandos, Wharncliffe, and Harrowby, should have continued
to harass a man who was undertaking so vital a task for his
Queen. Yet early in July, as soon as Lord Durham's despatch
had announced the appointment of Turton, they resumed their
role as the nation's conscience and renewed the attacks which
had been for a few weeks suspended. Once again Melbourne's
parliamentary skill won him a tactical victory, but once again
it was devoted to proving that he himself was not to blame and
that all the guilt was Lord Durham's. Melbourne had had a bad
fright as his letters to Lord Durham show. On 2 July he wrote:

'I have been questioned to-night in the House of Lords upon
the subject by Lord Wharncliffe, and I could not, of course,
say otherwise than that I had heard of the appointment with
great concern and surprise. . . . I could not say other nor less
than this, because I must own it appears to me so wonderful
that you should have done this so hastily so precipitately and
so entirely without consultation.'

Two days later Glenelg wrote more formally and at greater
length but in the same sense.

Lord Durham replied at once to both letters, though, unhappily his letter to Melbourne has been lost, or, more probably, destroyed by its recipient. His letter to Glenelg is

uncompromising. He does not try to shelve the responsibility for the appointment but reminds Glenelg that he had told Melbourne before leaving England that he had decided to make it; 'I am not, therefore, aware that Her Majesty's Government are called upon to take any cognizance whatever of Mr. Turton's appointment which, neither as to nomination or salary, can ever come under their notice.'

The claim that Turton's appointment was none of the Government's business has an agreeable touch of the old familiar arrogance, and he concludes with a stinging rebuke to them for their failure to give him the support which they had promised.

'You will allow me, my lord, to say that I also on my part, observe with great surprise and regret the tone which Her Majesty's Government adopted in the debates in the House of Lords to which you refer me. While the highest situations in the Empire have been and still are held by those who have had the misfortune to be convicted of adultery, it is most unjust to denounce and to devote to destruction the holder of a petty office, merely because he is without political friends of influence. I feel "surprise and regret" that Her Majesty's Government did not, at the outset, expose the hypocrisy of this proceeding and ascribe it to its true cause—the desire to embarrass political opponents and not a regard for that morality which has repeatedly been violated without compunction or remonstrance.'

As Lord Durham truly said, Turton's was a petty office and the whole affair was a petty one which Melbourne could have afforded to treat with contempt. It was not likely that the Government would have felt called upon to resign, even had they been beaten over so obviously trivial and factious a cause. But Melbourne saw danger to himself everywhere and continued to harass Lord Durham with letters about Turton written in terms of mounting anger and rebuke. 'Only consider,' he wrote on 18 July, 'how you injure your own private character by the association of such men with yourself and your family. Only consider how you injure the Queen, whose age and character demand some respect and reverence.' He added a plain warning that 'you must be prepared for the result of any motion in Parliament on the subject. I am prepared to resist such a motion; but if it should be carried, I hope that you will be prepared to acquiesce in it.'

Melbourne could hardly have made his meaning plainer. If a motion were introduced, he would make a formal resistance. If it should be carried Lord Durham would be expected to resign to save the Whig Government.

It is clear that the possibility of Durham's resignation was being openly discussed in London, hopefully by his enemies and with anxiety by his few friends. Joseph Parkes wrote to him at this moment:

> 'Under the circumstances of Lord Melbourne's last dis-
> claimer and rebuke of you the question with all your friends
> is what course you can wisely take—your enemies and
> political opponents hoping that you will throw up and
> return. We, who know you, know that you will disappoint
> them. . . .'

Lord Durham's friends were more right than his enemies. Many men might have felt themselves unable to stay at their work under such persecution from at home, and in face of such an obvious threat of betrayal by those who should have supported them. Durham's enemies relied on their memory of the old, haughty Radical Jack of a few years ago, not knowing how time and experience had altered him, and how adversity had taught him to subdue his natural resentment and curb his temper. Least of all did they guess how Canada now held him so that everything in him was devoted to the accomplishment of the work which he had set out to do. He had said what he had to say about the Turton business and now he dismissed it from his mind. There were greater things at stake than the appointment of a minor official, the danger of a political party or even than his own pride. On 9 August he sent home a preliminary report on all that he had done and observed since his landing in Canada. It was a long and detailed document and laid the foundations of his later Report, though it is more a narrative of events than a plan for future policy. The policy was taking shape in his mind but he felt that he had hardly gathered enough information to enable him to formulate one at this stage. Critics have found the despatch of 9 August incomplete, as indeed it must be, since he had only been two months in Canada and had spent nearly the whole of those, of necessity, in Lower Canada. They have found in it, too, the prejudice in favour of British over French methods, which is still evident in the Report. But the consideration of his policy is best left until it is time to consider the Report which was the final expression and explanation of it. The despatch of 9 August was meant to be nothing more than an interim report to keep the Home Government posted about the day-to-day condition of Canada, and of the matters which first needed attention. It was received with politeness rather than enthusiasm by the Government, who felt the uncomfortable danger of having to take some sort of action.

CHAPTER VII

On 28 July—and before the first mutterings of the trouble which was brewing in Parliament—Lord Melbourne wrote to Lord Durham a letter in which he warmly expressed his approval of the Ordinance:

'I am most obliged to you for what you have written to me, which is most distinct, clear and—to me—satisfactory. I have not time to do more than acknowledge it—I have nothing to express but the most entire approval and concurrence. I am very happy to hear that you have settled the very difficult affair of the prisoners and settled it so well.'

He mentioned that there might be some difficulty in dealing with the prisoners in Bermuda, where, as he truly said, 'Your Ordinance will have no validity nor confer any power', but treated it lightly, saying that, 'We must deal with them as well as we can there'. It is plain that the only difficulty which he anticipated would be in Bermuda itself, and that he had no idea of the impending attack at home. He even paid Lord Durham the great compliment of adding: 'There can be no doubt of the feeling of satisfaction that prevails in the province—it must be like a sudden transition from the discord of Hell to the peace of Heaven.' Glenelg too wrote on the 31st, the day after the first attack began in Parliament:

'You will see by the papers that our old enemies attacked your ordinance and proclamation last night. These attacks are after all impotent in this country. . . . All reasonable people approve your conduct. . . . My colleagues and I entirely approve—our opinion is that, although there may be some legal inaccuracies of form, the substance is entirely right and the result satisfactory. You have solved a very difficult question most judiciously and ably, in a way at once merciful and just, and equally grateful to rival parties and impartial judges. I congratulate you on this—and on the confidence which, I hear on all sides, all classes in Canada repose in you. Go on and prosper. . . .'

That was how they wrote when they had no reason to expect that the attacks on the Ordinance would be anything more than a party formality. It is interesting to note, in view of Melbourne's complaint later that Durham had kept him in ignorance of his proceedings, that at this time, his information is 'most distinct, clear and satisfactory'. Unfortunately both he and Glenelg were very soon to change their tune, when they found themselves involved in danger and in the possibility of defeat.

On 6 August, Brougham rose in the Lords to give notice of his intention to introduce a motion on the Ordinance and, two days later, he came forward with his Bill 'for declaring the true import of the Act . . . and for indemnifying those who have issued or acted under a certain ordinance made under colour of the said Act'.

Brougham, that experienced jurist, had chosen his ground well. The Act to which he referred was that which had defined the powers of Lord Durham and his council in Lower Canada. Ostensibly his was an offer to rectify any mistake that they might have made and to prevent any repercussions on them. Actually it amounted to a direct attack on Lord Durham and the freedom with which it offered pardon and oblivion to everybody could hardly have been exceeded had they all been conspiring to commit the most hideous crimes.

Also, that there might be no mistake about its real meaning, he inserted in the preamble, some recommendations for curbing Lord Durham's powers in the future, which would have reduced him to the status of a clerk and robbed him of all authority and initiative. On the following day, when the Bill came up for second reading, Brougham spoke at length and with all his old skill and force, asserting the illegality of the whole method of dealing with the prisoners and denying—in face of all the evidence—that they had pleaded guilty. He spoke of the illegality of using Bermuda as a place of detention and, most bitterly, of the threat that the prisoners would be executed if they returned to Canada.

The Government were in a difficult, but not by any means an impossible position, and, had they showed any real fight, they would probably have won. They were fortified by the opinion of the Law Lords who agreed that the whole Ordinance was perfectly correct with the small exception of the use of Bermuda—and this was a detail which could have been set right by a simple Bill to amend that part of the Ordinance. Brougham, in his anxiety to seem fair, had by accident been fair, and the Bill stated that the Ordinance was 'so much for the service of the public that it ought to be justified by Act of Parliament'. The Government could easily have accepted the principle expressed that the whole Ordinance was so merciful and just that they could only confirm it and at the same time introduce an amendment to regulate the purely formal mistake about Bermuda.

The lamentable fact is that they did nothing of the sort and the even more lamentable reason is that they were only thinking of their own safety. They would not risk a defeat which, since this was a matter of great importance, would have necessitated their resignation. Their defeat was not certain, not, at that moment, even probable. But had it been certain, it would not have meant the end of the world for them, only a temporary loss of power. It would surely have been more tolerable to men of spirit and decency than deserting the man to whom they had promised 'the most unflinching support'. Whatever they might have lost in power or place would have been a small thing in comparison with what they actually did lose, their reputation and their honour.

At the beginning of the debate it seemed that they were going to put up a good fight, for Glenelg, who followed Brougham, spoke with much more spirit than was usual and seemed to take the line that Brougham's Bill had admitted expediency and that all that Parliament had to do was to clear up the details and put them in order. The effect of his speech was spoiled on the next day by one of Melbourne's rare Parliamentary blunders. He was a good fighter for any cause—and there were not many—in which he believed, but he did not believe in Lord Durham and he was still only remotely interested in Canada. His great mistake was that he allowed his irritation with the Tory peers to overcome his prudence and attacked them in a personal and violent way which did no good to his own cause and stiffened the Opposition. The gravest consequence of it was that it brought the Duke of Wellington into the field against him, and the Duke still had enormous influence in Parliament and outside. Melbourne had told the peers that they had laid a trap for Lord Durham and went on: 'It is acting in a dangerous spirit; it is not acting like a high-minded and generous nobility, but more like a low and truculent democracy.'

The Duke had abstained from any of the petty attacks which had been aimed at Lord Durham, knowing, perhaps better than anyone, what a weight rested on the shoulders of a high official in a distant land. He had never had any taste for the guerilla warfare of party politics, but this was a matter of importance and he could hardly keep aloof from it. Great and good man though he was, there was always in his mind a trace of the military rigidity which makes a divine commandment out of a written order. If there had been an illegality, he would never favour an attempt to put it right in what he probably thought of as a hole-and-corner way. And, above all, he was not going to be accused of setting traps, still less of behaving like a 'low and truculent democracy'.

He had watched, with some misgiving but without criticism, some of Lord Durham's actions in Canada, especially his high-handed way of appointing his own council. But he knew the stories of Clive and Hastings, and his own brother had been Governor-General of India. He knew—and this made his intervention the more damning—that whatever happens abroad the responsibility rests with the Home Government in the first place for appointing the man abroad and in the second for the extent to which they have guided, helped, and supported him.

His speech was short and moderate in tone and he scrupulously refrained from criticism of Lord Durham. He explained his abstention from any earlier expression of opinion, but stated plainly that an illegality had been committed and must be annulled. The blame, he said, lay with the Government, who 'by themselves neglected to perform the duty which the Act laid upon them and which required them to superintend with care and attention the formation of the Council and the proceedings of the Governor'.

It was an honourable and characteristic point of view, based on a lifetime of experience and it carried more weight with the House than any other speech that was made. The Government had lost all hope of passing the illegality off as a trifling mistake which was all Lord Durham's fault. They knew that they must take responsibility for everything that had happened in Canada, because whatever he did, he had done in their name.

Melbourne knew that, unless he could contrive some unforeseen way of escape, he was beaten. In his reply, he contented himself with a hasty denial of having made any personal accusation against the Duke. Brougham knew better than to press the debate further. The Duke had done for him all that was needed and he was too shrewd a fighter to waste ammunition which might be needed at a later stage.

The House divided on the second reading, and, out of a total of ninety votes, there was a majority of eighteen in favour of the Bill. The news was given to the Press and caused a sensation in London and the country whence it travelled as fast as was possible in those days to the United States. But nearly a fortnight elapsed before it occurred to either Melbourne or Glenelg to write to Lord Durham to tell him the result.

CHAPTER VIII

On 19 August, Lady Durham wrote in her diary an unusually long and detailed account of a summer's day spent with her husband and family. 'We were a merry party . . . enjoying the little adventures and difficulties of crossing the ferry, laughing at Mr. Cavendish and his drag following us and delighted with the beauties of the scenery.'

As they drove homeward and climbed the heights above Quebec, they saw below them the whole width of the bay. A ship was coming in and someone remarked that it was probably bringing mail from England. The drive had been a long one and they were late. Lady Durham was expecting guests for dinner. She hurried upstairs to dress and, before she had finished, her husband knocked at her door and asked her to come into his room. There the official mail-bag lay on the table with a few folded newspapers beside it. Lady Durham knew that her husband was expecting trouble at home about his Ordinance and this must be the first news of it. She was reassured by the letters from Melbourne and Glenelg in which they stated their entire approval, but her comfort was to be short-lived. Lord Durham handed her one of the newspapers and she learned—as he had learned—for the first time of his defeat from the columns of an American journal.

'I can well remember now,' she wrote, 'the feeling of consternation which came over me on first hearing the news and then of grief for him and indignation and bitter resentment towards those who had so cruelly betrayed him. He said but little, but I was the more unhappy, and, when he finished his dressing and went with little delay to dinner, behaving as usual, my heart ached.'

Brougham's Indemnity Bill had passed its second reading, leaving Melbourne with a hard choice. He could introduce his own Bill to amend Lord Durham's technical errors and stand to fight on that ground, risking his own position on it; or he could throw Lord Durham over and save himself. The choice was, in fact, between the possible loss of his power and the certain loss of his honour. Being Melbourne, he did not hesitate.

On 9 August, speaking against the Bill, he had said:

'When I consider that the disallowing of the ordinances would be destructive of the Noble Lord's government and almost the same as pronouncing the termination of the connection between it and the Colony and throwing everything loose to every chance of confusion, I cannot, with my regard for the prosperity of the Country, be a party to that course. . . . I therefore cannot accede to the proposition of the Noble and Learned Lord and shall, most unquestionably, vote against the second reading of the Bill.'

Melbourne's regard for the prosperity of the country did not survive a night's reflection. On the following day, he announced that 'My colleagues and I have come to the determination to disallow the Ordinance'.

Parliamentary history provides few instances of so prompt and complete a volte-face. Brougham had defeated Melbourne and not only that but thoroughly frightened him, for he remarked to Russell: 'The fact is, my dear John, the fellow was in such a state that if I had opposed him, he would have gone stark, staring mad.' Not even Melbourne's skill could hide the contrast between his brave words of the 9th and his abject surrender the next day. If ever a Prime Minister betrayed a colleague to save his own position, it was Lord Melbourne. He pleaded for an alteration in the preamble of the Bill which would make it less offensive to Durham, and Brougham, who had won his battle and had no mind to insist on details, gave way.

There was a short and undistinguished debate during which Melbourne made one more half-hearted effort when he proposed an amendment which would strengthen Lord Durham's hand for the future and allow him most of the powers which had originally been granted to him. The House showed signs of objection, and again Melbourne cravenly capitulated: 'After what has fallen from Noble Lords, I shall not press my amendment.' The Bill had become a government measure and it fell to Russell, as leader of the Commons, to introduce it there. No man ever had to sponsor a measure more unwillingly, or did it with less conviction, and his speech was the most sincere and moving vindication of Lord Durham which was heard in either House.

'And I do say,' he ended, 'that if the province of Upper Canada is preserved to this country—that if, the insurrection being suppressed, the punishment of death can be altogether avoided in practice and that, if we shall be able to restore to that province the enjoyment of a free constitution—I do think that no invective—that no sophistry—that no accumulation of circumstances—that no bitterness of sarcasm—

accompanied by protestations of friendship and thereby attempting to disguise, but not, in fact, disguising the petty and personal feelings which are at the bottom of these attacks—will in the least degree affect the Noble Earl against whom they have been levelled, but that he will have deserved well of his country, well of his sovereign and well of posterity.'

It was a generous tribute from an old colleague who, though he had never been a close friend, had shared with Lord Durham the virtues of loyalty and courage, and later Durham wrote to him to thank him for his advocacy. (It was also perhaps one of the oddest methods of proposing a Bill which had ever been heard.)

The mail-bag which Lord Durham received on 19 August contained the American paper which gave him the first news of this betrayal, but there was no official news from Melbourne or Glenelg, other than their approving letters of the end of July.

As soon as he heard the news, Lord Durham realized that his usefulness in Canada was at an end. The Home Government had disallowed his first great act of public policy and there was no guarantee that they would not again act in the same way. As Melbourne himself had said, they had destroyed the Noble Lord's government. That night Durham told Buller that he would resign. It was the decision which any man might have made in the heat and humiliation of the moment and his enemies soon accused him of having acted through personal vanity and pique. Everything that he did the next day and until the day of his departure refutes the slander. On the 20th he wrote to Colborne and told him that he would resign as soon as he received official confirmation of the disallowance. Colborne would then be the senior British official in Canada, and it was only prudent and courteous to give him as much notice as possible. Two days later he announced his decision to a conference of representatives of the Maritime Provinces, which he had summoned some time before.

All the time, there was a clear distinction in his mind between resigning and leaving Canada. He would, of course, resign at once. No Governor-General could continue to hold office on terms which reduced him to the status of a clerk, as no gentleman could continue to serve a government which had proved itself so unworthy of trust. They had publicly shamed him and he would as publicly refute them, but he had no intention of leaving Canada until he saw fit.

Also his enemies overlooked the fact that he had a perfect right to terminate his mission whenever he thought proper. He had insisted when he undertook it that it should be only temporary and no time had been set for his stay in Canada. If, as he felt, he was useless out there, he was right in refusing to stay any longer.

And this was the most compelling reason of all, for his vision of Canada within the Empire was as strong as ever and he had begun to see that, while other men might finish in Canada what he had begun, no one but he could fight her battle in the home Parliament, and that this would be the most important and not the least difficult part of his task. Melbourne and Glenelg would be half-hearted if not worse. Russell would no doubt do his best, but he had no great knowledge of the subject and had in the past shown indifferent sympathy with the colonists. Only Lord Durham himself would avail, because only he had both the knowledge and the compelling desire to see justice done. And, whatever might be the cause which Radical Jack supported, it was never likely to be ignored, or to lack forceful advocacy. His place now, he realized, was in England, nor was he at all deterred, as many men might have been, by the storm which he had aroused there. Any storm was better than the flat torpor in which Britain had lately conducted her colonial affairs.

The storm in Canada which greeted the news of the disallowance of the Ordinance was far greater than the breeze at home. With hardly one exception, the whole Press of Upper and Lower Canada cried out in protest and in condemnation of the British Government. The colonists, being not at all concerned with the strife of parties in Britain, judged the Ordinance on its own merits and they found it to be an act of mercy and wisdom. They saw in the attitude of the home Parliament one more proof that it was futile to expect justice or even attention from Britain. It was one more repetition of the old story of Parliamentary obstruction and national indifference. The Quebec *Gazette* remarked that a prospect already gloomy had been made gloomier than ever: 'We see in the conduct of those noble Lords who supported Lord Brougham's bill, either an utter ignorance of the state of Canadas, or, worse, a disregard for the preservation of this important part of the Empire.'

The Montreal *Herald* said that, 'The Canadas appear to be a trump card in the hands of the political gamblers in the Imperial Parliament.' The Montreal *Gazette* commiserated with Lord Durham on serving a government who 'have neither the power to support him in the exercise of his public functions nor the courage to defend him and themselves from the factious insults of party politicians or the more infamous inroads of personal and jealous enemies'. *Le Canadien* spoke of 'noble Lords sitting tranquilly in their comfortable senatorial chairs, who have transformed the Canadian question into a plaything or weapon of party'.

In both the Canadas meetings were held and addresses sent to Lord Durham, begging him not to take the disallowance to heart and not to abandon his work, and letters flowed in from men of influence in local politics and business. The streets of the towns were crowded with marches of protest and on the evening of the 25th, Brougham was burned in effigy in the Place d'Armes at Quebec. (At the same time, the effigy of Lord Glenelg was displayed, not altogether unreasonably, as fast asleep.) Canada's anger was great in proportion as her hopes had been high. At last Britain had sent them a man who did more than sit in Quebec making vague promises, a man who went about and saw for himself and who had already done, on his own responsibility, more than any previous governor had attempted. Now Britain had disowned him. One most dangerous symptom of the general unrest was that several papers and assemblies said openly that, if this was all that Canada had to expect, she would be better off under the United States of America.

There seems to have been a general expectation both at home and in Canada that Lord Durham would refuse to stomach such an insult and that he would at once go home and wash his hands of Canada. The frequency and urgency of the entreaties which were addressed to him not to abandon the cause are a measure of the confidence which he had won in so short a time. He found himself even more popular than he had been in England at the time of the Reform Bill and it must have been a temptation to him to give way to the entreaties and to stay with the people who so sorely needed him. He could have done it. He could have submitted to the disallowance, knowing that no one in Canada would blame him for it, and that the Home Government would not recall him if they could help it. He could have gone on with his programme of reforms, his works of justice and economy, his roads and his canals, his schools and his immigration schemes. He could have done infinite good in Canada and have won for himself a name as the greatest and best-loved Governor that had ever ruled there. With such a wealth of support and confidence in the colony, he could have afforded to ignore the criticism and abuse of enemies at home.

But Radical Jack saw—had always seen—a little further than most of either friends or enemies, and his vision was not bounded by Canada's immediate prosperity or even happiness, but was of a free Canada. If he stayed with them and rode out the storm, he could give them almost any benefit except their freedom. That he could only win for them in the Imperial Parliament and among the people of Britain. It was the same cause for which he fought now as when he had won Reform at home— the right of a people to choose their own representatives, to be treated as reasonable adults and not as children to be rewarded with treats and presents.

He had already made up his mind to resign, but he took no official action until the 25th, when Melbourne's and Glenelg's letters telling him of the disallowance reached him. During that week he had written his own despatches to them telling them of his decision and most forcibly expressing his own view about their treatment of him. He sent these letters off to England on the same day as that which brought the official letters from the Prime Minister and the Colonial Secretary.

Glenelg's letter was brief and formal, but Melbourne allowed himself to indulge in his new taste for preaching. His letter was little more than an attempt to shift all the blame from his own shoulders, and he complained bitterly that Lord Durham had starved him of information about the prisoners who had pleaded guilty and about his own procedure—a complaint which accords strangely with his earlier remark that 'what you have written is most clear, distinct and—to me—satisfactory'. Now he wrote in quite different terms, that 'we laboured under great disadvantages from the very scanty information which you afforded us'; 'you could not fail to be sensible how much you were exceeding all former precedents.' He ended with an appeal to Lord Durham to 'persevere in it until you have accomplished the object of your mission'. One sentence in the letter is worth recording: 'We have,' Melbourne wrote, 'supported you with all our might.'

Melbourne's appeal to Lord Durham to stay in Canada was genuine enough. The last thing that he wanted was the return of an indignant and vengeful Durham, burning to overturn the Government and probably having enough following to do it. He wrote to Russell:

'Durham will either throw up at once, or he will hurry his measures very much, which he is otherwise inclined to do, and then insist on coming home immediately. He will concoct a general arrangement by the end of October, send it home, follow it himself, boast of the effect he produced while there and, if it is thrown out, will afterwards say that it is all owing to the manner in which he has been treated; in saying which he will have a good deal of colour if not of truth.'

Russell was an unsympathetic audience for abuse of Lord Durham. A few days later he wrote: 'No one can say that he [Durham] is not justified by the course of the House of Lords over the Indemnity Bill.'

On the 25th, 26th, and 27th, Lord Durham sent the three letters which he had already prepared while awaiting the official despatches from England. They are temperate in tone and confined to a factual account of all the actions which had led up to the Ordinance. No doubt it would have been better if he had sent them as soon as he had decided his course of action, though one may question whether it would have made any difference to the outcome or whether Melbourne would have tried to put up a better fight. In none of the three is there a trace of personal resentment or anger, but he would have been less than human—and certainly less than Radical Jack—if he had refrained from any word of his personal feelings, and he expressed them in a private letter to Glenelg, which accompanied the official despatches.

'I am bound to tell you privately that I never could have anticipated the possibility of such treatment as I have received. Having succeeded far beyond my most sanguine hopes, in restoring tranquillity and inspiring confidence, all over the Continent of North America, I little expected the reward I have received from home—disavowal and condemnation. . . . In these circumstances, I have no business here—My authority is gone—all that rests is military power, that can be better wielded by a soldier. . . .

'I shall appear in Parliament, not to defend my conduct, for it needs no excuse, but to expose the cruelty, injustice and impolicy of those who have trifled with the best interests of these Colonies for purposes of personal enmity or party hostility.'

Finally he expressed his intention of returning as soon as possible by way of America, 'where,' he adds, 'I hope my influence (which, permit me to say, is apparently greater than in the House of Lords or the Cabinet) may be beneficially exerted for the purpose of confirming and extending those friendly feelings towards England, with which I had, at some labour, succeeded in inspiring them'.

There could be no clearer proof of the breadth of Lord Durham's vision than this fact that, in the moment of defeat, he was thinking not only of Canada's problems but of her relations with her neighbour, with whom he had constantly striven to live at peace and on good terms It was one of his first thoughts when he landed in Canada and sent Grey to Washington to confer about the situation on the border. He had done much for it during those few days at Niagara.

He wrote now of returning home by way of America and he had been anxious to visit Washington and so to proclaim the friendship between the two countries. He had already been approached with the idea of a visit and, had he been able to make it, he would have been the first non-American to be entertained at the White House since Lafayette. It can hardly have been a pleasant prospect now, since he would have to appear as a disapproved and retiring official of his country, but that weighed nothing with him in comparison with the good that his visit would do. But the final act of his life in Canada was decided for him. The Government had decided that the disallowance of the Ordinance must be made by public proclamation.

CHAPTER IX

On 9 October Lord Durham issued his proclamation to the peoples of the two Canadas. It was perhaps the most open and honest form of words which had ever been offered to the people of a colony and it was a justification of all his actions and a refutation of all his accusers. He did not spare the Government and he did not try to hide the truth that all his work had been nullified by the petty partisanship of British politicians.

'From the very commencement of my task,' he wrote, 'the minutest details of my administration have been exposed to incessant criticism, in a spirit which has evinced an entire ignorance of the state of this Country.

'Those who have in the British Legislature systematically depreciated my powers, and the Ministers of the Crown by their tacit acquiescence therein, have produced the effect of making it too clear that my authority is inadequate for the emergency which called it into existence.'

He went on to defend his action in the matter of the Ordinance and of Bermuda, adding that he had 'expected the British Parliament to supply the insufficiency in case of need'.

Then followed the passage which aroused more controversy than all the rest, for Lord Durham asserted that, since his amnesty had been disallowed, 'no impediment therefore exists to the return of the persons who have made the most distinct admission of guilt'. In fact, the prisoners, whom he had exiled to Bermuda, had the right to return to Canada whenever they liked. His enemies made much of this permission, but it is hard to see on what grounds. If his Ordinance were to be disallowed, then all its consequences must be annulled and, if it meant the return to Canada of mischievous revolutionaries, it was not his doing but that of those who had gone against his decision. As he said: 'I cannot recall the pledge of Her Majesty's mercy.' It was said that this was an instance of his anxiety to embarrass the Government by giving a free hand to their enemies, when it was nothing but a simple act of justice.

For the rest he spoke in simple terms of all that he had hoped to do and of the obstacles which had been put in his way. Above all, he made it clear that he did not look on his work as finished, but that the most important part of it still lay before him.

'If I can carry into the Imperial Parliament a knowledge derived from personal inspection and experience of their interests, upon which some persons there are too apt to legislate in ignorance or indifference, and can aid in laying the foundation of a system of general government which, while it strengthens your permanent connection with Great Britain, shall save you from the evils to which you are now subjected, by every change in the fluctuating policy of distant and successive administrations.'

To Lord Durham's enemies at home the Proclamation was a godsend, since it gave them an opportunity of attacking him without seeming to be merely factious. Even the British Press, much of which had been inclined to criticize the Government for the Indemnity Bill, now rounded on Lord Durham. *The Times* went so far as to call him the 'Lord High Seditioner' and the *Standard* commented that, 'We cannot think that it has been made in the proper place. The whole paper looks like an appeal from the decision of the Queen and Parliament of Great Britain to the sense, if not the feeling of the people of Canada—surely an unbecoming character for a proclamation issued by the Queen's representative.'

Croker and Greville, both of whom hated Durham, wrote scathingly in their memoirs. 'Lord Durham,' Croker said, 'is coming home in dudgeon because, forsooth, he was protected from the consequences of his own indiscretion and his self-confessed illegal proceedings; but before he came away, he published a manifesto appealing from the Queen, his mistress, and arraigning the British Parliament, his masters, at the tribunal of the Canadian public.'

Greville was even more severe. 'Such an appeal to the people of the Colony over whom he is placed from the acts of the Government and legislature of the mother country is as monstrous as it is unexampled. The dignity of the Government now demands that his insolence and misconduct should be visited with the severest expression of disapprobation and reproof and the harshest measures, even an impeachment would be fully warrantable.'

It is idle to deny that the Proclamation was an appeal from

authority to good sense, from Philip drunk to Philip sober. The critics who made play with the Queen's name forgot that the Government had had small regard for her when they sent out Lord Durham to get rid of him and then betrayed him to save themselves. It can have been no surprise to him that his Proclamation should have been so ill-received at home, but he had long passed the point of thinking of his own position or reputation. He had seen his work in Canada threatened and likely to be nullified for purely party ends, nor was he likely to be impressed by a sudden access of noble sentiments on the part of men who had never hesitated to belittle him and whose interest in Canada was as newfound as it was insincere. What he had done was unprecedented and unconstitutional, but it was, in his view, the only thing to do to save Canada for the Empire and to realize his vision. History, seeing the results, will not hold him guilty.

Inevitably the Government adopted the view that Lord Durham's conduct deserved severe censure, even though they realized that an attempt at impeachment would be inadvisable. It was left to Lord Glenelg to convey their displeasure and, as far as was possible, to dismiss a man who had already resigned —and had indeed, with a touch of his old grandeur, told the Colonial Secretary to arrange for a ship to bring him home when he was ready to leave. Glenelg, in his official despatch, was no doubt inspired by Melbourne, who was going about London muttering threats about 'not truckling to Durham', and wrote with all the consciousness of carrying the heavy guns:

'The terms in which that appeal has been made appear to Her Majesty's Ministers calculated to impair the reverence due to the royal authority, to derogate from the character of the Imperial legislature, to excite amongst the disaffected hopes of impunity and to enhance the difficulties with which your Lordship's successor will have to contend. The ministers of the Crown, having humbly submitted this opinion to the Queen, it is my duty to inform you that I have received Her Majesty's commands to signify to your Lordship Her Majesty's disapproval of your proclamation of the 9th of October. Under these circumstances, Her Majesty's government are prepared to admit that your continuance in the government of British North America could be attended with no beneficial results.'

Melbourne had already been looking for a successor to Lord Durham and had decided to offer the post to Powlett Thomson, a Whig of old standing and a man of integrity and ability, who was also, by good fortune, a friend of Lord Durham. (Melbourne was also, though Glenelg did not yet know it, looking for a successor to Glenelg at the Colonial Office.)

For the present Glenelg was troubled by another problem, since Lord Durham, in his proclamation, had made it clear that the amnesty was to include the banished prisoners who were now free to return to Canada if they wished. It was obviously undesirable that they should do so, but difficult to avoid unless he liked to commit an even greater illegality than that attributed to Lord Durham. His not very honest or ingenious solution was that Durham should publish another proclamation, cancelling his permission and confirming the banishment. Lord Durham was in no mood for Glenelg's subtleties and replied coldly that the Queen's forgiveness had been granted and could not be recalled.

Though nearly all the Canadian papers had spoken in approval of the Proclamation of 9 October, there were a few who saw in it a proof that Lord Durham preferred British to French institutions and that he was unfair to the French part of the population. Even *Le Canadien*, which had approved of the mercy which he had shown, now turned against him and showed its anti-British bias. One or two of the lesser papers followed its lead and there were signs that the French-Canadians were dissatisfied with their prospects under future British rule and that they expected Lord Durham further to reduce their own rights. The feeling grew so rapidly that *Le Canadien* had completely turned against him before he left Canada and, on the day of his departure was to refer to him as 'envenomed by national distinctions', and said that 'he throws a burning brand' and 'declares himself for the national destruction of a whole people'. There is no doubt that Lord Durham had a preference for the institutions of his own country. The point aroused some discussion when his Report came to be published, and little need be said of it now, except that possibly his reference to British Institutions in the Proclamation lost him some of the goodwill which he had earned by his work for Lower Canada. The immediate result of this feeling, strengthened by the disallowance of his Ordinance, was a renewal of secret activity among the French-Canadians and signs that another outbreak of rebellion was possible. The movement was stronger in Lower than Upper Canada, but, in both provinces, it was poorly concealed and before the end of October both Lord Durham and Sir John Colborne knew all about it and were exchanging despatches about necessary precautions. Lord Durham reported the danger to Glenelg, adding, with some justice that 'the whole of this has been occasioned (You will excuse the frankness with which I tell it you) by your late proceedings in the Cabinet and in the House of Lords'.

Lord Durham was perfectly right in this opinion. Those in Canada who were still unfriendly to Britain had been vastly encouraged by the Government's Indemnity Act which they took to be a profession of lack of confidence in the Governor-General. They argued that since the last rebellion had been condoned and the exiles were free to return, a second attempt would not be likely to be dealt with more drastically. Letters could pass freely between Canada and Bermuda and the exiles had been in regular correspondence with their friends at home. Now they were beginning to creep back, riper than ever for sedition, since they believed that the British Government lacked the courage to punish rebels or to support their own side.

Later, when Lord Durham had returned home and any lie was useful to those who tried to discredit him, he was accused of cowardice in leaving his post when armed rebellion was threatening, and, alternatively, of incompetence for not having foreseen it. His own report to Glenelg and the despatches which he exchanged with Colborne are a clear refutation of the second charge. His decision to return and to leave Colborne to cope with the trouble was not only sensible but inevitable. It would be a soldier's business and Colborne and his troops were more than adequate to deal with anything that might happen. Colborne himself, when Lord Durham consulted him, said bluntly that, when it began, all power ought to be concentrated in the hands of the senior military officer, and that a civilian Governor-General would only be in the way.

Even so, Lord Durham came to his decision reluctantly and went so far at one point as to announce his intention of delaying his departure. A few days later, he cancelled the announcement. Colborne could do all that had to be done in Canada. No one but he himself could do any part of the far more important work which had to be done at home. By this time it was becoming an offence in the eyes of both Whigs and Tories to show any courtesy to Lord Durham, and Colborne was the next to incur their displeasure. Two battalions of the Guards, who were stationed in Montreal, asked for permission to invite the Governor-General to a farewell dinner. Their Brigadier approved but referred the request to Colborne who not only agreed but accepted an invitation for himself to be a guest. There were more than the usual number of speeches made and some of the speakers, while paying tribute to Durham allowed themselves to show more sympathy with him than was perhaps strictly correct—certainly more than was welcome to the growing numbers of his enemies. Durham spoke shortly at the dinner, and, with exquisite tact, did not refer at all to his own affairs but proposed the healths of the Duke of Wellington and Sir John Colborne. It was a genuine compliment to a man to whom he was politically opposed but whom he admired, and it was also a delicate hint to his fellow-guests that politics were out of place at a military function. Unfortunately the Duke held even stricter views on military etiquette, nor had thirty years of politics cured him of an innate dislike for politicians. He censured Colborne and the Brigadier for allowing the dinner to be held and especially for attending it. The Duke had no animus against Lord Durham, but he disapproved of politics in the Mess.

CHAPTER X

Lord Durham had fixed the date of his going for the early part of November and, through the weeks which remained, he worked steadily at the routine of administration and at such of his new projects as he had already put in hand. There was no lessening of activity at Fort St. Louis, no suggestion of the end of a régime. He might have been clearing up the last details before going on leave with the full expectation of returning. It was the only way in which he could ensure that his successor would find his work ready for the taking up and in which Canada could know that there would be continuity between one Governor and another. He had much to arrange for the transfer of power to Colborne, should it become necessary, much to discuss with Buller and Wakefield about his immigration schemes, about land tenure and schools and Church property. He had to answer the immense number of letters and addresses which came flooding in to tell him of the gratitude and admiration of Canada, and there were still interviews to be given and deputations to be received.

There was one thing on which all who worked with him through those last weeks agreed—however badly he knew himself to have been treated he made no complaint and spoke hardly at all of himself. He had no time and no thought to spare for his enemies at home, only for Canada, for his new vision of her, and for the infinite number of things that must be done before he could leave her.

The date finally set for his departure was 1 November. He had been at work until nearly midnight on All Hallows E'en and, when he had finished, one of his staff saw him wrap himself in a big military cloak and climb to the highest tower of the fort. He stood there for a long time, looking out over Quebec and its harbour, where the *Constant*, which had been sent to bring him home, lay at anchor. There were lights all over the city even at that hour and constant movement in the streets. All day long and for two or three days before, a steady stream of horsemen and carriages had been flowing into the town and now it was as crowded as though for some great festival. They had come from all over, from Montreal and the border country, from New Brunswick and Nova Scotia, to say Godspeed to the only Governor whom they had ever liked and trusted without reserve. As midnight sounded from the church steeples, there came the first flurry of snow carried on the bitter wind. It was midnight on All Hallows. God knows what ghosts walked with him on the battlements of Fort St. Louis.

All Saints' Day dawned cold and overcast with a further threat of snow. All morning, crowds filled the city and towards midday they stood close-packed along the streets which led from the fort to the harbour, where a battalion of the Guards in their heavy greatcoats and towering bearskins kept the roadway clear. In the open space before the fort a long procession was forming, made up of the Friendly Societies and more than 3,000 Canadian civilians. One of them wrote afterwards that, as they waited, he looked up and saw on the heights above the city a dense mass of spectators, dark against the white hillsides where more snow had fallen.

Shortly before two o'clock in the afternoon, the great gates were opened and the quarter-guard presented arms as horses' hoofs rattled on the stone of the courtyard, the first troop of the escort rode out and the long procession began to move. The drums of the Guards rolled beneath the shrilling of the fifes and, from the shore battery the first gun of the Governor-General's last salute boomed dully in the heavy air.

Lord and Lady Durham with their children rode in the first coach. He was muffled to the ears in a dark cloak and Lady Durham and the children were swathed in furs. His face was pale and showed no emotion as he sat looking straight before him, his white-gloved hand automatically acknowledging the salute of the quarter-guard. There was no cheering, hardly a sound in the streets except for the ring of hooves and the rattle of wheels. Many men's minds were carried back to that spring day when he had ridden up the hill from the harbour, mounted on his white horse, brilliant with silver and braid, while a hopeful and good-humoured throng cheered him. They were silent today as though they watched the passing of a funeral procession, and, indeed, many of the more thoughtful of them saw in his going the death of their hopes.

'The streets were crowded,' Buller wrote, 'the spectators filled every window and every house-top; and, though every hat was raised as we passed, a deep silence marked the general grief for Lord Durham's departure.' Lady Durham too described the scene with a more personal and intimate feeling for the man who rode beside her.

'The gloom which prevailed seemed indeed as if the people were parting with what was most near and dear to them. I never beheld any public ceremony so deeply affecting . . . there was now something so sad and solemn in the scene, so

274

heart-breaking in the unmerited disappointment which had fallen upon him and upon a great people, that a long life of happiness afterwards could never have effaced the impression made upon me at that moment. . . . I seem to have been speaking principally of myself—or my own sensations—but it was the sight of him, of his countenance which contributed to render them so intense.'

It had begun to snow again, fitfully and in gusts, as the carriage drew up at the quayside and Lord Durham's party went down into the boats which were to carry them out to the *Constant*. Every minute another saluting gun sounded from the shore and was answered by the shipping in the harbour. But the people of Canada had not yet taken leave of their Governor-General. A flotilla of small craft surrounded the *Constant* and the Friendly Societies had claimed the privilege of providing the tug which was to tow her out. The wind had whipped the sea into white crests which creamed away from the bow of the *Constant* as she began to move. The small boats were already bobbing and dipping and one by one, as she gathered speed, they began to fall behind and leave her. To the watchers on the shore it looked as though a line which had held the *Constant* to the shore was slowly parting, strand by strand.

As long as land was still in sight the Governor-General stood on the upper deck, huddled into his coat with his hat pulled down over his eyes. His face was towards Canada and his back towards the miles of desolate winter sea which separated him from England and from a welcome which would surely be as cold and harsh as the wind which filled the *Constant's* sails. He stood looking back on Canada until there was nothing left but a dim shape merging into the grey of sea and sky. Then the snow came down like a white curtain and hid even that from his sight.

EPILOGUE

'Le Jour Viendra'

1839-1840

Magnanimity in politics is not seldom the truest wisdom; and a great empire and little minds go ill together. If we are conscious of our situation and glow with zeal to fill our places as becomes our station and ourselves, we ought to auspicate all our public proceedings on America with the old warning of the Church, *Sursum corda.* . . . English privileges have made it all that it is; English privileges alone will make it all it can be.

EDMUND BURKE. *On Concilia-*
tion with the Colonies. 1775.

As for nobility in particular persons, it is a reverend thing to see an ancient castle or building not in decay; or to see a fair timber tree sound and perfect. How much more to behold an ancient noble family which hath stood against the waves and weathers of time. For new nobility is but the act of power; but ancient nobility is the act of time.

FRANCIS BACON. *Of Nobility.*

CHAPTER I

They had almost twenty-five days of continual wind and storm. There were nights of impenetrable darkness when the air was deadly cold and they could hear the creaking of masses of ice around them; days of fog, when all that they could do was to creep along close-hauled, hardly knowing when day changed to night and night to day. Twice there was a fire on board, and once they ran aground on a shoal, and always the *Constant's* top-hamper was so thickly coated with ice that she lost speed and threatened to become top-heavy until it seemed that one of the great rollers must overturn her. There was little rest or comfort for any of them until, towards the end of the month, they rounded the south point of Ireland and found shelter in pro-tected waters.

Lord Durham had been at dinner on the first night out, but it was to be almost his last appearance in public until the end of the voyage. He had gone aboard a sick man and all through the voyage, he suffered almost incessantly from his neuralgia. Lady Durham and Tommy Duncombe have both written in their memoirs of the horrors of those days and nights at sea, with an indifference to their own safety and comfort that is heroic and with an anxiety for Lord Durham which shows only too plainly how little they expected him to see England again. But their love and his own vision upheld him. On 26 November, the *Constant* dropped anchor at Plymouth.

In London the political clubs and the great houses were in a state of excitement which they had hardly known since the days of the Reform Bill, though it was a different excitement. Then a great cause was at stake. Now—though a cause as great was involved—there was a more personal feeling in the anticipa-tion with which political London awaited the great trial of strength between Durham, Brougham, and Melbourne. On the whole, England, apart from the few enthusiasts of the Coloniza-tion Society, knew and cared as little about Canada as did Melbourne. There was no thought but that Lord Durham had come home to attack the Government and possibly, with the help of the New Radicals, make a bid for the Premiership.

That was known to be a cause—perhaps the only one—for which Melbourne would fight as long as he could stand. Brougham could be relied upon to fight almost anyone and the novelty lay in his having two opponents who were also opposed to each other. Or so political England thought, having as yet no idea how far fighting for his own hand lay from Lord Durham's mind. Greville reported Brougham as 'in high spirits and looking forward with exceeding zest and eagerness to the fun he is to have in the House of Lords'. Greville also described Brougham as 'sitting every day at the Privy Council and growling at him [Durham] sarcastically'.

A more critical impression of Brougham comes from a letter which Lady Durham wrote to her mother at this time. Lord Durham had schooled himself not to criticize his opponents on personal grounds but, luckily for later historians, Lady Durham had imposed no such self-discipline.

She wrote: 'I admire Lord Brougham's impudence, but am not surprised for my part, considering him as a madman or a wild beast against whom one should be on one's guard. I do not feel the same resentment against him as I do against the others.' Lady Durham's opinion strengthens the impression gained from Joseph Parkes of a tiger in the jungle.

Up to this date, it would seem that the general feeling of the country, or at any rate of its politicians, was against Lord Durham. Melbourne and his Cabinet dreaded the attack which he might launch against them, which, if the Radicals would support him, might easily mean the end of the Government. The Tories had never forgiven him for his championship of Reform and saw in his recall a chance of 'dishing the Whigs'. The New Radicals, headed by such men as Parkes and Bulwer, were glad of his return but looked on him mainly as a prospective leader for their party ambitions. The Press, as a whole, were against him, but, two days before the *Constant* made her landfall, one paper, the *Spectator*, gave the first sign of the strength which was being mustered in his support. The leader of the new movement was John Stuart Mill, who commanded the more respect because he was not himself a politician and not attached to any party, though his sympathies were with the Radicals.

He was the Editor of the *London and Westminster Gazette*, but, since it was a quarterly paper and its next issue was not due until December, he had persuaded the *Spectator* to print his article, because he was determined that it should be read before Lord Durham's arrival in London. He wrote not only in defence of Durham's actions in Canada but in the assurance that he was the only man on whom England could rely to see her through the present times and to form a stable Government.

'He alone,' Mill wrote, 'was so marked out for the position by every consideration of character, situation and past services, that if he chose to assume it, he could do so without rivalry or dispute; and the whole of its effective strength would come forth at his voice and give him that decisive majority in the House of Commons with which he might break again the power of the aristocratic faction. . . . The battle for the good government of Canada, as well as for reform in Great Britain, will have to be fought here.'

'Few review articles,' Professor New observes, 'have exerted such an influence . . . and due largely to his eloquent advocacy, there was a widespread Durham movement by the time the Proconsul landed at Plymouth.'

Any man who had been treated as he had been treated might have been forgiven if he had resolved to deliver an open attack on the Government and, if he were successful, to make a bid for the Premiership. The Radicals and Mill expected it, and it was at the back of Melbourne's open pugnacity and secret panic. The Tory peers' virulence was the measure of their fear. But Radical Jack was thinking only of Canada. He had passed far beyond any personal ambition and beyond the heady excitement of party warfare.

There were many too in England, beside the politicians, who remembered Radical Jack and who welcomed him back. They were sick of both Whig and Tory, of parties who differed only in their speech and were alike in their indifference to the needs and rights of the ordinary man. There were the thousands to whom the Reform Bill had at last given a voice in the affairs of the country, and, behind these, the hundreds of thousands who knew that their only hope of getting the same thing lay in him. They had not forgotten him and now they came to meet him. While the *Constant* lay at anchor in Plymouth harbour, the roads which led to the port were filled with horsemen and carriages, as the roads leading to Quebec had been filled before his leaving. The men of the North, his own people, could not travel so far, but from the South and from the West, they streamed in, and all day long crowds stood on the cliffs looking out towards the harbour where the *Constant* swung at her anchor. There were hasty preparations made in the counties through which he would pass on his way to London. Already men were erecting triumphal arches and celebration dinners were on order at the inns in the towns. Earnest but not over-skilful mayors were composing addresses of welcome and town bands were painfully practising 'See the Conquering Hero'.

The *Constant* anchored on 24 November but it was not until four days later that Lord Durham landed. Though they were in harbour, the sea was rough and he was in no state to suffer any more discomfort. It would hardly seem unreasonable that a man who had endured the misery of that winter crossing should take his time in disembarking, but to the chafing Melbourne anything that Lord Durham did was an added irritation. On 4 December he wrote to Russell: 'This delay on the part of Durham appears rather strange, considering that he left Canada in such haste in order to give the Government information; but,' he adds with characteristic unfairness, 'I suppose he will say that his news was of the intended rebellion, which, together with its suppression outstripped him and rendered his intelligence of no value.'

The news of the failure of the second attempt at rebellion and of its suppression had reached England before Lord Durham had landed, to the intense disgust of Brougham who was heard to mutter: 'They'll soon break out again.'

Lord Durham, therefore, was in no great hurry to reach London, apart from the fact that it would have been discourteous to ignore the preparations which his friends had made to welcome him. Melbourne might be awaiting him impatiently, but that was of little importance, since Lord Durham had no intention of speaking to him. He had already decided upon his attitude towards the Government. He would not attack them or let himself indulge in personal recrimination, unless he were forced to do so in his own defence. He cared nothing whether they survived or fell except in so far as they would support his Canadian policy. In that case, he would support them, and no Radical blandishments, no thought of playing for his own hand would distract him. Canada was everything to him now and in the existing administration lay his best hope of a speedy fulfilment of his aims.

In any case his health was not such as to let him undertake a long carriage journey across mid-winter England without reasonable time for rest, and he was further delayed by the need to attend many of the festivities which had been got ready for him. Everyone who had known and liked him wanted to show some sign of gratitude and, with little regard for his comfort, they chose the form of interminable dinners at the towns on his route, at each of which he was expected to make one speech if not several. Late at night on 7 December the carriage drew up before the door of No. 13 Cleveland Row. Lord Durham went to his own room where the portrait of his dead son hung on the wall and sat down to read his letters. There was a big pile of them and, amongst them, was a copy of the letter which Glenelg had sent to Canada—the letter which was still in a westward bound ship now nearing the mouth of the St. Lawrence. Lord Glenelg, anxious that there should be no mistake about the Governor-General's recall—and perhaps fearing the Governor-General's anticipation of it—had sent the copy to his London House. There, in his own home, Lord Durham read that 'Her Majesty's Government are prepared to admit that your continuance in the government of British North America could be attended with no beneficial results'. He must have laughed as he read it. He was home again, the door was barred and, on the other side of it were Her Majesty's Government, wondering what he was going to do. *Le Jour Viendra*. It was never far from his mind. Perhaps his day had come at last, but it was not of his own day that he was thinking but of Canada's.

CHAPTER II

It is no exaggeration to say that, for the next two or three months, No. 13 Cleveland Row was the centre of political London, as it had been when the Committee of Four were drafting the Reform Bill. All through the December of 1838 and the first weeks of the next year, Lord Durham stayed at home, working steadily on his Canadian Report and received only those men who, like Buller and Wakefield, had worked with him and could now help him. Parliament was to meet again at the end of January 1839 and Lord Durham was determined to have his Report ready for the opening, so that there might be no delay in dealing with Canada's necessities.

Melbourne also was hoping for it by the same date, not because he or his colleagues cared about Canada, but because they sorely needed a new cause to buttress their tottering credit in the country. If the Durham Report should turn out well and if its author would support them, they might hope to gain a new lease of life while they introduced it or, at any rate, such parts of it as would cause them least trouble. But the difficulty was that the Cabinet could get no information about it or about its author's intentions. Lord Durham remained in his house and the door remained shut to them. Melbourne sought to gain entrance with all the persistence of a sales manager who is determined to get an order from an unfriendly firm. He sent his salesmen out, one after another, to try to force an entrance, but they all reported lack of success. The only one who penetrated beyond the front door was Mr. E. J. Stanley, whom Melbourne shrewdly selected because, though he was Patronage Secretary to the Government, he was not a member of the Cabinet and so might possibly escape Lord Durham's ban. Moreover Stanley had been an adherent of Durham and had once, for a time, been his secretary. Stanley indeed gained an entrance and was courteously received, but came away without any information about the Report or about Lord Durham's political plans. All that he could report was that 'Durham seemed quiet and calm enough', but did not attempt to conceal his resentment against the way in which he had been treated. 'He expressed no animosity against anyone, but said that he thought the Government had acted towards him with ill-will and that he had been made the object of persecution.' Stanley added that it did not seem to be Durham's object to embarrass the Government, but added, a little ominously, that 'he would defend himself'.

This, as far as it went, was good news to Melbourne, but it

did not go very far and he sent out other emissaries. He first tried the effect of family connection, by sending Duncannon, Lord Durham's brother-in-law, but Duncannon did not get past the door. Nor was even Lord John Russell more successful, when, very reluctantly, he yielded to Melbourne's pleading and tried his luck. Durham was friendly to Russell and had not forgotten his support; but Russell was a member of the Cabinet and he had said that no member of it would be received. Not for the first time Melbourne was made to understand that when Radical Jack said a thing he meant it. Lord Melbourne was left like a disconsolate Noah, contemplating the total failure of both raven and dove.

For a few weeks the deadlock was complete and it is impossible not to believe that Lord Durham must have derived some grim amusement from the Cabinet's situation. Yet it was characteristic of his new and mature wisdom that eventually the approach came from him. It was also characteristic of something which was not at all new in him that he left it until his work was practically completed and then summoned only his own kinsmen Duncannon and Howick. They called upon him, were kindly received and were even given some details of his plans for introducing his Report into the House, though of the contents of the Report they learned nothing. They discussed the probable tactics of the Opposition since it was notorious that those indefatigable moralists, Lord Wharncliffe and his friends, meant to renew their attack on the well-worn subject of Turton's appointment.

Duncannon and Howick, following their instructions, raised the point with Lord Durham and found less difficulty than they had expected, since he was thinking only of Canada and cared nothing for what Wharncliffe thought of him. He agreed easily enough to a form of words suggested by Melbourne which saved Melbourne's face and left the responsibility on Lord Durham, who had never attempted to avoid it. It was not the best course for him to pursue in his own interests, and his friends were disappointed that he did not take a stronger line over it and indeed over his whole attitude towards the Government. Charles Buller wrote:

'Many of those who enthusiastically rallied round him on his return, have since reproached him that he threw away the opportunity of complete justification and satisfaction and refused to take that position in the political world that seemed to invite him. But this course he took after full and anxious consideration and, I think, as wisely as I am sure he did honestly. Abstaining from all part in general politics, he reserved himself for Canada alone.'

There were some of those who had 'rallied round him' who did not know him as well as did Buller and among them were the new Radicals who hoped for him to lead them and to turn out the Whigs. Gibbon Wakefield had been active among them since his return and their leaders, such as Molesworth and Bulwer Lytton, were longing for Lord Durham to come out of his seclusion and take command. They were men of more enthusiasm than tact and, in December, committed a blunder which put an end to all their hopes of such leadership. The Westminster Reform Committee held a meeting at which they voted a complimentary address to Lord Durham and also asked him to receive a deputation. The address was not controversial and the deputation might have been received but for the extremely injudicious speeches which were made at the meeting and were reported in the papers. It was Lord Durham's habit to read several morning papers before beginning work every day and he was far from pleased to find that one speaker had referred to him as 'their trump card'. Hardly more happy was another who had said that 'he considered all great men humbugs, but Lord Durham was as little a humbug as could be found among them'. Two more speakers were even more inept, one of them promising that 'there was but little doubt but that the noble Earl would stand in opposition to the Ministers'. A third speaker, with remarkable lack of tact, advocated an alliance between the Noble Earl and Lord Brougham. Lord Durham was the last man to tolerate such an abuse of his name and when the Westminster Reform Association wrote to him to ask him to receive a deputation, he coldly declined in words which left them in no doubt as to his opinion of their manners or his awareness of their designs. 'I will not pretend ignorance,' he wrote, 'of ulterior designs on the part of those who agreed to the address, which are completely at variance with the objects to which I have adverted.'

The Association, shattered by this rebuff, pleaded abjectly

for a hearing and Lord Durham at last agreed to receive the deputation and the address, but the ceremony took place in an atmosphere of freezing formality, and they were made to realize that, if they had ever had any hope of Lord Durham's support, they had lost it. Many years before, Dr. Beddoes of Clifton had remarked that the young John Lambton could be led but not driven. This crude attempt to commit him to their cause put an end to the hopes of the Radicals for the time being, since they had no leader of their own with enough ability or standing to command respect in Parliament.

Lord Durham seems to have enjoyed this period of seclusion when he worked at his Report and saw no one except those of his own choice. 'Lambton,' Lady Durham wrote to her mother, 'has been very busy getting up his reports but he has been very happy and, I am glad to say, very well.' He himself wrote to Charles Grey: 'I am, and all my staff are working hard to get my report as High Commissioner ready for the meeting of Parliament.' He was determined that no time should be wasted in the presentation of Canada's case.

Parliament was to meet on 5 February and Lord Durham had completed the main body of his task by the end of January, though some additional matter, which his staff were preparing and which was to be printed as appendices, was not yet finished. He circulated proof-sheets to the Cabinet on 31 January and formally presented the document to the Colonial Office on 4 February.

Lord Durham made one of his rare appearances in the House of Lords on the day of the opening. He knew the Cabinet's habits of procrastination, and meant to see to it that there should be no undue delay in this case. Before even the Speech from the Throne had been read, he rose to ask the Prime Minister when his Report would be laid before the House. Melbourne replied that Ministers had only just received it and would need a little time to consider it, but that he would bring it before the House as soon as possible. Lord Durham, who took such promises at their face value, allowed the Cabinet three days for their deliberations and then renewed his demand.

But during those three days a misunderstanding, which has never been fully explained, forced the Cabinet's hand and gave to the Report an immediate interest which its intrinsic worth could not have commanded in so apathetic an atmosphere. On 8 February *The Times* printed a long extract from it and promised further instalments during the next few days. As it was, up to this point, a highly confidential document, there was tremendous political excitement in London, and the wildest rumours about the responsibility for the mistake were bandied about. Lord Durham himself was much annoyed and, when he spoke in the Lords to renew his pressure on the Government, said that 'he had seen with the deepest regret the publication of a part and a part only of the Report'. Melbourne, realizing that his hand had been forced, promised that Parliament should begin to consider the Report on the 11th. 'Since,' he said, '*The Times* obviously possessed a complete copy of the paper in question, the Government had no choice but to present it in full to the House.'

As this was what Lord Durham wanted, it is not surprising that one persistent rumour blamed him for the premature publication, but there is no justification for it. He of all men had least to gain by a partial publication made in such an unconventional way as to prejudice the public mind against the document. He himself denied it and even his most bitter enemies had never accused him of disowning his actions. In any case Brougham, who was also suspected, asked in the House: 'Would the Noble Earl do so injurious a thing to his own Report as to garble the questions which it contains?' Lord Durham would not be likely to oblige *The Times* which was opposed to him and had lately called him the 'Lord High Seditioner'.

One tradition has always blamed Gibbon Wakefield for the disclosure and he is supposed to have asked Lord Durham's permission first, to have been given it and then, when Lord Durham changed his mind and withdrew it, to have risked the publication without permission. Wakefield was selfish and impetuous enough but he was never actually disloyal; nor, it may be thought, was he so foolhardy as to risk his chief's formidable anger. It seems probable that the real explanation lay in the confusion which normally prevailed at the Colonial Office and which was at the moment acute. Besides the affairs of Canada, there was a crisis in Jamaica, and things were made worse by the impending change in control. Glenelg had been removed and Charles Grey was wrestling with a horde of problems which included all those which Glenelg had shelved during his last months of office. The Office had printed 2,000 copies of the Report and it is likely that one of these, through the dishonesty or perhaps only the carelessness of some official, went astray and was passed on to *The Times*. The point is of very little importance except in so far as it helped to prevent the Government from delaying publication.

As soon as they had read the Report they realized that it was not going to be a simple business from which they could profit. Lord Durham's recommendations were so drastic and so unprecedented that they amounted to a reversal of all the country's agelong ideas of Colonial Government. The Cabinet decided that their best policy was to provide for the immediate needs of Canada and to postpone the Durham Report until the next session. Lord Durham was not pleased, but could hardly disagree, since nothing much could be done until someone of industry and ability could be induced to take the Colonial Office. There was not much that he could do until his Report came up for discussion and he was resolute not to spoil its chances by airing any of his private grievances or by embarrassing the Government. He had always expressed his determination to defend himself if attacked and he was saved from inaction by the factious group of Tory Peers who had harassed him before he had left the country and had continued to snarl at intervals while he was away.

Westmeath, Harrowby, Wharncliffe, and their supporters chose this time to renew their personal attacks. They were somewhat taken aback on 8 February, when he anticipated them. He had spoken shortly, asking for a date to be set for the discussion of his Report, and, before sitting down, surprised the House by adding:

'Permit me to say one word on a subject which it is very painful to me to refer to. My Lords, I am made acquainted that, in other quarters an attempt has been made to prejudice me in the public mind with reference to the expenses incurred in my mission to Canada. I beg to have no mystery on that point. I beg to state most distinctly that every shilling of expense which could relate to me—everything referring at all to this subject on which so much calumny has been indulged in—has been defrayed by myself. My position with regard to the mission will be this—that I shall not only not have received a salary but shall have incurred a loss of nearly ten thousand pounds.'

Lord Westmeath affected great concern for the noble Earl's position and tried to give the impression that his remarks had constituted a request for repayment.

'I am of opinion,' he said, 'that whatever is due to the noble Earl ought to be paid and that that account be made perfectly square, if nothing else is done about Canada. . . . Now it may be said that the report which the noble Earl had drawn up and laid before the Government is cheap at that sum; but, be that as it may, if the country do owe the noble Earl the amount stated the sooner the debt is discharged the better.'

There were men in the House who had known Radical Jack in his more tempestuous days who gasped at Westmeath's impudence and waited for the storm to break on his head. But Lord Durham's rebuke, when it came, was delivered in a quiet voice and without any appearance of the old anger. It was the more devastating for that and for its courtesy:

'My lords, I wish to set the noble Marquis right—if he is willing to be set right, on the matter to which he has just referred. I never did say that the country owed me £10,000 or any sum whatever. What I did say was that the cost of my outfit and of everything relating to myself was borne at my own expense. . . .'

Then he turned contemptuously from Westmeath and spoke in moving words to the whole House.

'I have only one word more to add. I would ask your Lordships whether the discussion of this great question to which the papers on the table refer is to be disfigured by personalities such as we have tonight heard? My Lords, I am perfectly ready to answer any objections or to enter into any explanations on any and every part of my conduct, as fully as any of your Lordships can desire. Let noble Lords condemn or blame or praise any part of my conduct as they may think fit; but when all that is past, let us, I beg, go to the discussion of the great question to which the papers before us refer, with that calmness and dignity which become a subject of such importance to the Empire at large and to our North American Colonies in particular. Such a subject ought not to be mixed up with any low personalities or petty personal feelings.'

Westmeath could only achieve an inaudible mutter in which he referred to his lack of personal feelings and, not very lucidly, to 'a public question' and 'public grounds'. For once the whole House was in sympathy with Lord Durham and even those who hated him looked at him with a new respect, sensing a new depth of feeling in him and a hard-won restraint.

Wharncliffe was to be even more surprised. He had been speaking loftily of the purity of private morals needed in men who hold public positions, a proposition which was both new and distasteful to their Lordships, when he found his suggestion warmly adopted by his intended victim. Lord Durham agreed in glowing terms to the principle of private morality in public men and announced his intention of calling for a formal inquiry to ensure that all of them were free from even the suspicion of adultery.

It was not a proposition which commended itself to many noble Lords who realized that they would be lucky if they had to appear before the commission only as witnesses. Even the Duke looked sour, though he said nothing, and there was a tacit understanding that the subject of Turton had become a bore. It was well known that Lord Durham was quite capable of doing what he so willingly offered to do, and sleeping dogs, wherever they had slept, had better be allowed to stay undisturbed.

CHAPTER III

'The Durham Report', Sir Reginald Coupland writes, 'has long been considered as the greatest state document in British Imperial history. It became, to use a cant phrase, the Magna Carta of the Second British Empire.' He adds that its immense historical importance lies 'in the fact that it established the principles on which the British Commonwealth of Nations has been built'. Sir Reginald was writing almost 100 years after the first publication of the Report. Time and the facts of history have obliterated all the factious criticism of Lord Durham's contemporaries and have proved the irrelevance of much of the later objections, reasoned and just though some of them were. If the Report was at fault in some matters of detail, as it may well have been, considering the political turmoil which surrounded its writing and publication, its main principles have been shown to be as sound in practice as they were magnificent in conception. The astonishing thing is, not that it should have been imperfect but that its faults should have been so few and so trivial. Lord Durham spent only five months in Canada and, of these, less than three weeks away from Quebec. He was often ill and more often harassed by the men who should have supported him. His elaborate plans for collecting information were curtailed and, for much of the detailed work, he had to rely on Wakefield and Buller. They served him well in nearly every respect but he had to rely on second-hand information where he had wished and intended to make his own inquiries. He never went to the Maritime Provinces or to Newfoundland and he spent only a few days in Upper Canada where the French interest predominated.

This lack of personal touch, though it was through no fault of his, led him into what has generally been held to be the weakest feature of the Report: its unquestioning acceptance of British principles and customs as better than French. It has been held against him that, whereas in one province the French settlers predominated, he so manœuvred the union of Upper and Lower Canada as to give the British all their own way after the amalgamation of the two. It seems an odd criticism of the Radical Jack whose first public speech was on behalf of an oppressed minority and whose whole life was a struggle for freedom for the less privileged in his own country and in many others. Yet there is some truth in it. One of the main principles of his scheme was Union, but his own words and writings and the testimony of Buller show how late and reluctantly he adopted it and abandoned the idea of Federation which had been his earlier wish. As we know, he had thought much about the choice on the voyage to Canada and had decided that Federation would be fairer to both parties than a complete union in which the British were bound to be better off than the

French. 'On my first arrival in Canada,' he wrote in the Report, 'I was strongly inclined to the project of a federal union.' Yet, after only a short investigation and relying partly on the judgement of his assistants, he did not shrink from changing his mind and preferring complete Union. It might bear hardly on the French—that he realized and accepted—and he was not indifferent to their feelings.

But, in taking his decision, he remembered—what can have been seldom from his mind—that he had a double task to do. He had to pacify a Canada which had just been distracted by a rebellion and therefore had to produce a prompt and efficient plan for the immediate future; and, beyond that, he had to plan for a lasting and just settlement which should be as nearly permanent as any human plan can be. Someone would have to take second place for a time for the sake of later unity and peace. It was inevitable that it should be the French and it is hardly possible now to think that he was not right. A federation of provinces, in either of which one nation held the ascendancy, could only have been a source of later trouble. Nor is it possible now to ignore his real reasons for making the choice. He was sympathetic to the French, but not to their institutions. He had, after all, grown up during the days of the French Revolution and had seen the horrors of the Bourbon restoration, and there was little in either to give him confidence in the French genius for politics or government. 'The institutions of France', the Report says, 'during the period of the colonization of Canada, were, perhaps more than those of any other European nation, calculated to repress the intelligence and freedom of the great mass of the people. These institutions followed the Canadian colonist across the Atlantic. The same central, ill-organized despotism extended over him.' For, as Lord Durham soon found, the government of Upper Canada was at fault not only in being French but in having survived, almost without alteration, from the France of the years before the Revolution. He observed the corruption of municipal affairs, the seignorial system of land-tenure and the pervasive power of the Roman Catholic priest.

Radical Jack was the last man to see without impatience such an anachronism. He had watched, in 1815, the Bourbons' determined attempt to put back the clock and to pretend that the Revolution had never been; and here, beyond the Atlantic, the clock was ticking as sleepily as though it have never stopped and the New World might never have heard of the fall of the Bastille. It is not to be wondered at that Lord Durham should have preferred the institutions of his own country.

Yet it was not out of blind prejudice that he took this decision, and there were other reasons which made the dominance of British ways desirable, even necessary. 'The French,' the Report says, 'regarded with jealousy the influence in politics of a daily increasing body of the strangers whom they so much disliked and dreaded.' The French, as Durham admitted, could justly claim to be the original settlers, but they were rapidly becoming a minority and the process was bound to continue. There was no longer even a trickle of emigrants from France while the stream which came from Britain was becoming a flood. Not only was the French culture obsolete but they were a dying race, while the strength of the British was being constantly renewed. The Union which he proposed might bear hardly on the French at first but he was looking to the day when there should be neither French nor British but only Canadians. (He had promised as much in his speech in the House of Lords before he sailed for Canada.) The history of the last 100 years can only be held to have justified his vision—and confounded his critics—and not only that but to have proved the wisdom of his first intention, for in 1867 the Union of Canada was dissolved into a Federation.

The Government accepted without hesitation this recommendation which had cost Lord Durham so much heartsearching, yet they refused to consider the principle of representative government about which he had no doubts at all. Most of them, and especially Melbourne, were only interested in a palliative, short-term policy which would dispose of the present trouble and enable them to claim the credit for a solution. It does not seem to have occurred to them—certainly it did not worry them—that neither Federation nor Union would endure for long without a complete revision of the whole method of government. As long as they could hold on to office and repel the Tories, they were quite happy to gamble with Canada's future. So, in 1840, they passed the Act which united the two provinces, but it was not until six years later, when

Durham's brother-in-law, Lord Grey, was at the Colonial
Office, that the full principle of the Report was adopted, and
made effective by Lord Elgin, Durham's son-in-law, as
Governor of United Canada. Even then it was only gradually
developed and the Imperial Government tried to keep control
over Canada's right to impose import duties and to regulate
her foreign affairs. The turning-point in the fiscal question came
in 1859 when Canada repudiated the new imperial doctrine of
Free Trade and refused to withdraw her protective tariffs. It
took longer to reach agreement on foreign affairs, though from
1887 onwards colonial representatives were called into conference with ministers at home, a step which soon led to the
creation of the Committee of Imperial Defence. Even these
conferences were limited to colonial foreign problems. As late
as 1910 Dominion Premiers were kept in ignorance of the secret
facts of the European situation and when, in 1911, they were
informed, they were not asked to give an opinion on the proposed British measures. When the First World War began
three years later, the Dominions were still without a voice in
the direction of general foreign policy.

Lord Durham never used the phrase 'Responsible Government'—it only became fashionable after his death—but he
asserted the principle of it without equivocation and with all
his considerable force and eloquence. Once more he found his
model in the institutions of his own country.

'It needs no change,' he wrote, 'in the principles of government, no invention of a new constitutional theory to supply
the remedy which would, in my opinion, completely remove
the existing political disorders. It needs but to follow out
consistently the principles of the British constitution and
introduce into the Government of these great Colonies those
wise provisions, by which alone the working of the representative system can in any country be rendered harmonious
and efficient.'

His outline of the ideal government for Canada was traced
from the picture of Britain. The Governor represented the
Crown, but, the Report says, 'must be given to understand that
he need count on no aid from home in any difference with the
Assembly that should not directly involve the relations between

the mother country and the Colony'. For the Governor in his province,' Coupland comments, 'as for the Sovereign in Britain, there could be no appeal beyond the vote of the electorate. If that failed, he must make his peace with the Assembly. Otherwise, he might be coerced by a refusal of supplies or his advisers might be terrified by the prospect of impeachment.' It was plain speaking and it was meant to be. 'I admit,' says Durham, 'that the system which I propose would in fact place the internal government of the Colony in the hands of the colonists themselves.'

But the colonists, too, had to listen to some equally plain words, for, if Durham proposed to give them responsibility for their own affairs, they must understand that it involved duties as well as privileges and that, for them as for the Governor, there could be no running to the Mother Country if things went wrong. 'If,' the Report says, 'the colonists make bad laws and select improper persons to conduct their affairs, they will generally be the only, always the greatest sufferers; and, like the people of other countries, they must bear the ills which they bring on themselves, until they choose to apply the remedy.'

It was unfortunate for the immediate prospects of the Report (as it was ironical in the light of past history) that much of the opposition should have come from Durham's old colleague, Russell, now at the Colonial Office. Russell was sympathetic towards Durham himself, but not noticeably so towards the colonies, and his mind was not of a type to approach any problem in the same way as Durham's. During the preparation of the First Reform Bill their methods had been complementary, Durham supplying the broad sweep of the design and Russell the essential detail, rather as Napoleon had been used to lay down the main strategy and leave Berthier to write the orders.

Since those days, though they had always remained on good terms as colleagues, their natural differences of outlook had widened, and their nicknames of Radical Jack and Finality John were typical of the distance which now lay between them. Durham saw further ahead and was always ready to take a risk for the sake of the future. Russell liked to see every detail settled and written down and abhorred risk of any sort. Detail was never Durham's strongest point, as he had shown in his use of Bermuda as a place of exile, and it was nothing but Russell's plain duty to scrutinize the new proposals with the utmost care to prevent any more trouble arising from a like piece of carelessness. He thought that he had found a possible source of trouble in what he called in his letters to Melbourne the device of 'dyarchy' or 'dualism', which Durham had apparently adopted in his combination of the Crown as represented by the Governor with responsible government in the Assembly. He could visualize a situation in which the two might come into irreconcilable opposition, but he could not see how to provide for it. Few men had a greater knowledge of British constitutional procedure than Russell, but it failed to provide him with an answer to this dilemma.

Durham could not see how to provide for it either, and he knew less about procedure than Russell, but what he did know was that in British affairs there are many things which look dubious on paper and are found to be effective in practice. There might be technical blemishes on his plan for Canada, but he was not drafting a constitution for some theoretical Utopia but a practical code for a contemporary colony which was in trouble and had lately been in greater. He may have known less than Russell about written codes but he knew the working of them, and above all he knew men and trusted them on the whole to be fair and reasonable. He had to provide a code, and that at very short notice. It was for the Government and the colonists to apply energy and goodwill to make it work. If they could do that, any legal defects or omissions could be easily corrected later, but unless goodwill and energy were forthcoming, it mattered little what form of government was suggested. Canada would be lost and there was not likely to be a third chance.

Durham's approach, as ever, was the human one. In Canada, he saw a loved daughter who had come of age and wanted to live her own life, and, like a wise parent, he was ready to give her a latch-key and trust her. Russell was willing, with due safeguards and on special occasions, to lend her the back-door key, but when she came home Russell would be sitting up for her.

Whatever else may be said of Lord Durham, he was a willing and a generous giver and he was not the man to impose conditions when he made a gift. His vision found perfect expression, over fifty years after the date of his Report, in Kipling's poem, *The Lady of the Snows*, written in 1896:

> *A nation spoke to a nation*
> *A throne sent word to a throne,*
> *Daughter am I in my mother's house,*
> *But mistress in my own.*
> *The gates are mine to open*
> *As the gates are mine to close*
> *And I abide by my Mother's House*
> *Said our Lady of the Snows.*

CHAPTER IV

The Cabinet's anxiety to postpone the Canadian debates was helped by the breakdown of Lord Durham's health which began within a few weeks of his completion of his Report. While he was working on it, he had been unusually well and cheerful, but, once again he had taxed his strength and he had little in reserve. In London the Government were busy with the reconstruction of the Colonial Office, which Lord Normanby had just taken over and was now anxious to leave as soon as possible. The crisis in Jamaica persisted and once the Government were beaten in a division by a narrow margin, and nearly had to resign. Melbourne was pressing Russell to take over Colonial Affairs and Russell, though he found the leadership of the House occupation enough, reluctantly agreed to do so later in the year. Melbourne's happiest idea was the appointment of Mr. Powlett Thomson to the Governor-Generalship of Canada, a choice which Lord Durham warmly endorsed.

Normanby was still in office when the first effort to deal with Canada was discussed in the House, but it was only a pale shadow of Lord Durham's plan which appeared. Normanby moved two resolutions: one a temporary measure to continue the suspension of the Lower Canadian constitution; the other in favour of Lord Durham's proposal to unite Upper and Lower

Canada into one province. It was a pitiful attempt to cope
with the situation and at the same time to give away as little as
possible, but the Government took fright even at that and,
soon after its introduction, announced that it was to be postponed until the next session. Their ostensible reason was the
hostility of Upper Canada to the idea of Union, though in fact
some section or other was bound to oppose it and the Colonial
Office had known all about the objections before they framed
the resolutions. The real reason, as Brougham in a characteristically penetrating speech made painfully clear, was their
recent defeat over Jamaica and their reluctance to risk another
over Canada. Even Melbourne could hardly have clung to
office after two such failures.

Lord Durham had spent the spring months at Cowes where
he still had a house and where he had in the past enjoyed so
many weeks of yachting with Tommy Duncombe. He was
taking life very quietly there, spending hours of every day in
bed, reading books from the parcels which came regularly from
London. His spirits were improved and he felt himself so much
better that he began to think about buying another yacht, but
it was too much trouble or perhaps he knew that he would
never sail again. In a gesture of friendship to both Canada and
her new Governor, he sent his old yacht to Plymouth for
Thomson's departure and she sailed out of the harbour ahead
of the ship which was carrying him. When she returned to
Cowes Lord Durham had other schemes for refitting her and
sailing again later in the year; or perhaps next year, when he
would undoubtedly be strong again, and with Duncombe,
would be able to renew their old pleasures. His room was full of
plans and estimates, but somehow it was hard to concentrate
on them. It was easier to turn to the parcel of books which had
just arrived, and only too easy to lie thinking about Canada and
wondering, with decreasing hope, when, if ever, the Cabinet
were really going to do anything to help her.

When he felt well enough he went up to London and tried
to be in his place in the Lords whenever Canadian affairs were
on the order paper. He spoke briefly on 3 June when Normanby
introduced his abortive resolutions, making a plea for his
Report to be postponed no longer than until the next session.
But every effort of this sort was a strain and had to be followed

by complete rest. So the year dragged on and the Report was postponed again and then once more, so that it could not possibly be discussed before the early months of 1840. While the Whigs, who were in office again after the brief interlude of Peel, were inactive from choice and indolence and Lord Durham from necessity, his enemies were still busy. Nothing was too mean for them to use in an attempt to discredit him and they began while he lay ill at Cowes to deny his authorship of the Report, saying that he had only signed it and that all the work had been done by Buller and Wakefield. Tradition assigns the discredit of this canard to Brougham, who undoubtedly described it publicly as 'a third-rate article for the *Edinburgh Review*' and who is supposed to have added: 'The matter comes from a felon, the style from a coxcomb and the Dictator contributed only six letters D.U.R.H.A.M.' It was perhaps the inevitable result of the seclusion in which Lord Durham wrote the Report that doubts should have been thrown on its authorship by his insatiable enemies, but later opinion has unanimously accepted as fact that he himself wrote the body of it, leaving only some of the detailed work to Buller and Wakefield. 'Careful research,' Coupland writes, 'has put it beyond question that, though certain sections of the Report may have been drafted by other hands, the main parts of it, and especially the section on Lower Canada and the vital conclusions were written by Durham himself.' In any case it hardly seems to matter now. The incident only has importance as proving that there were no depths to which Lord Durham's enemies would not descend to harm him.

During his rare visits to London in the summer of 1839 some of the Whigs tried to persuade Durham to renew personal contact with the Government. He met these overtures without enthusiasm but not with an absolute refusal. He had kept his word and had not received any of the Ministers nor spoken to them apart from the barest and most formal discussions in the House, but, now that his work was done, he was too good-hearted to keep up the full rigour of his aloofness and perhaps too tired to care whether he met them or not. Early in the summer, he went so far as to accept from Lady Blessington an invitation to dinner at her house to meet Brougham, but Brougham failed to appear. Next Hobhouse resolved to renew what had once been a friendship and went up to Durham at a reception and offered his hand. Hobhouse tells the story with all his usual self-admiration and seems surprised that, after such generosity on his part, Lord Durham should have accepted his hand 'rather formally'. It was not until later in the year that the two greatest breaches were, at any rate in appearance, healed. Lord Durham was alone in London and at a party at Lady Tankerville's came unexpectedly face to face with Brougham. Lord Durham described the meeting in a letter to his wife: 'Shortly after in marched Brougham. Of course I took up my hat and coat to be off, after bowing to him. He walked up to Lady Tankerville and said, "Do be the peace-maker between us and let us shake hands." I thought it was as well not to make a scene before Lord Canning, so I took his offered hand and sat down again. He was in great spirits.'

It was—it could be—no more than the most formal reconciliation, though Hobhouse tells of an occasion when Brougham seeing Lord Durham walking in London, crossed the street to talk to him. The last gesture was made in the autumn when he and Lady Durham dined with Lord Melbourne.

When Lord Durham was well enough he spent much time with Powlett Thomson before he sailed for Canada, giving all the help and information which he had gained there by experience, and as the year went on, he still tried to attend Colonial debates in the House and waited and hoped for the debate on his Report. After the Government had withdrawn their resolutions in June, they made no further move until the beginning of the year 1840, when Russell introduced the Canada Act 1840. It was far less than Durham had hoped for since, though it reunited the two Canadas, it refused Responsible Government. He was too ill that winter to think of coming up to London, but, as he lay in bed in his house at Cowes, he followed the progress of the Bill and was generous enough to write to Russell a letter in which he spoke of his congratulations and concealed his disappointment.

That spring he made one last attempt to keep up his connection with Parliamentary affairs and took a house at Putney, where he could find more quiet and better air than in Cleveland Row. He had hoped too much and he hardly had the strength to leave it, but his friends came there to see him and to tell him about the passage of the Bill through the Houses. Now that the affairs of Canada were out of his hands his thoughts turned a little nostalgically to the old days of Home politics and he dreamed of a new Whig Cabinet with Earl Grey as Prime Minister. It could never have been possible, for Earl Grey, who was then seventy-three, was happily living at Howick and had no intention of leaving it again for Westminster. It only represents Lord Durham's last tribute to the man whom he had always admired and in his way loved; with whom he had quarrelled in private as hotly as he had defended him in public; and whom he had tried to put in the place of the father whom he had never known. Grey was always in his thoughts as winter faded and he talked to Lady Durham of the green beginning of spring at Lambton, the new beauty of the larches on the slopes below the Castle and of how—quite soon now, for he would surely be strong again when summer came—they would go back there and renew the old friendly visits between Lambton and Howick. In a letter which Lady Durham wrote to her daughter immediately after his death, she told how his last talks with her had run on the same idea.

He was still in Putney on 12 April, his forty-eighth birthday, when he seemed fairly well and very gay and there was a little family party, but almost at once he began to fail and his doctors decided that he must be moved to a warmer climate. They recommended, as they had to his father, Italy, and he languidly agreed, since, if it could not be Lambton, he cared little where he went. When he arrived at Dover, he was too ill to go on board, and, while he lay in bed there, he longed again for his own home at Cowes. If he could not see the woods above the Wear he could at least look out on the blue water of the Solent and see the white sails of the yachts and remember happy days with Tommy Duncombe in the *Louisa*. His family were constantly with him and Lady Durham seldom left his room. He was failing rapidly and on 23 July, when they told him that the Canada Bill had received the Royal Assent, he scarcely seemed to understand.

Lady Durham slept in his room and early in the morning of the 28th, she heard a sound from his bed and ran to him. He was trying to say something to her but he was past speech and the doctor told her that he could not live more than a few hours more. The children came to his room but he did not regain consciousness and at nine o'clock, he died.

Lord Durham's yacht, the *Albatross*, which had brought his body from Cowes, anchored off Sunderland on 3 August and the slow journey overland to Lambton began. The funeral was arranged for 10 August and when, on the previous day, the cortège drew near to the Castle, all the countryside had turned out to see its passing. When Radical Jack had come home after the triumph of the Reform Bill, his miners had taken the horses out of the shafts and had drawn the carriage through the streets of the villages to his home. Now they stood before their cottage doors with bared heads and many of them were weeping openly—and those not only women and children. Behind the bier rode an escort of black-clad horsemen, for everywhere that they had passed, the country gentlemen had joined the procession and Lambton of Lambton was followed by many of the famous names in Durham history—Williamson, Ridley, Thurloe, Liddell, White. The riders halted at the foot of the hill which leads to the Castle and the miners, bareheaded and wearing their carefully tended best suits, fell in behind it and escorted it for the last short stage.

At the Castle the hatchment was over the door and the sable and argent of Lambton flew at half-mast above the roof. A party of estate workers took the coffin on their shoulders and carried it into the great hall. It was covered with crimson velvet ornamented with gold—Radical Jack had always liked splendour—and all the rest of the day and far into the night his people filed past it. Many of them again were in tears and a bystander heard from many the supreme tribute of a north-countryman—'He were an honest man, he were.' And once, one of them answered that with, 'Aye. He cared about us, he did.'

On 10 August the Castle opened its doors to receive Radical Jack's last guests. They stood eating and drinking in silence, while those who had come from far went into the Hall to pay their respects to the dead. All the time there was a sound of horses' hoofs and carriage wheels as the funeral procession formed up outside. When, early in the afternoon, it began to move, it was over a mile long and more than 50,000 people walked or drove in it. The column was so long that Lady

Durham, standing at a window, could see that its head was among the trees on the far side of the valley of the Wear—just at the point where she had been used to catch a last glimpse of her husband's grey horses when he drove away from her on the road to London. At the head of the column walked 140 tenants and workers on the estate, who were followed by the hearse and the mourning coaches. Behind them came 300 of the Free-masons of Country Durham and 175 carriages of friends and neighbours. Slowly the procession went on its way to the Collegiate Church of Chester-le-Street, where the boy Charles William had lain these eight years.

All the county mourned on that 10th of August 1840. In Durham, Sunderland, South Shields, the shops were shuttered and the streets were empty. The sound of tolling bells rolled over the countryside from Cathedral to parish church till it reached the border and was echoed by the bells of Gateshead and Newcastle. Among them were the bells which, eight years ago, had for the last time rung Triple Grandsires for the birthday of the heir to Lambton.

At the door of the church the choir and the priest, a kins-man, Charles William Grey, stood waiting. When the service was over, the bearers carried the coffin into a vault and laid it beside the smaller one which held the remains of the eldest son. A handful of earth rattled on the lid and the priest's voice spoke the last words. 'In sure and certain hope of the Resur-rection to Eternal Life.' It was the last and the most triumphant assertion of Radical Jack's motto, *Le Jour Viendra*.

INDEX

INDEX